THE SUPPLY MANAGEMENT ENVIRONMENT

Stanley E. Fawcett
Brigham Young University

Published by: National Association of Purchasing Management, Inc.
Paul Novak, C.P.M., A.P.P., Chief Executive Officer

© 2000 National Association of Purchasing Management, Inc.
P.O. Box 22160 Tempe, AZ 85285-2160 USA
www.napm.org

INTRODUCTION

Supply management professionals provide many valuable and important contributions to organizations throughout the world, whether they are public, for profit, or non-profit, and across all sectors. The field is quickly evolving and changing, reflecting the evolution of technology, the Internet, heightened professional standards, and increased collaboration between different internal departments, between suppliers, between customes, and between organizations. Supply management is affecting the bottomline more than ever before, and is "value added" for all companies and their financial success.

This new environment, however, requires all supply management professionals to stay on top of the tools, practices, policies, and knowledge relevant not only to supply management, but to the business environment as a whole. NAPM is dedicated to building the professional through education and professional development. The NAPM Supply Management Knowledge Series (previously known as the NAPM Professional Development Series) was developed to assist the supply management professional do this.

The Series has been updated to include an analysis and discussion of newly emerging trends and the new tools, practices, policies, and knowledge that have developed from these trends. Our goal in publishing the Series is to encourage and support your professional growth and contribute to the image of the profession, and to assist you with learning about and mastering these new skills . . . basically, to help you do your job the best you can.

In addition, the books are a resource for preparing for the C.P.M. and A.P.P. certification exams. The exams were also recently updated and many of the topics addressed in this four-volume series appear on these new exams.

It is my intention that NAPM will not only continue its efforts to support and build the supply management profession, but will also add to it. The NAPM Supply Management Knowledge Series is a part of these efforts.

Paul Novak, C.P.M., A.P.P.
Chief Executive Officer
NAPM
August 2000

i

NAPM – Your Source for Supply Management Resources

Since 1915, the National Association of Purchasing Management (NAPM) has served thousands of supply management professionals from around the world. Domestically, NAPM works with affiliated associations across the country to continually keep its members well informed, and trained on the latest trends and developments in the field.

The information available from NAPM is extensive. One of the greatest resources is the NAPM Web site, www.napm.org. In addition to general information, this expansive site features a vast database of supply management information, much of which is available solely to members. Information includes a listing of general supply management references as well as an extensive article database, listings of products and seminars available, periodicals listing, an Online Career Center with job listings and resumes posted, contact information for NAPM affiliate organizations nationwide, and links to other related Web sites.

The monthly Manufacturing and Non-Manufacturing *NAPM Report On Business®*, including the Purchasing Managers' Index (PMI) in the manufacturing survey, continues to be one of the key economic indicators available today. NAPM members receive this valuable report in the pages of Purchasing Today® magazine, one of the many benefits of membership.

The quarterly publication *NAPM InfoEdge* is also included in membership. *NAPM InfoEdge* provides unique, how-to approaches on single supply management topics.

NAPM also publishes *The Journal of Supply Chain Management*, a one-of-a-kind publication designed especially for experienced supply management professionals. Authored exclusively by accomplished practitioners and academicians, this quarterly publication targets purchasing and supply management issues, leading-edge research, long-term strategic developments, emerging trends, and more.

Members also enjoy discounts on a wide variety of educational products and services, along with reduced enrollment fees, for educational seminars and conferences held throughout the country each year. Topics cover the entire supply management spectrum.

For executives interested in professional certification, NAPM administers the Certified Purchasing Manager (C.P.M.) and Accredited Purchasing Practitioner (A.P.P.) programs. Members receive discounts on test preparation/study materials and C.P.M./A.P.P. exam fees.

To provide a forum for educational enhancement and networking, NAPM holds the Annual International Purchasing Conference. This is a unique opportunity for members and non-members alike to learn from each other and share success strategies.

To learn more about NAPM and the many ways it can help you advance your career, or to join online, visit NAPM on the Web at www.napm.org. To apply for membership by telephone, please call NAPM customer service at 800/888-6276 or 480/752-6276, extension 401.

THE NAPM SUPPLY MANAGEMENT KNOWLEDGE SERIES

Volume 1
THE SUPPLY MANAGEMENT PROCESS
Alan R. Raedels

Volume 2
THE SUPPLY MANAGEMENT ENVIRONMENT
Stanley E. Fawcett

Volume 3
SUPPLY MANAGEMENT FOR VALUE ENHANCEMENT
Lisa M. Ellram and Thomas Y. Choi

Volume 4
THE SUPPLY MANAGEMENT LEADERSHIP PROCESS
Anna Flynn and Sam Farney

SERIES OVERVIEW

In the past decade, purchasing has moved to the center stage of the organization as it has become increasingly clear that purchasing and supply management can make a significant contribution to organizational success. Beyond simply reducing prices for purchased goods and services, purchasing can add value to organizations in many ways, including supporting organizational strategy, improving inventory management, forging closer working relationships with key suppliers, and maintaining an active awareness of supply market trends. The ability of purchasing to significantly contribute to organizational success is the core of this four-book series.

While differences exist among various types of organizations, industries, business sectors, regions of the world, and types of items purchased, these books provide an overview of current issues in purchasing and supply management. The topics covered in this series range from the basics of good purchasing practice to leading-edge, value enhancement strategies. These four books provide an excellent survey of the core principles and practices common to all sectors within the field of purchasing and supply management.

These four volumes were designed to support the National Association of Purchasing Management (NAPM) certification program leading to the Accredited Purchasing Practitioner (A.P.P.) and Certified Purchasing Manager (C.P.M.) designations. They also provide practical and current coverage of key topics in the field for those interested in enhancing their knowledge. They also can serve as useful textbooks for college courses in purchasing.

The textbooks are organized around the four modules of the C.P.M. exam as follows:

1. *The Supply Management Process* (for C.P.M.s and A.P.P.s)
2. *The Supply Management Environment* (for C.P.M.s and A.P.P.s)
3. *Supply Management for Value Enhancement Strategies* (for C.P.M.s only)
4. *The Supply Management Leadership Process* (for C.P.M.s only)

Volume 1, *The Supply Management Process*, focuses on the overall purchasing process and its major elements. It looks at the requisitioning process, sourcing, bidding, and supplier evaluation, and offers an overview of cost and contract management. This volume also examines how technology has changed procurement techniques and provides a summary of the key legal issues facing purchasers.

Volume 2, *The Supply Management Environment*, explores how the ever-changing environment in which purchasers operate is affecting their roles today and in the future. Volume 2 provides an overview of purchasing's role in strategy and looks at how globalization, just-in-time/mass customization are affecting purchasing. This volume also explores issues related to negotiations, quality, reengineering, and supply chain management. It examines the increased role and impact of information technology on purchasing, and looks at what skill sets will be required for success in purchasing in the future.

Volume 3, *Supply Management for Value Enhancement Strategies*, explores a number of traditional and leading-edge approaches for increasing purchasing's contributions to organizational success. The volume begins by looking at outsourcing and lease versus buy issues. It then delves into the many issues associated with inventory management, including inventory classification and disposal. Specific value enhancement methods, such as standardization, value analysis, early supplier involvement, and target costing, are also presented. The volume closes with a discussion of developing and using forecast data, and offers an overview of specific strategies to apply in various purchasing situations.

Volume 4, *The Supply Management Leadership Process*, provides an overview of key general management issues specifically applied to purchasing activities and purchasing's role in the organization. It begins with an overview of strategic planning and budgeting processes, and continues by presenting specific issues related to effectively recruiting, managing, and retaining good employees. Volume 4 then discusses the role of operating policies and procedures, tools to manage workflow, and performance monitoring. It ends with a presentation of how to most effectively present purchasing performance results within the organization.

It has been a privilege to edit this series for NAPM and to work with an excellent group of authors. The authors' practical and theoretical knowledge has contributed to the quality of these books. I hope you find them both useful and interesting.

Lisa M. Ellram
Series Editor

PREFACE

This book considers those issues in the supply environment that are influencing today and tomorrow's purchasing strategy and practice. Its goal is to provide the purchasing professional with an overview and foundational understanding of critical issues that impact purchasing decisionmaking. The hope is that a better understanding of today's complex, dynamic, and evolving supply environment will help purchasers help their companies compete more effectively. This book, like the other three in this series, is based on the newly revised ninth edition of the *C.P.M. Study Guide* and is intended to assist purchasing managers prepare to take and pass the C.P.M. examination.

I wish to thank Alan Raedels for the many hours he dedicated to the development of the latest edition of the *C.P.M. Study Guide.* I would also like to thank Lisa Ellram, series editor; Scott Sturzl, NAPM Vice President of Certification; and Cynthia Zigmund, project coordinator, for their editorial insight and patience throughout the process of writing this book. Their timely and helpful feedback improved the quality of this publication. Of course, any errors in reason are the responsibility of the author.

Stanley E. Fawcett

This book is dedicated to Amydee Mackley Fawcett, A.B.O.: my partner, my friend, my love.

Stanley E. Fawcett

CONTENTS

Chapter 1: Strategic Purchasing and the Supply Environment

Chapter 2: The Globalization of the Supply Environment

Chapter 3: The Affect of Time Compression on the Supply Environment

Chapter 4: Rising Expectations: Meeting the Quality Challenge

Chapter 7: Information Technology in Purchasing

Chapter 8: The Art and Science of Negotiation

Chapter 9: Purchasing's Role in the Learning Organization

Chapter 1

Strategic Purchasing and the Supply Environment

*As a purchasing manager, can I really impact strategic
results in today's supply environment?*

Chapter Objectives

This chapter is designed to help the purchaser:

- Understand how today's supply environment affects each step in the purchasing process.
- Understand how today's supply environment affects purchasing's strategic significance.
- Understand the elements of strategy and why the supply environment is so important.
- Recognize the key forces that influence today's supply environment.

What is Purchasing?

To fully understand purchasing's unique ability to affect not only an organization's P & L statement but also its long-term competitive posture in today's dynamic and intensely competitive global marketplace, we must start with the basics and then review the role and nature of purchasing.

Every organization, whether large or small, profit or non-profit, service or manufacturing oriented, purchases materials, supplies, and services from outside suppliers to support its own internal operations. Of course, the nature, quantity, and dollar value of purchases vary greatly from organization to organization. For most organizations, the financial and operating affect of these purchased goods and services is substantial and influences both short-term profitability and long-term survivability. The challenge of managing this acquisition process generally rests on the shoulders of the purchasing organization. This challenge is exacerbated by constantly rising performance expectations placed on purchasing managers, increasing environmental uncertainty, and diminished managerial control. These are the natural outcomes of globalization and shifting channel power. Meeting this challenge requires that purchasers efficiently and effectively acquire inputs to support an organization's efforts to manufacture a world-class product and/or deliver unparalleled service.

The Purchasing Process

The purchasing process varies considerably depending on what an organization is purchasing. Services are managed differently from raw materials and MRO items as are sophisticated technological components. Each organization performs the basic nine steps of the purchasing process at varying levels of sophistication and formality. This formality depends on the items being purchased, the skills of the purchasing managers, and the resources dedicated to the purchasing process. The steps of the purchasing process are discussed below.

Recognition of need – The purchasing process begins when someone within an organization identifies a need to acquire some input, such as materials, supplies, or services, for use in the transformation process or in support of the organization's day-to-day business activities. Recognizing that a need exists is the responsibility of the user of the item to be purchased. For example, a production manager would be responsible for knowing how much and when each component is needed. The production manager's responsibility is to identify and communicate needs to purchasing in an accurate and timely manner. The well-managed organization typically uses a purchasing policy or procedure handbook to establish guidelines for the interaction between internal users and the purchasing group. Today, many standard production needs are communicated automatically through a computerized production control system that monitors inventory levels and reorder points. However, a clear and precise set of guidelines must be in place to facilitate communications regarding new, unique, or one-time purchases.

Description of need – To make sure that the right items are available at the right time, the user must clearly communicate specific needs to purchasing, usually through a purchase requisition. The purchase requisition contains the following information: the item description; requisitioning department; authorizing signature; purchase quantity; and delivery date and location. The information should be stated clearly to assure that the purchasing process is as smooth as possible. For example, the delivery date should be specific to a day and time and not "ASAP". If the item isn't needed for four weeks, the user should indicate four weeks and not two weeks just to make sure the item is available "on-time". The two-week cushion might require a higher price than necessary to get the item delivered "on-time." Realistic and accurate information is needed to reduce confusion and establish good working relationships. The item description is particularly critical since purchasing must have a clear understanding of what is needed to identify the appropriate supplier and then communicate the needs to the supplier. The less experience purchasing has with an item, the more clear and specific the description must be.

Supplier selection and development – Once purchasing understands the needs of the user regarding the item to be purchased, the next step is to find the best supplier possible. Supplier selection is an important step in the purchasing process: "the success of the purchasing department depends on its skill in locating or developing suppliers, analyzing supplier (vendor) capabilities, and then selecting the appropriate supplier (vendor)."[1] Because purchasing's objectives include providing the highest-quality product at the lowest total cost supported with the best service, a supplier should be selected based on the ability to meet these requirements.

The actual process used to identify good suppliers varies a great deal depending on the importance of the item being purchased. The same basic relationships hold true for most organizations, suppliers of MRO items receive less attention than suppliers of major components such as engines or flat panel displays that are carefully analyzed. In general, the higher the dollar value or the greater the affect of the purchased item on the end product's performance, the more important and resource intensive the supplier selection process. The basic supplier selection process is characterized by four stages: identification, evaluation, approval, and monitoring. Identification involves making a list of all potential suppliers and begins with a review of the purchasing database, which contains information on all suppliers used in the past several years. Supplier names often come from contacts, such as purchasing and sales managers, within and outside the organization. Additional sources of information include trade publications and supplier directories such the *Thomas Register of American Manufacturers* (www.thomaspublishing.com) which includes almost all American manufacturers by type of product, and contains almost 50,000 pages listing over 150,000 companies. Such directories do not contain any performance information, nor do they include international suppliers. In today's global marketplace, the best supplier might be located outside the United States.

Determining the performance potential of the companies on the supplier list is the primary task of the evaluation stage, which takes place in two steps. First, a list of supplier selection criteria is put together. These criteria include quality, price, delivery dependability, both current and future capacity, service responsiveness, technical expertise, managerial ability, and financial stability. The second step in the evaluation stage is to gather performance information that can be used to evaluate possible suppliers. After the purchasing manager assembles the necessary information for each supplier under consideration, comparative analysis is then performed. An interesting development in the area of supplier evaluation is the use of expert systems to help make supplier selection decisions.[2] An expert system is a tool that combines the knowledge of "experts" with decisionmaking logic to help managers take a systematic approach to decisions such as supplier selection. A supplier selection expert system would contain not only an extensive set of questions that incorporate the appropriate selection criteria, but also relative weightings or priorities for each.

After carefully evaluating potential suppliers, purchasing must reduce the selections to an approved list of suppliers. This process is the focus of the approval stage. Suppliers that remain on the approved list are eligible to receive an order if their price and other terms are competitive at the time the order is being placed. If the organization has a policy of sourcing from multiple suppliers to assure competition in the hope of getting lower prices, then several suppliers for each item will be maintained on the approved list. If the organization seeks to consolidate all of its purchases for an item with a single supplier, then the approved list must be reduced to a single or sole source. This sole source is usually determined through the negotiation of a partnership relationship.

Monitoring supplier performance is the final stage in the selection and development process. Many purchasing departments now use performance scorecards to evaluate supplier performance. The scorecard is a report card that identifies and weighs the critical performance criteria, evaluates the supplier's performance on each criterion, and provides an overall supplier rating. Some organizations use the scorecard rating to categorize suppliers. For example, a leading manufacturer of transportation equipment places suppliers into one of four groups: partner; key approved supplier; approved supplier; or conditional supplier. Regardless of categorization, all suppliers are expected to use the scorecard information to drive continuous improvement. Most organizations update the scorecard on a quarterly basis.

Determination of price – Price is only one factor in the supplier selection decision, but it is the factor used most frequently to evaluate the purchasing group's performance. Thus, purchasing actively pursues the "best" possible price using one of three primary approaches: purchasing at list price; competitive bidding; and negotiation.

Purchasing at list price – For many items, the best approach is to comparison shop and then purchase the item at the published asking price. Lower-volume or lower-valued items often do not merit the managerial time and effort needed to obtain a lower-than-list price.

Competitive bidding – Competitive bidding relies on market forces to get prospective suppliers to offer a low price. Because potential suppliers are competing for the order, they will offer a price that will allow them to cover the costs of production and distribution as well as make a small profit. Because the order typically goes to the supplier with the lowest reasonable bid, competitive bidding has often been viewed as the most efficient means of obtaining a fair price.

Negotiation – Negotiation is used when the dollar value of the purchase is large, high uncertainty exists, or a long-term relationship is desired. Negotiation generally goes beyond price determination to develop an overall agreement that is mutually beneficial to both negotiating parties. Typically issues included in a negotiation are price, delivery, continuous improvement, product specifications, warranty, and financial terms. Organizations like Wal-Mart and Toyota are known for their ability to use negotiation to obtain the lowest possible costs combined with high levels of service.

Preparation of purchase orders – After a need has been recognized and described, a supplier selected, and all of the necessary details regarding quantity, quality, price, and delivery are determined, a purchase order (PO) is issued. A purchase order specifies the terms and conditions of the purchase agreement and initiates supplier action. Assuring that every purchase order is filled out correctly is important because of the potential costs associated with fixing problems that result from inaccuracies in purchase orders. For example, the time and effort required to make up for mistakes such as filling in the wrong part number or specifying the wrong delivery time and place drives up purchasing costs and can negate the benefits of careful supplier selection and astute negotiating. Efforts to streamline the purchasing process have focused on reducing the paperwork associated with purchase orders and have led to the use of blanket orders. A blanket order specifies the overall terms of agreement for a given time period, usually one year, and covers the entire quantity to be purchased even though smaller quantities may be delivered periodically during the agreement. Once the blanket order is on file, the purchasing organization issues a materials release to trigger a new shipment. Because a blanket order promises the supplier future business, the purchaser often qualifies for a quantity discount. Today, purchase orders can be sent electronically by either an end-user or the purchasing department. The use of corporate procurement cards is another approach to reducing paperwork costs.

Follow-up and expediting – Purchasing must routinely follow-up with suppliers to make sure that they live up to the terms in the purchase agreement. Regular follow-up with suppliers helps identify quality or delivery problems as they arise. When problems occur, purchasing might increase the frequency and noise level of follow-up efforts; send personnel to work with the supplier; use higher-cost emergency transportation; arrange for delivery from an alternative supplier; or alter the purchasing organization's production schedule. Purchasing should consider the problem type, the order importance, and the nature of the purchaser/supplier relationship before deciding what action to take.

Expediting refers to efforts to speed up the delivery of an order. Expediting is necessary when an order is behind schedule but needed as originally promised or when the purchasing organization needs the order to be delivered ahead of schedule. A well-managed organization expedites only a small percentage of total shipments. If purchasing performs well, only suppliers capable of delivering as promised will be selected, and if production adequately plans its materials requirements, requests for early shipments should be rare. To avoid late delivery problems, many organizations now build penalty clauses into the purchasing agreement. One organization charges $5,000 for the first late delivery; $50,000 for the second late delivery; and removes the supplier from the approved list for a year after the third late delivery. Another organization has written its penalty clause so that suppliers have an incentive to communicate when problems arise so the two organizations can work together to eliminate the source of the delay. When a supplier fails to notify the organization of delivery problems, the monetary penalty is quite severe.

Receipt and inspection – When an order arrives at the purchasing organization, it must pass through a receiving process. The receiving process requires matching the invoice to the order contents. This involves a physical count and quality inspection. The objective is to make sure that the purchased inputs are fit for use. In most organizations, the receipt and inspection is actually managed by a separate organizational unit to assure an accurate and objective inspection. Purchasing is notified when an incoming shipment fails to pass inspection. Two primary reasons for failure are either too much or not enough was shipped, resulting in an incorrect count, or that the inputs do not meet quality standards. When an order does not meet specifications, purchasing must work with the supplier to correct the problem.

At many organizations, the use of certified or preferred suppliers has changed the receiving process. Purchasing works closely with key suppliers to help them achieve certification. Most certification programs focus primarily on improving the supplier's ability to produce high-quality products so that quality inspections can be eliminated. Making sure the supplier has the procedures and skills in place to deliver the right quantities on time is also a primary consideration in the certification process. Once the supplier achieves certification, incoming inspection is eliminated and incoming orders are moved immediately to incoming storage or directly to the production area where they will be used – from dock to stock. Inspections are only performed if problems occur at some point in the future. The benefits of certifying suppliers and streamlining receiving are better quality and reduced cycle times.

Invoice clearance and supplier payment – Suppliers deserve to be paid on time. Moreover, timely payment is critical to building good relationships with capable suppliers. In addition to helping maintain good purchaser/supplier relationships, developing efficient procedures for invoice clearance makes good financial sense because payment terms often include discounts for prompt payment. Actual payment is done by accounts payable, but purchasing should design a system that clears and submits the invoice to accounts payable as quickly as possible. Supplier certification combined with information technology can streamline the invoice clearance and payment process. When Ford redesigned its accounts payable process in the early 1990s, it adopted "invoiceless processing." When an order arrives, a computer database is checked to make sure that a corresponding order is expected. If a record of the order is found on the database, the order is accepted and accounts payable issues payment directly from the purchase order.

Performance monitoring and database management – Supplier performance should be tracked carefully and the purchasing database updated to provide purchasers with good information for future decisionmaking. Four types of information should be maintained in the database: the current status of all purchase orders; performance information for selected evaluation criteria for all suppliers; information on each part type or commodity; and information regarding all contracts and relationships. If a volume contract is in effect that commits the organization to a total annual volume, purchasing needs to know how much has been ordered to date. If a contract stipulates that the supplier will reduce the item price by 3 percent a year over the life of the relationship, purchasing needs to know whether or not the supplier is adhering to the contracted discount. Because information is critical to purchasing success, care should be given to designing and maintaining a database capable of providing accurate, relevant, and timely information.

When all nine steps in the purchasing process are performed well, purchasing can have a powerful competitive affect on an organization.

Why Is Purchasing Important? A Strategic Perspective

For much of the twentieth century, the process of acquiring materials was considered as somewhat of a nuisance. However, purchasing's role has had significant importance in recent years as its competitive affect has become more visible. For example, purchased inputs from raw materials to overnight mail now represent the single largest cost category for most organizations. Most manufacturing firms spend about 55 cents of each sales dollar on purchased goods and services.[3] This translates to approximately 60 to 80 percent of an organization's operating expenses. Table 1.1 shows that purchased inputs represent a sizable cost element in many industries. By comparison, direct labor costs have decreased to 5 to 10 percent of total operating costs in many industries. In some cases direct labor accounts for as little as 2 percent of operating costs. Purchasing decisions play an important role in determining the relative cost position of most organizations.

TABLE 1.1
Importance of Purchased Items – Purchased Inputs as a Percent of Sales, 1997

NAICS Code	Industry	Cost of Materials (1,000's)	Capital Expenditures (1,000's)	Materials & Capital Expenditures (1,000's)	Industry Shipments (1,000's)	Material Sales Ratio	Purchase Sales Ratio
311991	Perishable Prepared Food	1,357,722	124,723	1,482,445	2,740,447	0.50	0.54
313221	Narrow Fabric Mills	606,166	72,537	678,703	1,390,642	0.44	0.49
314992	Tire Cord and Tire Fabric	790,743	70,152	860,895	1,207,840	0.65	0.71
316992	Handbags and Purses	158,768	8,336	167,104	372,430	0.43	0.45
321211	Hardwood Veneer and Plywood	1,755,698	71,682	1,827,380	2,856,487	0.61	0.64
321991	Manufactured Home	6,105,063	137,052	6,242,115	10,167,746	0.60	0.61
322226	Surface-coated Paperboard	800,159	14,137	814,296	1,155,716	0.69	0.70
322232	Envelope Mfg.	1,882,776	145,487	2,028,263	3,582,016	0.53	0.57
325920	Explosives Mfg.	542,828	34,009	576,837	1,318,404	0.41	0.44
327113	Porcelain Electrical Supply	355,681	68,329	424,010	1,167,201	0.30	0.36
331511	Iron Foundries	5,174,792	512,167	5,686,959	12,266,373	0.42	0.46
332313	Plate Work Mfg.	1,190,533	78,103	1,268,636	2,707,463	0.44	0.47
333313	Office Machinery Mfg.	1,180,516	97,724	1,278,240	2,667,886	0.44	0.48
334111	Electronic Computer Mfg.	40,239,744	1,053,379	41,293,123	65,923,736	0.61	0.63
334417	Electronic Connector Mfg.	1,818,892	237,872	2,056,764	5,666,430	0.32	0.36
334419	Electronic Component Mfg.	4,385,786	424,939	4,810,725	10,375,635	0.42	0.46
335221	Household Cooking Appliance	1,754,600	120,678	1,875,278	3,540,221	0.50	0.53
335911	Storage Battery Mfg.	2,238,893	171,434	2,410,327	4,422,702	0.51	0.54
336212	Truck Trailer Mfg.	3,764,716	88,895	3,853,611	5,500,475	0.68	0.70
336611	Ship Building and Repairing	4,286,697	241,691	4,528,388	10,441,434	0.41	0.43
339920	Sporting and Athletic Goods	4,679,110	345,602	5,024,712	10,458,222	0.45	0.48

Source: U.S. Bureau of the Census, 1997 Economic Census (Washington, D.C.; U.S. Government Printing Office)

Service industries tend to be less materials dependent than manufacturers and often spend less on purchased inputs than manufacturing firms. However, service industries such as telecommunications still purchase material items such as, office supplies, maintenance, repair, and operating (MRO) items, clerical help, computer programming, overnight mail, and other services. The cost of these purchased inputs is often substantial. For example, purchased inputs represented 30 percent of AT&T's 1994 sales. Purchased services and MRO items accounted for 60 percent of AT&T's total purchasing bill.[4] The importance of purchasing extends beyond manufacturers to include service and non-profit organizations.

Clearly, the dollar value of purchased inputs is substantial. Equally important, the value-added affect of these goods and services has recently increased.[5] Today's manufacturers not only purchase raw materials and basic supplies but also purchase complex fabricated components and finished goods to which the organization's branded name is added. A focus on core competencies has also led many organizations to outsource value-added activities such as light assembly, inventory management, and distribution services.

The affect of purchasing on competitiveness in other areas is also significant. For example, quality expert Philip Crosby [6] claimed that up to 50 percent of an organization's quality problems could be traced to defective purchased materials. Likewise, in today's time-sensitive environment, purchasing has a huge opportunity to reduce replenishment cycle times and help an organization take time out of the new product development cycle through early supplier involvement. Clearly, in today's competitive supply environments, purchasing is well positioned to help an organization achieve greater strategic success. To better understand how purchasing can do this, a brief review of the nature of strategy is valuable.

What is Strategy?

The original Greek verb *stratego*, means, "to plan the destruction of one's enemies through the effective use of resources." Unfortunately, strategic management often yields less than the desired results because strategy is often defined and measured in terms of the competition. Competitive strategies become reactive in nature as they are always responding to the actions of key competitors. If using the organization's resources to beat the competition is not an effective strategy, then what constitutes an appropriate strategic mindset?

Perhaps the answer lies in looking forward to the customer instead of sideways at the competition. A real and effective strategic focus helps the organization meet the needs of customers; not just beat the competition. Sun Tzu observed that the smartest strategy in war is the one that achieves key objectives without having to go to battle. More recently, Kenichi Ohmae[7] noted,

> The visible clashing between companies in the marketplace – what mangers frequently think of as strategy – is but a small fragment of the strategic whole. Like an iceberg, most of strategy is submerged, hidden, out of sight. . . . most of it is intentionally invisible – beneath the surface where value gets created, where competition gets avoided.

The Elements of Strategy

Reviewing the elements of strategy helps to fully understand the relationship between strategy, value-addition, and meeting the real needs of customers. In a comparison of the duties of a military general and a business manager, Socrates showed Nichomachides that in each case the role of strategy is to plan the use of resources to meet objectives. Socrates thus identified the two central elements of strategy, resources and objectives, along with the elements of the environment and feedback.

- **Objectives** – An organization's foremost objective should be to create customer value. This requires that questions such as "What does our product do?" and "What are customers really looking for?" be revisited. After all, when customers purchase a product, the real intent is to purchase a set of satisfactions. Satisfactions emerge in two areas. First, satisfaction results from the interaction between the customer and the product's service component (this includes both the service used to deliver the product and the services that support the product after the sale). Second, the feelings engendered as the customer actually uses the product determine the level of satisfaction. Only by "getting into the minds" of customers can a manager discover the best approaches to delivering real value and real solutions that not only satisfies customers but helps them achieve higher levels of success.[8]

• **Resources** – The days when an organization's "brick and mortar" assets provided the best path to delivering customer value are long past. Today, investments in knowledge, technology, and processes hold the key to success. Truly hard-to-replicate capabilities are built on value-added processes that integrate human and technology resources. Wal-Mart, the world's largest retailer with 1998 sales of approximately $140 billion, established an inventory replenishment system that combines human resources, technology, and unique processes to meet customer needs.[9] Via cross-docking, Wal-Mart is able to purchase in economical lot sizes without incurring traditional inventory and handling costs. The resulting lower costs allow Wal-Mart to advertise "everyday low prices." However, cross-docking would not be possible without extensive infrastructural support, including a fleet of company-owned trucks and a satellite system that directly links Wal-Mart's retail outlets, distribution centers, and suppliers. This information and logistics capability also allows Wal-Mart to replenish its stores twice as often as its major competitors.

• **Environment** – Managers of value-added processes do not make decisions in a vacuum. Indeed, the need for strategic management emerged as the competitive environment changed from a relatively stable to a dynamic and intensely competitive environment. This same environmental change propelled purchasing from its historical clerical role to a more valued, more strategic function. Most managers implicitly consider external issues that arise from the competitive, economic, financial, and political environments. A fifth factor, national culture, plays an important role in international operations. While each of these areas affects performance, emphasis is usually placed on the competitive environment (see Figure 1.1). As organizations evaluate their competitive environment, most of the evaluation is directed toward understanding the industry structure and the affect of competitive drivers like quality and cost on the environment.[10] While the external environment is almost always considered in the strategy formulation process, the influence of the organization's internal environment is often overlooked. Company culture, functional relationships, and measurement systems affect an organization's ability to implement a value-added strategy. Indeed, these issues greatly influence the visibility of purchasing and its role in creating customer value.

FIGURE 1.1
Environmental Considerations

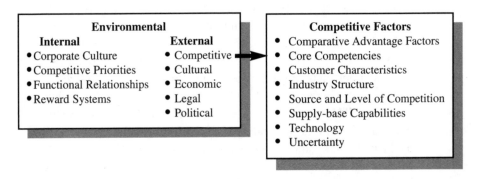

© Stanley E. Fawcett, Ph.D., C.P.M.

- **Feedback** – The fourth element of strategy emerges from the fact that internal capabilities develop and decline; customers' expectations change; competitors act and react; and the external environment changes quickly and often unpredictably (i.e., exchange rates fluctuate, governments enact new policies, technologies change, natural disasters strike). To help managers evaluate emerging threats and changing opportunities, a feedback mechanism is needed. Feedback allows purchasers to monitor the progress of the organization as it moves from its current competitive posture to its desired position, and allows an organization to modify its competitive approach to meet the demands of a changing world.

Competitive strategy has the following characteristics: an environmental analysis is performed to determine the organization's position in its field, and then the organization's resources are used to achieve key objectives. These same principles apply to purchasing strategy. When purchasing strategy is formulated and implemented appropriately, purchasing is able to mobilize its value-added capabilities to help the organization meet and exceed customer expectations.

Environment as a Driving Force in Purchasing Strategy

The development of a purchasing strategy that supports and advances corporate competitiveness depends on purchasing's ability to understand the organization's overall strategy and to analyze the affect of the four elements of strategy on purchasing decisions (see Table 1.2). For example, a premiere objective of purchasing organizations is to reduce costs. Extensive benchmarking is performed to assure that both the cost of goods purchased and purchasing administrative costs are in line with industry standards. Purchasing managers are then rewarded based on their ability to reduce costs to world-class levels. Much less managerial attention is focused on how purchasing can create unique customer value. Likewise, purchasing controls a large and important set of resources and capabilities that reside in the supply base. As outsourcing and supply chain integration initiatives gain momentum, purchasing's approach to developing and leveraging the supply base will influence, and in some cases determine, the organization's competitive viability. Unfortunately, while feedback involving purchasing is important, the excessive focus on costs has been too unidirectional. Purchasing has not played a strong enough role in sharing information and expertise with the rest of the organization. This limited-feedback position is changing as purchasing plays a more visible role in new product development, outsourcing, supply chain integration, and other value-added decisions. While the preceding issues must be factored into the development of a cohesive purchasing strategy, the supply environment's affect on purchasing strategy cannot be underestimated and merits specific attention.

TABLE 1.2
Aligning Purchasing to the Four Strategy Elements

Strategy Element	Common Purchasing Posture	Strategic Purchasing Focus
Objectives	Reduce purchase price Minimize administrative costs Meet needs of internal customers	Obtain lowest total cost of ownership Reengineer purchasing processes Act as a boundary spanning function Look to create customer value
Resources	Purchase the best inputs available Maintain appropriate supplier relationships	Purchase supplier capacity Develop supplier capabilities Build world-class supply base
Environment	React to environmental changes – view change largely as a challenge	View changes as both challenge and opportunity – leverage relationships and technology to create value
Feedback	Monitor supplier performance Maintain purchasing database One-way flow of information from users One-way flow of information to suppliers	Use performance data to help suppliers improve Data mining helps standardize and consolidate Actively participates in product design Two-way information and idea sharing

The evolution of purchasing strategy – Changes in the supply environment have propelled purchasing's emergence as a valued contributor to organizational success. (See Figure 1.2.) Before World War II (WWII), purchasing was viewed as a necessary but non-glamorous activity. For an organization to produce a product it had to have materials to use in the production process, but materials were widely available and labor represented the most important cost of doing business. Purchasing was viewed as a clerical activity in that orders needed to be processed to trigger the inflow of materials. During WWII, scarcity prevailed and greater emphasis on securing a steady flow of materials was needed to keep production lines running. Purchasing gained recognition as a legitimate managerial activity. For the next two decades, relatively little change occurred in the way organizations viewed their purchasing activities. Most organizations recognized that planning was essential to purchasing success. However, most of the planning activities were driven by events outside of purchasing. Purchasing operated on a largely reactive basis.

FIGURE 1.2
Timeline of Purchasing's Strategic Emergence

- **Pre World War II ▸▸ Purchasing was viewed as a clerical function**

- **WW II ▸▸ Purchasing receives increased emphasis**

- **1950-early 1970s ▸▸ Purchasing becomes a managerial function**

- **1973-mid 1980s ▸▸ Scarcity & inflation increase purchasing visibility**

- **1985-1995 ▸▸ JIT partnering makes purchasing quasi-strategic**

- **1995-Today ▸▸ Outsourcing and SCM make purchasing strategic**

Changes in the supply environment in the 1970s brought renewed interest to purchasing management. Perhaps the single most visible event in the early part of the decade was the Middle East oil embargo in the summer of 1973. The embargo exacerbated existing raw materials scarcity problems. In fact, scarcity combined with dramatic price increases provided purchasing an opportunity to show that it could have a positive affect on performance. Purchasing's challenge was to identify new sources of supply and manage increasingly complex purchaser/supplier relationships. Top management began to view purchasing's value in a competitive market, placing it in a new, more favorable light.

The perception of purchasing as a competitive weapon continued to emerge gradually throughout the 1980s and early 1990s as purchased inputs became a primary operating cost. The transformation of purchasing into a strategic function was promoted by two important developments. First, better trained and more competent managers began to enter the purchasing arena. Second, the advent of new information technologies made it possible to store and track the large amounts of information needed to strategically manage purchaser/supplier relationships. The combination of more highly trained managers, better technology, and greater organizational support allowed purchasing to assume a proactive role in helping organizations meet new competitive challenges.

Purchasing strategy as a competitive weapon – The supply environment of the 1990s continued to pressure purchasing strategy to add even greater value. Purchasing's ability to successfully manage four trends elevated purchasing strategy to a higher profile position. The four trends that redefined purchasing strategy are the reduction of the supplier base; an increase in purchaser/supplier partnering; an expansion in the range of purchased items; and the increased involvement of suppliers in new product development programs. Each of these issues has influenced the management of purchasing activities by changing both what purchasing must do as well as how well purchasing must perform to help the organization compete. These trends are briefly discussed below.

- **Supply-base reduction** – During the late 1980s, purchasers began to consider the costs of competition-based relationships and realized that purchasing from a single source could provide substantial benefits. By reducing the size of the supply base and working closely with the remaining suppliers, total cost could be reduced, quality enhanced, service responsiveness improved, and product design time reduced. To ensure that single-source suppliers are capable of meeting required performance levels, rigorous supplier screening and certification almost always accompanies supply-base reduction. Organizations can dedicate the resources to develop high-performing suppliers because they dramatically reduce the total number of suppliers they work with. For example, Xerox reduced its global supply base by 90 percent from about 5,000 suppliers to just over 400 suppliers, saving $100 million annually on purchased inputs.[11] A major challenge is to establish the right type of relationship with individual suppliers to meet the needs of an ever-changing competitive environment.

• **Supply partnerships** – The success many organizations experienced with improved purchaser/supplier relationships led them to develop more fully integrated supply partnerships. Some of the characteristics of purchaser/supplier partnerships are contrasted with the characteristics of more-traditional relationships in Table 1.3. These characteristics point out that a high degree of planning and cooperation is required to build successful alliances. Alliance building implies very close working relationships. The boundaries between the purchaser and supplier tend to become blurred as the value-added processes of the two organizations become integrated. A clearly defined approach to sharing risks and benefits has been identified as critical to establishing a strong alliance foundation. Realistic alliances look to the future to consider the circumstances that might call for the end of the alliance and include provisions for terminating the alliance.[12] Many analysts suggest that alliances will become critical to long-term survival in today's intensely competitive and dynamic marketplace. Boston Consulting Group's Harold Sirkin observed that competition among supply alliances is becoming the norm. "As the economy changes, as competition becomes more global, it's no longer 'company versus company' but 'supply chain versus supply chain'."[13]

TABLE 1.3
Characteristics of Supply Partnerships

Characteristics of Partnering	Characteristics of Traditional Relationships
Continual improvement	One contract at a time
Win-win	Win-lose
Long-term perspective	Immediate returns emphasized
Trust/sharing	Secretive/little or no sharing
Proactive, problem-solving orientation	Crisis-driven interaction
Top management involvement	No top management involvement
Frequent interaction	Interaction at contract time or when problems arise
Strategic fit exists	Current needs can be met
Total cost approach	Lowest purchase price directive
Emphasis on technology development	Technology is closely guarded
Emphasis on training	Skill building not actively supported
Constructive performance evaluation	Little evaluation except for criticism
Strong commitment to the relationship	No commitment to the relationship
Supply-base reduction	Multiple suppliers
Safety in knowledge	Safety in numbers and contracts
Use cross-functional teams	Focus only on purchaser-sales relationship
Early supplier involvement	No early involvement
Quality at source	Quality inspected in
Information replaces inventory	Inventory used as safeguard

- **Expanded range of responsibility** – Purchasing's expanded responsibility has occurred because organizations have more closely defined their own core competencies. Some organizations, like athletic footwear giant Nike, have decided that what they do best is design and market products. These organizations purchase most or all of their product line. Nike does not manufacture any of the athletic shoes that it sells. Other companies purchase finished goods to round out existing product lines. An organization that has expertise in design and marketing but no control over production must manage the purchaser/supplier relationship very carefully to assure high quality and outstanding customer satisfaction. Throughout the 1990s organizations began purchasing a wider range of services including accounting, advertising, communications, computer programming, consulting, customs brokerage, freight forwarding, insurance, janitorial, legal, research, security, secretarial, transportation, and third-party logistics. While the techniques used to identify and select service suppliers are similar to those used in the purchase of physical goods, purchasers had to develop new knowledge in order to make good purchase decisions. The fact that services cannot be inventoried greatly increases the importance of making good purchasing decisions.

- **Involvement in new product development** – The ability to bring new products to market quickly became a vital component of many organizations' competitive strategies during the 1990s. To reduce concept-to-market time, many organizations implemented integrated product development teams that brought marketing, manufacturing, and engineering together to develop superior products. The use of teams gave purchasing an opportunity to be more involved in the new product-development process. Many organizations have sought to get both customers and suppliers involved in the early stages of product development. Customers are included in the process to generate better and more timely feedback related to the product design. Suppliers are included in the development process because they frequently possess design and technology expertise. Purchasing must work closely with suppliers to leverage suppliers' involvement on these new product design teams. Purchasing's facilitator role has strengthened because competition has continued to place a premium on more rapid innovation. This trend is likely to continue into the foreseeable future.

To summarize, purchasing's ability to scan the environment and take on new roles and responsibilities that help the organization meet customers' demands for high-quality, innovative products at lower prices has led purchasing to be recognized as a critical value-added activity. Senior corporate managers now realize that purchasing managers must possess highly developed skills and substantial managerial judgment to not only build and manage a world-class supply base, but to work closely with other areas within the organization. Successful purchasing managers must grasp the ramifications of a constantly changing supply environment; recognize sourcing alternatives; assess a wide range of tradeoffs; and balance both the short- and long-term requirements of the organization. Now that purchasing is recognized as a value-added activity, its future evolution will depend on how purchasers manage the challenges and opportunities of a constantly changing supply environment.

Forces Driving the Supply Environment

Purchasing's new found credibility as a competitive weapon comes at an opportune time because today's competitive environment is as challenging as ever. The competitive and supply environments share several characteristics that require adept management and careful resource allocation. Simply stated, the environment is increasingly global, intensely competitive, extremely dynamic, intractably complex, and incredibly uncertain. Within this environment, managers must spend considerable time in scanning and planning activities. Scanning is vital for purchasers to understand evolving competitive, industry, and supply environments. Planning is necessary to create a common vision and to marshal resources in a way that mitigates threats and capitalizes on opportunities. In short, organizations must scan and plan in order to select and build the right competitive capabilities. This endeavor is the essence of strategy, and strategic purchasing can help an organization survive and prosper in an ever-changing world.

The following six forces are influencing the supply environment and altering the way purchasing managers do business. Table 1.4 matches the six forces with the steps in the purchasing process.

- **Economic globalization** – Purchasers have more options but face new challenges in the form of communication, culture, distance, and documentation. They must be globally knowledgeable and very flexible to succeed in a global environment.
- **Time compression** – The just-in-time revolution that began in the 1980s lives on and is embodied in several popular strategic initiatives: quick response, efficient consumer response, continuous replenishment programs, supplier managed replenishment, and concurrent engineering. Each of these techniques is founded on

the JIT philosophy of eliminating waste. Wasted time and effort are the primary targets of the improvement efforts. Purchasing mangers possess the knowledge, skills, and external relationships needed to eliminate waste and compress cycle times.

- **Rising customer expectations** – Customer expectations have steadily increased over the past decade. Customers throughout the supply chain expect near perfect quality, immediate responsiveness, universal availability, and continual innovation. Moreover, they expect all of this at the same or lower cost levels. Meeting expectations while overcoming or mitigating inherent performance tradeoffs will be a huge challenge for purchasing managers.

- **Process management** – Business process reengineering was perhaps the hottest management tool of the early 1990s. Reengineering promised more effective and efficient processes through the application of new information technologies and the breaking down of functional silos. While reengineering per se has lost some of its momentum, emphasis continues to be placed on cross-functional process integration. Purchasers need to understand when and how they can participate in effective process integration to advance the development of unique value-added capabilities.

- **Supply chain integration** – Supply chain integration is the design and management of seamless value-added processes across channel members and is vital to meeting the competitive and market demands present in a global economy. In such a world, where competition is no longer "company versus company" but "supply chain versus supply chain," purchasing mangers take on a key role in bringing together the best possible supply team. Purchasers must learn to interface better with other channel members as well as governmental and other agencies that influence supply chain design.

- **Technological innovation** – Technological innovation is one thread that ties the other environmental forces together. Technology has helped to shrink the world, facilitated time compression, driven customers' demands for superior performance, propelled reengineering, and enabled supply chain integration. Unfortunately, the rapid nature of technological change has created one fundamental challenge for purchasing mangers – how can they harness technology in each step of the purchasing process to achieve the greatest competitive edge?

TABLE 1. 4
Tomorrow's Supply Environment and the Purchasing Process

Steps in the Purchasing Process	Supply Environment Forces
Recognition of Need	Cultural differences require product customization Technology enables the automation of routine purchases Consolidate common parts via purchasing database analysis Better internal coordination leads to reduced communication cycle times Better external coordination leads to reduced fufillment cycle times
Description of Need	Language and culture make communication more difficult in global purchases Time compression requires better information sharing Early supplier involvement creates better understanding of needs Technology facilitates the sharing of information such as blueprints
Supplier Selection and Development	Must identify and examine suppliers from around the world Must evaluate suppliers' capacity and ability to meet global needs Performance expectations are constantly increasing Greater emphasis on time and value-added capabilities More active involvement in developing supplier capabilities Suppliers are increasingly viewed as part of an extended enterprise
Determination of Price	Better understanding of exchange rates is needed Greater emphasis on total cost of ownership The cost versus value relationship requires more tradeoff analysis Cross-cultural negotiation skills become more important Global consolidation increases volumes and leverage
Preparation of Purchase Order	Language and cultural differences require greater clarity Greater use of blanket orders with localized materials release The preparation of purchase orders is computerized Orders of standard items are placed automatically via EDI or Extranets
Follow-up and Expediting	Global purchasing often increases distances and leadtimes Time compression requires just-in-time delivery Ever shorter fulfillment cycles and greater responsiveness are desired Technology enables better product tracking and expediting
Receipt and Inspection	Global purchasing places premium on accurate documentation Supplier certification eliminates need for incoming inspection Receiving process reengineered to enable "dock-to-stock" capability Technology makes receiving process transparent Closer supply chain relationships allow supplier-managed replenishment

8. Blackwell, R.D. *From Mind to Market: Reinventing the Retail Supply Chain*, Harper Business, New York, NY, 1997.

9. Stalk, G., P. Evans, and L.E. Schulman. "Competing on Capabilities: The New Rules of Corporate Strategy," *Harvard Business Review*, (70:2), 1992, pp. 57-69.

10. Porter, M. *Competitive Strategy*, The Free Press, New York, NY, 1980; Hayes, R., S.C. Wheelwright, and K.B. Clark. *Dynamic Manufacturing: Creating the Learning Organization*, The Free Press, New York, NY, 1988.

11. McGrath, M. and R. Hoole. "Manufacturing's New Economies of Scale," *Harvard Business Review*, (70:3), 1992, pp. 94-102.

12. Bowersox, D.J., R.J. Calantone, S.R. Clinton, D.J. Closs, M.B. Cooper, C.L. Droge, S.E. Fawcett, R. Frankel, D.J. Frayer, E.A. Morash, L.M. Rinehart, and J.M. Schmitz. *World Class Logistics: The Challenge of Managing Continuous Change*, Council of Logistics Management, Oak Brook, IL 1995.

13. Henkoff, R. "Delivering the Goods," *Fortune*, November 28, 1994, pp. 64-78.

CHAPTER 2

THE GLOBALIZATION OF THE SUPPLY ENVIRONMENT

What do I need to know to succeed?

Chapter Objectives

This chapter is designed to help the purchaser:

- Understand the implications and imperatives of a global supply environment.
- Recognize purchasing's role in global network design and management.
- Understand how to organize purchasing to leverage global volumes while achieving flexibility.
- View the world as a global market where the best source can be found outside the home country.
- Develop more effective global sourcing strategies.

The Globalization of Markets

Globalization has been described as one of the most important and dramatic changes in the business environment this century. Globalization is likely irreversible and the idea that a domestic entity can exist in isolation, unaffected by the other players in an increasingly global supply environment, has all but disappeared. For example, the U.S. economy sustained growth without inflation throughout the economic expansion of the 1990s in part because of a huge influx of low-cost imports. At the same time, U.S. steel and apple producers faced some of the fiercest price competition in memory because low-

29

cost apples and steel were readily imported from global suppliers. Elsewhere, macroeconomic events such as the introduction of the Euro as the European Union's single currency and China's entry into the World Trade Organization influenced government policy and corporate strategy. These events affect consumer and supply markets worldwide. Globalization has changed the nature of industrial competition and the role of purchasing in providing a competitive advantage. As globalization progresses, new rules have emerged and purchasing mangers need to adopt a more global perspective to meet new competitive challenges.

Forces Driving Globalization

The rate of transition to a global economy has been increasing for many years as technological advances have made the world smaller. The first pervasive technology to propel globalization was the television. As early as 1983, Theodore Levitt,[1] a Harvard marketing professor, argued that television had changed the world, "It has made isolated places and impoverished peoples eager for modernity's allurements." Levitt obviously overstated the extent to which technology had overcome cultural influences; nevertheless, he did correctly forecast that worldwide consumers would soon expect the latest innovation coupled with superior quality and low cost. By the 1990s, consumers' experiences, vicarious through television and via personal travel, had led them to want the best that was available anywhere in the world. It has even been said that the Eastern Block's thirst for Coca-Cola and Levi's brought down the Berlin Wall.

The world has become more accessible over the past 25 years, and the process of globalization continues. Today, as in the past, the pace of economic globalization depends on three principal forces: the ability to share information, the availability of reliable transportation, and the extent of regulation.

Information as a driving force – Today, telephones, faxes, satellites, and e-mail make worldwide communication common and relatively inexpensive. The Internet is gaining popularity and will eventually live up to its moniker and become a truly World Wide Web bringing the latest news, fads, and fashions into homes and businesses worldwide. As communication systems improve, organization's can better coordinate operations in multiple locations around the world. Managers are better able to track competitors' actions and purchasers are better able to comparison shop. The time between first action and competitive response is drastically reduced. Digital communication is changing capabilities.

Logistics as a driving force – Today's logistics systems provide more consistent, reliable, and timely service at known, affordable prices. The selective use of air freight, the development of "fast ships," better service from third-party intermediaries, and streamlined customs clearance have all reduced the uncertainty and variability both in scheduling and in transportation costs. Information technology has also greatly enhanced logistical coordination. Advanced shipping notices, global geographic tracking systems, and electronic customs clearance all increase the manageability of logistics operations. Organizations can more accurately and affordably schedule the movement of physical goods to and from diverse locations around the world. Better logistics have greatly lowered the barriers to a globally integrated economy.

Government intervention as an impediment – While economic borders have eroded, political borders remain. Organizations continue to rely on their home governments for assistance as they seek advantage in a global marketplace. While government intervention remains as the last great structural impediment to a global economy, the long-term trend has been to reduce protectionist practices. Since World War II, the General Agreement on Tariffs and Trade (GATT) has been effective at reducing tariffs and other barriers to the free flow of goods. By the beginning of the 1990s, worldwide tariffs averaged less than 5 percent (down from 40 percent in 1947). GATT's successor, the World Trade Organization (WTO), has continued to work to reduce tariffs and other protectionist practices among its 130 plus signatory countries. However, the WTO has yet to prove that it can effectively resolve disputes and pave the way to lower levels of protectionism.

Competitive Implications of Globalization

It has become apparent that the world's economies are more integrated and therefore more interdependent. Purchasers who correctly identify and understand the immediate and longer-term implications of globalization will be in position to help their organizations achieve unparalleled success. By contrast, those managers who do not anticipate the affect of globalization are likely to be overtaken by the challenges of globalization and miss out on its opportunities. At least three implications should be recognized by purchasers and factored into their strategic thinking: competition will intensify; global markets will become increasingly important; and domestic and global business is different.

Intensified competition – The most visible implication of globalization is intensified competition. The threat of global competition became apparent in the late 1970s as the U.S. consumer electronics and steel industries came under siege from international rivals. By the early 1980s, the automobile industry was also under attack. The term "rust belt" emerged to describe America's decimated industrial heartland where tens of thousands of American workers had lost their jobs because their organizations could not compete with global rivals. From the perspective of U.S. industry, organizations like Nippon Steel, Sony, and Toyota were unbelievably efficient and produced high-quality products; but they also resorted to "unfair" advantages such as low-cost labor and low interest rates. The competitive threat spurred a debate on free versus fair trade that continues to this day.

By the 1980s, international competition had arrived. In 1990, 70 percent of all U.S. industry had competition from foreign rivals. Today, serious global competitors exist in almost every industry. International competition comes from several different sources. Global competitors like Nokia and Unilever possess the capital and technology needed to challenge U.S. organizations in markets around the world. Competitors from less developed countries typically have access to incredibly low-cost labor. Because industrialization and export-led growth provides needed employment, these foreign competitors often receive some form of government support. Leading organizations from around the world have learned to succeed in this new competitive environment by increasing productivity, enhancing quality, compressing cycle times, and emphasizing innovation. Intense competition is the one constant in a global economy. Andrew Grove, former CEO of Intel, has noted:

> Business knows no national boundaries. Capital and work – your work! – can go anywhere on earth. The consequence of all this is painfully simple: If the world operates as one big market, every employee will compete with every person in the world who is capable of doing the same job. There are a lot of them, and many of them are very hungry.[2]

Globalized markets – Globalization has changed consumer behavior, leading to the creation of global market segments that cross geographic and cultural boundaries. Educational background and disposable income are now pervasive drivers of consumer behavior, often eclipsing cultural and ethnic characteristics as factors that motivate purchase decisions. This affect is particularly prevalent among the educated and affluent market segment of over 700 million consumers who live in industrialized nations with per capita gross domestic products approaching $20,000 or more (see Table 2.1). Highly educated and affluent consumers in Europe, Japan, the United States and elsewhere form a market with very similar wants and needs. The commonality of wants is strongest in high-tech, durable, and consumer packaged products. Because the spending potential of this affluent global market dwarfs that of any single home-country market, managers must consider approaching these markets simultaneously to capture the scale economies needed to secure a competitive position. This reality has led many companies like Procter & Gamble to reorganize in order to develop truly global brands.[3]

Given the affluence of the industrialized nations combined with the sheer size and rapid growth of the emerging markets, it is not surprising that many organizations now find that much of their sales and profit growth comes from global markets.

Even as global consumer markets have emerged, global supply markets have come into existence. Purchasers now scour the world looking for the best possible mix of inputs. For many years, the emphasis was on finding low-cost labor. Organizations would "island hop" from country to country in search of lower labor costs. With Mexican labor costs below $2 per hour, Mexico became host to over 2,000 Maquiladoras (low-cost assemblers of components and finished goods.)[4] Even lower wage rates in China, Thailand, Vietnam, and other Asian countries have attracted large amounts of foreign direct investment. Almost all of Nike's contract manufacturing capacity is located in Southeast Asia. The quest for the best inputs extends beyond labor to raw materials, technologically sophisticated components, and capital equipment. General Motors recently used a global target costing campaign to obtain the lowest price for critical die tooling for its stamping operations. After completing a world negotiating tour, GM sourced its dies from a new Korean supplier as well as an established German supplier.[5] As leading organizations now know, the failure to look to worldwide sources for labor, materials, and technology deprives an organization of the resources needed to compete.

The Supply Management Environment

TABLE 2.1
Demographic and Economic Statistics for
Countries Around the World (1997)

Industrialized Economies:

	Area (km sq)	Population (x1,000)	GDP ($Billion)	GDP/ Capita	Exports ($Billion)
Australia	7,686,850	18,613	394	21,400	68.0
Austria	83,850	8,060	206	21,395	57.1
Belgium	30,510	10,157	242	21,856	168.4
Denmark	43,070	5,262	163	22,418	50.7
Finland	337,030	5,125	117	18,879	40.6
France	547,030	58,380	1,393	20,533	284.0
Germany	356,910	81,877	2,115	21,200	512.7
Hong Kong	1,040	6,706	175	26,800	180.7
Ireland	70,280	3,621	72	18,988	48.2
Italy	301,230	57,473	1,146	19,974	250.8
Japan	377,835	125,864	4,223	23,235	410.9
Luxembourg	2,566	418	15	32,416	168.4
Netherlands	37,290	15,494	362	20,905	177.4
New Zealand	268,680	3,625	63	17,700	18.5
Singapore	632	3,490	84	24,600	125.6
Sweden	449,964	8,901	229	19,258	82.9
United Kingdom	244,820	58,782	1,278	18,636	258.9
United States	9,372,610	265,557	7,819	27,821	582.1
Total	**20,212,197**	**737,405**	**20,104**	**23,959**	**3,486**

Emerging Economies:

	Area (km sq)	Population (x1,000)	GDP ($Billion)	GDP/ Capita	Exports ($Billion)
Argentina	2,766	36,265	348	9,700	25.4
Brazil	8,512	169,807	1,040	6,300	53.0
Chile	756	14,788	168	11,600	16.9
China	9,596,000	1,236,914	4,250	3,460	182.7
Czech Republic	78	10,286	111	10,800	21.7
Hungary	93	10,208	73	7,400	16.0
India	3,287,000	984,004	1,534	1,600	33.9
Indonesia	1,919,400	212,941	960	4,600	53.4
Korea	98,480	46,416	631	13,700	129.8
Malaysia	329,800	20,933	227	11,100	78.2
Mexico	742,486	98,000	694	7,700	110
Peru	1,285	26,111	110	4,420	5.9
Philippines	300,000	77,725	244	3,200	25.0
Poland	312	38,607	280	7,250	26.4
Russia	17,075	146,861	692	4,700	86.7
Slovakia	48	5,393	46	8,600	8.8
Taiwan	35,980	21,908	308	14,200	122.1
Thailand	514,000	60,037	525	8,800	51.6
Uruguay	176.2	3,285	29	8,900	2.7
Venezuela	912	22,803	185	8,300	20.8
Total	**16,855,163**	**3,243,292**	**12,459**	**3,908**	**1,071.5**

Source: Central Intelligence Agency, The World Factbook, 1998; OECD in Figures, Statistics on the Member Countries, 1998 Edition.

Domestic and global business are different – The fact that global and domestic business are conducted differently too often escapes the thought process behind the design of a global network or the decision to source globally. The real challenge is in the intricacies involved in managing across borders. Four areas provide much of the difference and the detail that must be understood and managed by the purchasing organization for lasting global success.

- **Political issues** – Political issues vary dramatically from country to country. The most important political issue is political stability. The violence in Indonesia that resulted from the currency devaluation of 1998, and the 1999 India/Pakistan confrontation over Kashmir highlight the need to assess current stability while examining the undercurrents that might suddenly put a global business strategy in jeopardy. Another vital political issue for purchasers involves establishing the right contacts and relationships to facilitate business. The Chinese word "quanchie" means relationship and suggests reciprocity at the highest levels. If senior management is not willing to invest the time needed to build the right relationships, bureaucratic hurdles can stop business in its tracks. Building the right relationships is critical to success in many parts of the world including Asia, Central Europe, and South America.

- **Legal issues** – Legalities differ from country to country. For example, in France, English advertising is banned and in Singapore, chewing gum is prohibited. Such details increase the emotional and monetary costs of doing business globally. A more substantive legal issue involves bribery. In some countries, bribery is a prerequisite to relationship building. A purchaser would want to know this before selecting a supplier in such a country. Other legal issues that complicate global business include diverse product liability standards, unique documentation requirements, confusing labor laws (it might be impossible to fire an employee), domestic content regulations, and confounding advertising laws (direct product comparisons might be illegal). Obtaining competent legal counsel is vital to the success of an organization's global endeavors.

- **Financial issues** – Financial differences can determine the profitability of global operations. Exchange rates are the most visible financial issue. Because every international transaction is susceptible to fluctuating exchange rates, purchasers should establish a reasonable currency strategy to reduce the organization's exposure to exchange rate risk. Taxation is another issue that can make or break the profitability of global operations. The complexity, nuance, and vagary of national tax laws require expert assistance. Currency convertibility and repatriation of profits also need to be considered.
- **Cultural issues** – Cultural norms vary dramatically from country to country and pervade every aspect of behavior. Cultural differences affect the way people view time, personal space, communication, worker/manager relations, and individual accountability. Global communication and travel have reduced behavioral gaps. However, cultural norms are deeply imbedded and change slowly. Understanding cultural issues, especially as they undergo constant transition can be a difficult challenge. Purchasers who do their homework up front, are constantly observant, and are willing to adapt, find that cultural quagmires can be safely navigated.

When purchasers understand the difference between domestic and global business, they are more fully prepared to face the challenges of globalization, find opportunities, and help their organizations gain a sustainable competitive advantage.

The Affect on the Purchasing and Supply Manager

Purchasers need to recognize the pervasive influence of globalization, develop new knowledge sets, and act proactively and globally to support their organization's competitive efforts.

- Purchasing's main role is to acquire the best set of materials and services to support the organization's operations and strategy, regardless of where these resources are found.
- Sometimes the best suppliers, newest technology, or most advanced processes are found outside the home market. The

quest for core competence and operational excellence means that an organization must have access to these resources.

- Organizations are increasing their manufacturing and marketing activities in countries outside their home markets.

Supporting a Global Network

In today's world, organizations must establish some semblance of global presence, if only to protect home markets from global rivals. If an organization is going to enter the global arena, managers should look at how specific investments support the overall competitive strategy as well as how they affect the organization's global operating network. The success of any global network depends on how effectively the organization rationalizes its productive activities; that is, how well the organization assigns each value-added activity to the appropriate area of the world. Appropriateness is defined in terms of either comparative advantage or market access.

Most global strategies can be classified as either factor-driven or market-driven (see Figure 2.1). Factor-driven strategies seek to gain access to worldwide resources – often inexpensive labor – in order to improve the organization's overall cost position. A classic U.S. example of rationalization involves the electronics organization that moves assembly and production activities of labor-intensive components to another country with abundant and inexpensive labor such as Malaysia or Mexico. Knowledge and capital intensive activities are maintained in the U.S. market. Market-access strategies seek to increase the organization's global market share. Organizations do this by overcoming the physical and emotional barriers that impede international market entry and development. For example, Honda, Nissan, and Toyota established assembly facilities in the U.S. in order to establish a local presence and circumvent the quotas that had been established in the early 1980s. In the longer term, these Japanese automakers hoped to be perceived as local organizations and thus mitigate the negative feelings sometimes associated with global organizations. Most organizations incorporate aspects of both strategies in their worldwide operations – using a "best mix" of worldwide resources to deliver distinctive products to worldwide customers.

FIGURE 2.1
Global Network Design

Factor-Input Strategy

Objective — Access low-cost inputs

Example — Technology organizations (i.e., HP, Intel, and TI)

Implication — Manage functional performance tradeoffs

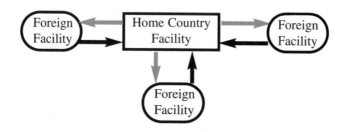

☐ Information, Raw Materials, Components or Capital

■ Finished Goods or Acquired Inputs

Market Access Strategy

Objective — Avoid tariffs and establish presence

Example — Automobile manufacturers (i.e., Honda and Toyota)

Implication — Provide materials support to the transplants

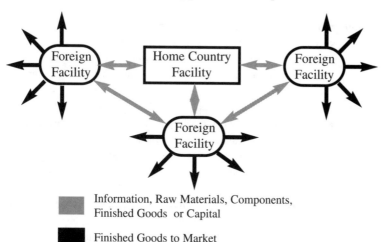

☐ Information, Raw Materials, Components,
Finished Goods or Capital

■ Finished Goods to Market

© Stanley E. Fawcett, Ph.D., C.P.M.

Whatever the strategic nature and complexity of the global network, purchasing should participate in the network design because purchasers will ultimately have to provide materials support to the resulting global operations. And a well-designed network is much more easily and efficiently supported than a tangled web of operations dispersed across the world. Unfortunately, many organizations have established tangled networks by default – they have built their networks incrementally without fully considering the interconnectedness and tradeoffs inherent in global operations. Purchasing's involvement in four specific decision areas related to network design and management can help the organization achieve efficient and competitive global operations. The four decision areas are Compatibility, Configuration, Coordination, and Control. Table 2.2 highlights some purchasing issues that should be factored into global network design and management decisions.

TABLE 2.2
Purchasing and the Four Cs of Global Network Design

The Four Cs	Purchasing Decisions
Compatibility	• Is direct investment really needed or can a virtual solution work? • Can purchasing support the new operation efficiently and effectively? • Can existing suppliers be used? Should co-location be considered? • Can a local supply base be developed? Can domestic content rules be met?
Configuration	• Should the organization make or buy a given component? • Where should decisionmaking authority reside? • How many suppliers should be used worldwide? • What type of relationship is going to be used with foreign suppliers?
Coordination	• What are the most appropriate supplier selection criteria? • How is market and/or commodity knowledge going to be transferred worldwide? • How can commonalities be leveraged across dispersed operations? • How are materials going to be shipped to and from each operation? • Can purchasing realistically manage and develop suppliers worldwide?
Control	• What is the total cost of providing materials support for the global operations? • Can quality be maintained and improved across a global supply base? • Can delivery be assured given the nature and location of the supply base? • How are orders going to be released? Tracked? Resolved when necessary?

Compatibility – Compatibility needs to be assessed from a more holistic view than many organizations currently employ. Is the investment really needed and is there a close fit between the organization's rationale for making the investment and the country's inherent advantage? Can the operation be efficiently integrated into the existing network? Purchasing's primary contribution to the compatibility decision is to determine whether or not purchasing can provide cost-effective support for the proposed operation. Strategic compatibility is the first test of viability.

Configuration and coordination – Configuration focuses on the location of manufacturing and marketing operations. Coordination involves the linking or integration of the operations into a unified system. Synergies occur when configuration and coordination issues are considered simultaneously. Experience has shown that network performance declines when configuration issues take precedence in the design process.[6] Purchasing issues, including the number and location of suppliers, can be dramatically affected by a decision to locate a facility in a given country. As a result, the cost, quality, and delivery of inputs can be adversely affected. Purchasing administrative costs might also escalate. The ability to work with suppliers to build close partnerships and to help them achieve world-class performance can also be hindered. Because purchasing's performance influences the success or failure of a global network, purchasers should be proactively involved in configuration and coordination decisions.

Control – The success of global operations depends on the ability to obtain high levels of operational performance on a daily basis. Poor on-site control can lead to disappointing results. Global operations are generally more difficult to manage than domestic operations because of cultural and other environmental differences. Purchasers face serious challenges as they manage suppliers worldwide and work to support day-to-day operations of geographically dispersed activities. For instance, differences in language, reward systems, workforce relations, and infrastructure are among the issues purchasers must deal with on a daily basis to ensure delivery of world-class inputs throughout a global network.

By systematically assessing the issues associated with the four Cs of network design, purchasers can gain the understanding necessary to help design superior networks. Purchasing managers can then deliver exceptional value as they provide materials support for the organization's global operations.

Establishing a Virtual Network

While organizations of all types use global networks to enhance competitiveness and gain market access, such operations require extensive financial investment and can be difficult to manage. Global networks can also limit flexibility – once a facility is built, it cannot be easily moved to the newest, best location. Further, once an investment is made, the organization loses its primary source of negotiating leverage with the host-country government. Therefore, more and more organizations are turning to global sourcing to allow them to take full advantage of worldwide resources while maintaining maximum flexibility and avoiding large up-front investments. Developing a global supply network also helps the organization gain valuable experience in a given region without incurring the risk of foreign direct investment.

The amount of global outsourcing organizations engage in varies greatly. Some organizations source only one or two raw materials or components from global suppliers; others outsource almost all of the value-added manufacturing to the best suppliers available worldwide. For example, Deere & Company has generally relied on a domestic supply base, using global suppliers sparingly in an effort to contain costs. By contrast, Boeing outsources nose, fuselage, and tail assemblies to Korean and Chinese suppliers. Boeing has adopted this strategy in part to reduce costs but also to gain orders from government-owned airlines throughout Asia. This strategy is leading Boeing to become an engineering design and final assembly organization. Nike represents an extreme. Nike does not operate any significant manufacturing or assembly capacity of its own. Rather, Nike outsources all of its manufacturing requirements to a few Asian subcontractors that operate manufacturing facilities throughout Asia. Having made the decision to be a virtual manufacturer, Nike has become a design and marketing organization.

The challenge for most organizations is to decide what mix of value-added activities they need to perform and then to design a global network that efficiently brings the correct resources together. For most organizations, the right global network will be part physical and part virtual. Existing trends suggest that all non-core activities will be performed by someone else, often somewhere else in the world.

Organizing for Leverage and Responsiveness

One of the great challenges of global operations is that of organization. With facilities located in diverse countries around the world, and each facility having its own purchasing requirements, where should purchasing decisions be made to achieve maximum value? Three primary options exist. Purchasing decisions can be made at the local facility level, at the strategic business unit level, or by a central purchasing group based at corporate headquarters. Pros and cons exist for both decentralized and centralized purchasing organizations. The primary benefits of decentralization are increased facility control over purchases; better responsiveness to facility needs; and more effective use of local suppliers. No one knows the needs of the unit better than managers in the unit. Likewise, no one is in better position to know the local supply base better than a purchasing manager at the facility. The principal drawbacks of decentralized sourcing are the loss of leverage with suppliers because smaller volumes are purchased, and the duplication of purchasing efforts throughout the organization.

Consolidated purchase volumes through centralized purchasing create leverage and allow suppliers to take advantage of production economies of scale, which create savings that can be passed on to the purchaser. Thomas Stallkamp, the former Chrysler procurement head, noted the importance of centralization, "The advantages of decentralization don't show up in purchasing. We centralize purchasing to get the best prices from suppliers." [7] Administrative duplication is also reduced through centralization. Only one purchase order needs to be filled out for any item such as light bulbs, memory chips, or plastic tubing. Further, purchasers can develop specialized knowledge in purchasing techniques as well as in commodity or technology areas. Another benefit of consolidation is the opportunity to reduce the number of items purchased through greater standardization. Centralization makes it much easier to establish and manage a common database of purchased items and capable suppliers. Finally, centralization makes it easier to build supplier-partner relationships. Through greater coordination of requirements, a centralized purchasing organization can reduce the total number of suppliers used. Supply-base reduction frees up time to spend on key relationships. Suppliers also benefit from larger volumes and better coordination, which helps build closer relationships.

For several years, the trend has been toward centralization Some organizations have bounced back and forth between centralized and decentralized organizations as they have sought to obtain the benefits of both. The challenge encountered is one of coordinating and consolidating requirements while maintaining maximum flexibility without disrupting the smooth inflow of materials to each facility. As modern information technology reduces this challenge, more organizations are implementing hybrid organizations (see Figure 2.2).

FIGURE 2.2
Managing the Hybrid Global Organization

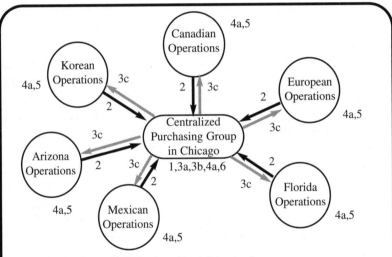

Managing the Center-Led. Decentralized Organization

1. Database of all preferred or certified suppliers is established.
2. Requirements are reported to the center purchasing group.
3. All requirements are compared:
   a. Standardization occurs where possible.
   b. Common requirements are assigned to the center to take advantage of scale economies.
   c. Unique requirements are assigned to the individual facility to achieve responsiveness benefits.
4. Purchasing agreements and buyer-supplier relationships established.
   a. For common items: center purchasing group selects supplier and negotiates agreement based on combined volumes.
   b. For unique items: individual facility purchasing manager selects best supplier and negotiates agreement.
5. For common items: individual facility purchasing manager schedules receipts based on volume contract.
6. Database is updated based on supplier performance and environmental changes.

The hybrid approach requires the use of a real-time communication system and a common database that tracks worldwide supplier performance. Once the database and communication links are in place, each facility or operating unit communicates its requirements to the center group where the requirements are compared. Opportunities for standardization are evaluated, common requirements are consolidated, and unique items assigned to the individual facilities' purchasing managers. New ideas and successful experiments can also be shared through this information network. After consolidating the common requirements, the center group selects the most appropriate supplier and negotiates an overall contract based on the total worldwide volume. The larger volume almost always achieves lower per unit costs. Information regarding the contract is then communicated back to the individual units. Working within the blanket purchasing agreement, the operating units' purchasing managers place orders and schedule receipts based on their specific needs. In effect, the center group contracts for capacity and the purchasing managers at the individual operating units manage the actual flow of materials. Supplier performance is constantly updated and tracked using the common database. This monitoring helps the center group allocate resources to work with suppliers so that continual improvement is obtained and the best suppliers are consistently used. Hybrid global purchasing helps the organization achieve the efficiencies of centralization and the responsiveness of decentralization.

The Evolution of Global Sourcing

Most of the preceding discussion has focused on globalization's affect on the supply environment. Clearly, intensified competition and the emergence of global consumer markets will affect the way organizations do business. Purchasing managers need to adjust, building new skills and competencies to help support the organization's manufacturing, marketing, and competitive strategies. The most important skills that purchasing managers will need are the following:

- Purchasers need to be more aware of the global political environment. Political stability in a country can be very important to the ability of a supplier to fulfill its contractual obligations.

Purchasers need to be able to assess both the immediate and the longer-term political stability of countries where qualified suppliers are found.

- Purchasers need to become more culturally sensitive, recognizing that cultural differences influence the way managers think and act. American managers, in particular, need to become more familiar with cultural norms and more flexible in their own approach to business. Cultural understanding is particularly critical in negotiating contracts and in supplier development initiatives.

- Purchasers need to be familiar with complex and dynamic international and national laws that affect the purchasing and selling of materials. Laws that might affect a purchase decision include domestic content regulations, tariff restrictions, health codes, product safety requirements and liability issues, countertrade policies, and antitrust considerations. Every purchaser should be familiar with the Foreign Corrupt Practices Act, which prohibits U.S. organizations from engaging in bribery.

- Purchasers must be more cognizant of fluctuating exchange rates. In recent years, the Brazilian Real lost 40 percent of its value in a month, the Mexican Peso devalued by half overnight, and the Russian Ruble and Indonesian Ringgit devalued by 70 percent in a period of a couple of weeks. Even stable currencies of industrialized countries fluctuate in value. For example, the Euro declined by over 10 percent in eight months following its introduction in January 1999 and the Japanese Yen appreciated by 20 percent against the dollar from Fall 1998 to Fall 1999. Purchasers need to learn how and when to use different hedging mechanisms.

- Purchasers must become more logistically proficient. Longer supply lines that use multiple modes of transportation and cross international borders can create chaos with just-in-time delivery schedules. Global supply lines can also be quite costly. Further, some issues such as carrier liability are quite different in international shipping. Unforeseen events including storms at sea and hijacked carriers also change the dynamics and certainty of global logistics. Purchasers need to be conversant with all of these issues as they negotiate with international carriers and manage global supply lines.

Fortunately, the foundation for future purchasing success is already being established at many organizations. Basic skills in each of the above areas have been built over the past 25 years as purchasers have engaged more intensely in global sourcing to obtain unique items and reduce the total purchasing bill. In 1973, only 21 percent of organizations sourced from foreign suppliers. Foreign sourcing, as it was then called, was a limited and reactive effort to neutralize the threat of low-cost foreign competition. By 1987, the percentage of organizations engaged in international sourcing had increased to 71 percent.[8] The increased popularity of international sourcing corresponded to a changed mindset among purchasing managers, international sourcing had become a proactive strategy capable of creating competitive advantage. Today, the need to leverage world sources of supply is vital to remain competitive, and almost all major manufacturers and service providers global source to some degree. The term coordinated global sourcing now "refers to the integration and coordination of procurement requirements across worldwide business units, looking at common items, processes, technologies, and suppliers."[9]

Just as the percent of organizations involved in worldwide sourcing has increased, the extent of international purchasing activity has risen. In the early 1980s, international purchases represented 5 percent of every purchased dollar with raw materials representing the largest dollar volume of inputs sourced internationally.[10] International purchasing was also viewed as something only large, resource-rich organizations could do. Today, organizations of all sizes source internationally. Small organizations have been a beneficiary of new information technologies and the assistance of third-party service providers that reduce the up-front costs of going international. By the early 1990s, the typical small to medium-sized organization spends about 13 percent of every purchase dollar on globally sourced items.[11] Larger organizations (those with more than 5,000 employees) spent close to one in five purchase dollars globally. The value-added nature of items sourced from worldwide suppliers had also changed, fabricated components were the most frequently sourced items followed by raw materials and finished goods.

The nature of worldwide sourcing activities varies greatly. Some organizations continue to source on a strictly reactive, as-needed basis. Others have made coordinated global sourcing from the world's best suppliers, regardless of location, a central element of their competitive strategies. The critical question in determining the correct global sourcing posture to pursue is, "what level of global sourcing activity is needed for the organization to remain competitive?" To answer this question, purchasers need to understand customer requirements; the competitive forces that drive success in their industry; and the overall level of global competition. Once these issues are clearly defined and understood, purchasers should perform a comprehensive cost/benefit analysis for each major transaction as well as for the overall global purchasing strategy. Table 2.3 identifies some of the issues that should be considered as the organization gauges its ability to effectively pursue global sourcing.

TABLE 2.3
Benefits, Barriers, and Bridges to Global Purchasing Success

Benefits	Barriers	Bridges
Access to lower priced goods	Diverse political environments	Top management support
Access to worldwide technology	Diverse business practices	Developing communication skills
Access to higher quality goods	Nationalistic attitudes/behavior	Establishing long-term relationships
Better delivery performance	Culture/language differences	Knowledge of exchange rates
Better customer service	Volatile exchange rates	Understanding global opportunities
Help meet countertrade obligations	Logistics support	Knowledge of foreign business practices
Help develop a foreign presence	JIT sourcing requirements	Foreign supplier certification
Improved competitive position	Finding qualified sources	Obtaining expert assistance
Increased number of suppliers	Duty/customs regulations	Planning for global sourcing

Benefits of Global Sourcing

Why do organizations initially begin to global source? The primary catalyst is the opportunity to secure lower-priced materials. The availability of unique products is the next most common reason for initially looking to global suppliers. Another common driver is the belief that worldwide operations need to be supported by worldwide purchasing. Other reasons for starting to purchase internationally include

- Access to advanced technology
- Access to higher-quality products
- Intensification of international competition
- The opportunity to develop a foreign market presence
- The opportunity to fulfill countertrade or local content obligations
- The availability of better delivery or service

Organizations begin to source globally because they believe that the use of global suppliers will provide some form of competitive advantage.

What benefits do organizations actually obtain through global sourcing? According to purchasing managers, the single most important benefit of sourcing globally is reduced product cost. Experience has shown that after taking into account all of the added costs of purchasing from foreign suppliers, savings of 20 percent or more are not unusual. These cost savings come from lower labor costs, access to lower-cost raw materials, tax incentives/subsidies, more efficient production processes, and exchange rate differentials. There is an important caveat to consider. While item price differentials can make a foreign supplier look attractive, the purchase price is just one component of the product's actual "in-use" cost. Some of the costs incurred in purchasing globally include tariffs, documentation, global transportation, and international shipping insurance. One manufacturer expects these ancillary costs to be substantial and therefore only looks seriously at foreign suppliers that offer prices at least 20 percent lower than comparable domestic suppliers.[12] Even when the total landed cost is favorable, price alone should not be the sole motivation behind a sourcing decision.

Two other benefits have also played a key role in the growth of global sourcing – quality and product technology. No country has suppliers that have cornered the market on quality or innovative technology. Purchasing managers need to seriously consider global suppliers that bring new and valuable technologies to market. In a world where a fascination for the newest and latest technologies often propels products to commercial success, gaining access and exposure to leading product and process technologies is an important benefit of global sourcing. A corollary benefit is product availability – sometimes a product is only available from a global supplier. Better delivery performance and better customer service are also benefits that occasionally accrue from global sourcing. Some suppliers have developed products and processes that allow them to provide unparalleled delivery and service to almost any location around the world. The opportunity to obtain the world's best set of resources is a highly regarded benefit of global sourcing.[13]

Barriers to Global Sourcing

Challenges encountered in global sourcing can be categorized as strategic, tactical, and environmental. Strategic barriers include the coincident use of JIT sourcing strategies, the qualification of suppliers, and developing logistics support for longer supply lines. An increased emphasis on lean production and continuous replenishment has only increased the tension created by integrating global and JIT strategies. Similarly, supply-base reduction and closer purchaser/supplier relationships place stress on global sourcing strategies. It is simply more difficult and more costly to develop close, productive relationships with geographically distant suppliers. The challenge begins with identifying and qualifying capable suppliers from regions of the world where purchasers have relatively little experience. Purchasers need to recognize that supplier visits and other communication is going to be more time consuming and costly. Supplier development initiatives are also more challenging. These barriers must be proactively and systematically resolved for the organization to use global sourcing as a strategic thrust.

Tactical barriers encompass daily operating procedures such as duty/customs regulations, fluctuations in currency exchange rates, and knowledge of foreign business practices. Of these, gaining a complete knowledge of global business practices is the most difficult barrier to overcome. This knowledge is vital in the supplier selection and contract negotiation process. Purchasers acknowledge frustration with these issues, but they generally note that most of these barriers are manageable, especially as education and experience are gained. When enhanced in-house capabilities are added to the selective use of third-party service providers, purchasers can overcome the administrative hurdles posed by global sourcing.

Environmental barriers consist largely of cultural and language differences, nationalistic attitudes, and diverse political environments. Of these, only culture/language differences are consistently viewed as a substantial impediment to global sourcing success. Cultural and language barriers can make it difficult to accurately ascertain the real capabilities of a supplier, magnify the challenge of negotiating a favorable contract, and hinder efforts to manage suppliers up to world-class performance levels. Language is perhaps the most visible challenge for American purchasing managers. In many parts of the world, it is common for managers to be conversant in three or more languages. By contrast, Americans often rely solely on English (fortunately, English is typically the second language of choice around the world). Even when negotiations are conducted in English (or with the aid of a competent translator), U.S. purchasers often know less about what is going on than their counterparts. Further, American managers have earned a reputation for being quite ethnocentric; that is, of thinking that managers throughout the world do business in the same way that it is done in the U.S. Ultimately, the barriers to effective global sourcing are substantive and make careful assessment a key to global sourcing success.

Bridges to Successful Global Sourcing

The benefits of global sourcing can be dramatic; yet, barriers to success are real. Purchasing managers must therefore ascertain whether their organizations possess the wherewithal and the determination to bridge the barriers to achieve global sourcing success. Three critical success factors have been identified: top management support, highly developed communication skills, and a strong focus on a few key long-term relationships. Global sourcing requires extensive time and resource commitments to overcome the obstacles found in this complex purchaser/supplier environment. Therefore, a long-term perspective must be adopted and supported by top management to assure that the foundation for success is established. Without top management support coupled with patience, it is difficult to move beyond ad hoc, reactive sourcing practices. The education and skill building efforts needed to develop cross-cultural communication abilities and specific global sourcing skills can only thrive with top management approval and investment. Managerial support is also needed to build strong purchaser/supplier relationships globally. Not only is supplier development expensive in a global setting but the personal friendship between senior managers often becomes the foundation for the working relationships.

Purchasers view three other practices as important to global sourcing success: an effective methodology for identifying and understanding sound international opportunities; a systematic supplier qualification program; and a consistent approach for gaining knowledge of foreign business practices. Each of these practices focuses on supplier selection and development – purchasing's most important responsibility. If the global sourcing team possesses the skills to find, evaluate, select, and certify the best suppliers worldwide, then the barriers to global sourcing can be effectively mitigated. Other important facilitators include the following:

- The appropriate use of experts such as international freight forwarders, customs house brokers, and third-party logistics service providers can reduce the challenges created by longer supply lines.
- The effective use of hedging instruments such as forward contracts, futures, and options can eliminate the risk of currency swings.
- The establishment of international purchasing offices, staffed with experts on the local or regional marketplace, can compensate for a lack of market experience.

Global Sourcing Implementation

Global sourcing requires substantial resource dedication and considerable effort. Purchasing managers must clearly define the organization's purchasing needs and objectives before venturing into the complex global environment. A follow-the-leader mentality almost always leads to poor performance and costly mistakes. Figure 2.3 is a flowchart that can be used to guide efforts to assess global sourcing needs and establish an effective global sourcing strategy.

FIGURE 2.3
Assessing the Organization's Global Sourcing Needs and Strategy

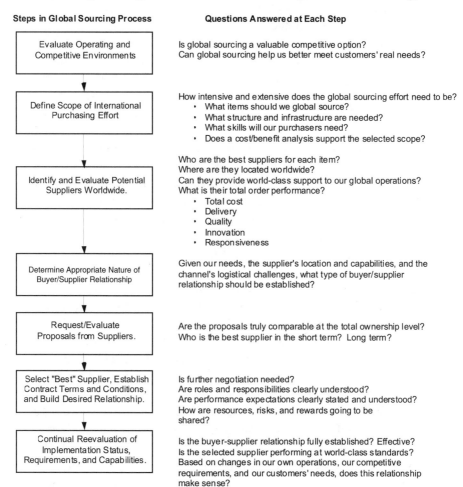

Steps in Global Sourcing Process

Questions Answered at Each Step

Evaluate Operating and Competitive Environments

Is global sourcing a valuable competitive option?
Can global sourcing help us better meet customers' real needs?

Define Scope of International Purchasing Effort

How intensive and extensive does the global sourcing effort need to be?
• What items should we global source?
• What structure and infrastructure are needed?
• What skills will our purchasers need?
• Does a cost/benefit analysis support the selected scope?

Identify and Evaluate Potential Suppliers Worldwide.

Who are the best suppliers for each item?
Where are they located worldwide?
Can they provide world-class support to our global operations?
What is their total order performance?
• Total cost
• Delivery
• Quality
• Innovation
• Responsiveness

Determine Appropriate Nature of Buyer/Supplier Relationship

Given our needs, the supplier's location and capabilities, and the channel's logistical challenges, what type of buyer/supplier relationship should be established?

Request/Evaluate Proposals from Suppliers.

Are the proposals truly comparable at the total ownership level?
Who is the best supplier in the short term? Long term?

Select "Best" Supplier, Establish Contract Terms and Conditions, and Build Desired Relationship.

Is further negotiation needed?
Are roles and responsibilities clearly understood?
Are performance expectations clearly stated and understood?
How are resources, risks, and rewards going to be shared?

Continual Reevaluation of Implementation Status, Requirements, and Capabilities.

Is the buyer-supplier relationship fully established? Effective?
Is the selected supplier performing at world-class standards?
Based on changes in our own operations, our competitive requirements, and our customers' needs, does this relationship make sense?

In the minds of most purchasers, developing a well-defined understanding of the organization's purchasing needs and objectives is clearly the most important step. Some organizations only need to look globally from time to time for unique and specific items or services. These organizations do not need to invest a lot of time or money in training programs, information systems, or dedicated global sourcing personnel. Top management support is generally not needed for such ad hoc global sourcing. Other organizations find that they must support production operations scattered around the world, as well as consistently find the lowest-cost, highest-quality, and most technologically advanced products available worldwide. These organizations often find that tremendous synergies can be generated by coordinating worldwide sourcing strategies, pooling purchase requirements, and negotiating long-term contracts with the world's best suppliers. This type of intensive and integrated global purchasing strategy requires that organizations invest heavily in systems, skills, and support.

After establishing the scope of the international purchasing strategy, emphasis shifts to supplier selection and development. Longer, international supply lines place a premium on meticulous supplier evaluation. During the selection process, purchasers need to evaluate international suppliers more thoroughly than their domestic counterparts because redressing conflicts and resolving problems in a global environment can be complicated, if not impossible. Purchasers need to look at total order performance. That is, how do total landed costs, quality levels, delivery performance, total cycle responsiveness, and other key performance areas compare from one supplier to another. Significant differences in total order performance arise because different delivery channels are used. Experienced global purchasers note that purchaser/supplier contracts should be written with clear and concise specifications. Performance expectations, roles and responsibilities, arrangements on the sharing of risks, rewards, and resources should be clearly stated and understood. Taking time to develop a clear and specific contract can mitigate future compliance problems. Overall, purchasers concur that rigorous supplier screening and development; good communications and information sharing with international suppliers; and the establishment of close purchaser/supplier relationships are important steps in implementing a world-class global sourcing program.

Of course, in order to identify potential suppliers on a worldwide basis, evaluate their capabilities, and build strong relationships with selected suppliers, the purchasing organization must create a global mindset, establish a knowledge base regarding international sourcing, and build global purchasing capabilities. Not all purchasers are equally well suited to work in a global environment. Cultural sensitivity, global awareness, language skills, adaptability, and commitment to the global coordination process are all attributes that a global purchaser should possess. For purchasers who lack the needed experience and expertise in a given region, obtaining expert assistance in developing or extending the international sourcing strategy can be highly beneficial. However, organizations should put in place a mechanism to ensure that knowledge is transferred from the outside expert and assimilated by the organization's own purchasing personnel.

Finally, experienced global purchasers point to the need for follow through. Purchasers almost always encounter problems in their initial efforts to go global. This experience is hard to avoid as purchasers get acquainted first hand with the hurdles that are found in global sourcing. Because of the obstacles and the expense incurred in the learning process, purchasers need to have an ability to learn and move forward with dogged perseverance. The negative affect on organizational support of a major miscue early in the implementation process highlights the need to achieve early successes. Initial success helps solidify top management support. This reality points to an important implication for the worldwide sourcing champion – he or she needs to select and structure early efforts to achieve positive results and then work diligently to make sure that early successes are realized. The task is not complete, however, until the early successes are made highly visible throughout the organization. In effect, early success stories are needed to build managerial commitment and move from a "testing the waters" scenario to a fully established worldwide sourcing program. As this occurs, worldwide sourcing activities move from reactive to strategic and provide the organization with a sustainable competitive advantage.

A Global Marketplace

As a rule, local suppliers are easier to manage and the on-time delivery of materials is easier to ensure. Dealing with the language, legal, and logistical barriers that are inherent in global sourcing greatly exacerbates the challenge of providing an uninterrupted flow of materials to the organization. Even so, purchasers often have little choice but to look to global sources of supply. Local suppliers do not always have the necessary technology and often cannot compete at world-class levels in the areas of price, quality, delivery, or service. Bringing the "best mix" of inputs together to support the organization's operations requires that purchasing managers expand their horizons beyond their home country's border. Recognizing this fact is absolutely critical in an environment where rivals already look at the world as a single marketplace, obtaining vital resources from the best suppliers available regardless of where they are located. To stay competitive in today's global supply environment, purchasers need to adopt a global mindset supported by worldwide information and logistics systems as well as comprehensive training and educational programs.

Key Points

1. Economic globalization is one of the most important forces affecting today's supply environment. Advances in information exchange and logistics facilitate globalization; government intervention is the primary impediment to globalization.

2. Purchasers need to recognize the three implications of globalization: intensified competition; the emergence of global consumer and supply markets; and the fact that domestic and global business is different.

3. The purchasing function will increasingly need to support global manufacturing and marketing networks as well as provide a virtual extension of these networks. Hybrid centralized/decentralized organizations are needed to provide the efficiency and flexibility required in global networks.

4. Purchasers need to build new skills to succeed in a global supply environment. Important skills include more awareness of the global political environment; greater cultural sensitivity; greater understanding of international and national laws; more proficiency in the use of currency hedging instruments; and greater logistical knowledge.

5. Global sourcing will continue to increase in importance as an important competitive strategy. To effectively implement a winning global sourcing strategy, purchasers need to understand the benefits, barriers, and bridges to global sourcing success. Well-designed strategies can deliver the best mix of goods and services available worldwide and provide the organization with competitive advantage.

Questions for Review

1. What are the primary forces driving globalization? Which forces are most prevalent in your industry?
2. How has your organization's purchasing strategy changed over the past five to10 years to help the organization achieve higher levels of global competitiveness?
3. What are the pros and cons of centralized and decentralized structures for global sourcing? Is a centralized or decentralized structure more appropriate for your organization? What would the ideal purchasing structure look like for your organization? What capabilities would such a structure deliver?
4. What percent of your organizations purchase dollars are spent globally? From how many countries does your organization source products?
5. What are the most important benefits of global sourcing? What are the critical barriers your organization has encountered? What are the most important bridges to successful global sourcing?
6. What are the most important skills purchasers need to develop to successfully source from global suppliers? Evaluate the level of skill development in your organization.

Endnotes

1. Levitt, T. "The Globalization of Markets," *Harvard Business Review*, (61:3), 1983, pp. 92-102.
2. Grove, A.S. "A High-tech CEO Updates His Views on Managing and Careers," *Fortune*, September 18, 1995, p. 229.
3. Fairclough, G. "P & G to Slash 15,000 Jobs, Shut 10 Plants," *Wall Street Journal*, June 10, 1999, pp. A3, A4.
4. Fawcett, S.E. "Purchasing Characteristics and Supplier Performance in Maquiladora Operations," *International Journal of Purchasing and Materials Management*, (29:1), 1993, pp. 25-34.
5. Simison, R. "General Motors Drives Some Hard Bargains With Asian Suppliers," *Wall Street Journal*, April 2, 1999, pp. A1, A6.
6. Scully, J.I and S.E. Fawcett. "International Procurement Strategies: Opportunities and Challenges for the Small Firm,"

Production and Inventory Management Journal, (35:2), 1994, pp. 39-46; McDonald, A.L. "Of Floating Factories and Mating Dinosaurs," *Harvard Business Review*, (64:6), 1986, pp. 81-86.

7. Tully, S. "Purchasing's New Muscle," *Fortune*, February 20, 1995, pp. 75-83.

8. Monczka, R.M. and R.J. Trent. "Global Sourcing: A Development Approach," *International Journal of Purchasing and Materials Management*, Spring 1991, p. 27.

9. Monczka, R.M. and R. Trent. "Worldwide Sourcing: Assessment and Execution," *International Journal of Purchasing and Materials Management*, October 1992, pp. 9-19.

10. Monczka, R.M. and L.C. Giunipero. "International Purchasing: Characteristics and Implementation," *Journal of Purchasing and Materials Management*, Autumn 1984, pp. 2-9.

11. Birou, L.M. and S.E. Fawcett. "International Purchasing: Benefits, Requirements, and Challenges," *International Journal of Purchasing and Materials Management*, (29:2), 1993, pp. 28-37.

12. Dobler, D.W. and D.N. Burt. *Purchasing and Supply Management*, McGraw-Hill, New York, NY, 1996.

13. Min, H. and W.P. Galle. "International Purchasing Strategies of Multinational U.S. Firms, *International Journal of Purchasing and Materials Management*, Summer 1991, pp. 9-18; Birou, 1993; Handfield, R., "Global Sourcing: Patterns of Development," *International Journal of Operations and Production Management*, (14:6), 1994, pp. 40-51.

CHAPTER 3

THE AFFECT OF TIME COMPRESSION ON THE SUPPLY ENVIRONMENT

What really matters in a time-centric world?

Chapter Objectives

This chapter is designed to help the purchaser:

- Understand the contribution that purchasing can make to time-based competitive strategies.
- To be able to redesign the purchasing organization to support time-based sourcing.
- To be able to design the purchasing organization to promote continuous improvement.
- Understand the role of suppliers and the importance of collaboration in time-based sourcing.
- Recognize the need to integrate global and time-based sourcing strategies.

The Currency of Time

The accelerated pace of business has had a dramatic affect on today's supply environment. In today's dynamic world a new customer mindset has emerged – a mindset that emphasizes time as a competitive weapon.[1] Time has always been a valued commodity for managers. Even company slogans have changed in recent years to emphasize time as the source of value: United Parcel Service's switched its emphasis from productivity - "The tightest ship in the shipping business" — to time — "Moving at the speed of business."

The recognition of the importance of time is not new. Frederick Taylor's scientific approach to management, which incorporated the intensive use of time and motion studies, dominated management practice for much of the twentieth century. Just-in-time placed a new emphasis on time and on the synchronization of processes throughout the supply chain. The key elements of the Just-In-Time (JIT) philosophy were waste elimination and employee involvement. High productivity, quality, and responsiveness made possible through JIT enabled Japanese organizations like Sony and Hitachi to take market share from their less time-conscious U.S. counterparts.

Today, the value of time has made continual, synchronized replenishment a goal of purchasers in a variety of industries from grocery retail (Kroger) to fashion (The Gap) to heavy manufacturing (Ford). To achieve this goal, purchasers must reengineer processes, learn constantly, and eliminate waste everywhere. They must also work more closely with other organizations in their supply chain. This chapter explores the affect of time-based strategies on the supply environment and on purchasing strategies.

A Just-in-Time World

In the early 1900s manufacturing made a leap forward when Henry Ford moved automobile production from the job shop to the assembly line. Mass production on assembly lines continued to be viewed as the best way to produce high-volume products until the late 1970s. Japanese manufacturers, with a strong belief in continuous improvement and under tremendous competitive pressure, sought to improve on the efficiencies of assembly-line production. At that time the most efficient production occurred in process industries like oil refining where continuous production is the rule. An attempt was made to pattern the production process, as closely as possible, to those found in the process industries. The result was Just-In-Time (JIT) manufacturing. In JIT, inventory is reduced to minimal levels and the flow of material through the manufacturing system is synchronized so that as one item moves out of a work station, another is ready to move in.

By altering the cost structure of the manufacturing process, the cost/volume relationship changed. The experience curve (also known as the learning curve) for JIT manufacturing dropped beneath that of the standard volume-dependent experience curve. An experience curve expresses the cost relationship between the number of items produced and the cost per item, every time the cumulative production volume doubles, the cost of the nth item produced decreases by a certain percentage. For example, if an organization is on a 90 percent experience curve and production of the hundredth unit cost $10, then the production of the two-hundreth part will cost only $9. The decrease in cost is brought about by improvements in the production process and by the worker's increase in ability.

Using the volume-dependent relationship, the key to low-cost production was to increase volume and build large factories to capture economies of scale. However, on the JIT experience curve, volume was only important in the early stages because the curve flattens out, most of the economies were achieved by the time production reached 200,000 cars per year. While American carmakers were willing to settle for a 5 percent to 15 percent improvement rate, JIT organizations were able to achieve a 33 percent rate.[2] JIT provided a solid competitive foundation, outstanding productivity, exceptional quality, compressed cycle times, and tremendous responsiveness. Organizations worldwide sought to adopt JIT and attain these competitive benefits.

The Essence of JIT

Many of the early JIT adopters found that its implementation was seldom easy. By the early 1990s, after years of working to implement JIT, many organizations began to abandon their JIT initiatives.[3] Managers frequently misunderstood the nature of JIT or underestimated the amount of work required to support JIT. When JIT benefits were quantified in terms of reduced inventories, they were viewed as insufficient to justify commitment to JIT implementation. Other organizations aggressively attempted to implement JIT without adequately planning for or supporting JIT operations. The failure to carefully weigh the requirements of JIT led firms to reduce inventories prematurely, leading to work stoppages and frustration. Successful JIT implementation required more than just reducing inventory levels. It required reengineering the entire value-added environment.

Only when the requirements and benefits of JIT are mutually understood is it possible to implement JIT (see Figure 3.1).

FIGURE 3.1
Alternative Views of JIT Implementation

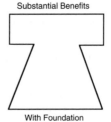

Scenario 1	Scenario 2	Scenario 3
Strictly quantify benefits of JIT based on forecasts of inventory reduction. Recognize that JIT is not easy and requires signficant investments of time and capital.	View JIT as a competitive panacea. The envisioned productivity, quality, and responsiveness benefits lead to rapid adoption. Fail to recongize the required extent of process change.	Correctly assess wide ranging benefits that arise in a JIT setting. Recognize that JIT is not easy and requires significant investments of time and capital.
Minimal Benefits	Substantial Benefits	Substantial Benefits
With Foundation	Without Foundation	With Foundation

	Scenario 1	Scenario 2	Scenario 3
Decision:	Not Worth the Effort	Worth the Effort	Worth the Effort
Outcome:	Maintain the Status Quo	Attempt, but Fail	Attempt and Succeed

Requirements	Benefits
Inventory Reduction	Reduced Capital Investment
Process Development	Enhanced Product Quality
Workforce Training	Enhanced Responsiveness
Worker Participation	Improved Flexibility
Managerial Support	Improved Production Process
Synchronized Manufacturing	Reduced Manufacturing Costs
Long-term Management Support	Better Facility Layout
Logistical Support	Better Facility Utilization
Supportive Measures	Reduced Confusion

© Stanley E. Fawcett, Ph.D., C.P.M.

The initial JIT hype focused on inventory reduction. In fact, the term JIT was often considered to be to be synonymous with "zero inventories" and "stockless production." By the end of the 1980s, JIT thinking had transitioned to emphasize a set of related practices that when jointly implemented would simplify and streamline the manufacturing environment, enabling reduced cycle times, greater productivity, and enhanced quality. The generally accepted components of a JIT strategy included total quality management, set-up time reduction, uniform workload, cross-trained workers, focused factory, group technology, JIT purchasing, total productive maintenance, and the kanban or pull system. This more holistic approach to JIT implementation set the stage for current thinking regarding JIT practice, with JIT now viewed as a philosophy of continuous improvement. Perhaps the best way to understand the logic of JIT is to look at the adaptations to the operating environment that are required for JIT success.

Inventory reduction – Inventory reduction's true role in JIT is as a tool to expose problems in the value-added process so that they can be removed. Inventory covers up many problems in the value-added system that if removed, would improve quality, increase productivity, and shorten leadtimes. Therefore, JIT organizations work constantly to reduce inventories in a systematic way that brings problems to light and allows their resolution. The key is to build constant learning loops into the system.

JIT's approach to quality improvement illustrates the basic JIT learning loop. Because JIT operates without buffer stocks, an individual's ability to be productive is hindered if defective parts are received from the preceding workstation. When defective parts are received, the worker communicates the problem back to the source where the problem is resolved. If the problem cannot be resolved quickly, the entire production line is stopped until the source of the disruption can be eliminated. The key to this improvement process is that the consequences of each team member's efforts are quickly seen and feedback is provided immediately while the team member still remembers what was done that might have caused the problem. Individual responsibility is critical to improvement. However, feedback should focus on the problem itself, without placing blame. Rapid feedback, responsibility, and urgency drive improvement. This approach can and should be extended upstream through the supply chain.

Inventory reduction also impacts cycle time. Replenishment cycle time is the time between when an order is received and when the order is shipped. This time is roughly equivalent to the time it takes to run the order through production, which depends directly on the amount of work already on the production floor. Large WIP inventories not only extend cycle times but also create variability. In non-JIT settings, up to 90 percent of the time an order is in production can be non-value-added queue or wait time. Interoperation time comprises most of the cycle time and accounts for almost all of the leadtime uncertainty. Reducing WIP leads to a dramatic reduction in cycle times and allows for much greater customer responsiveness.

Process control and development – Effective process management begins with process control (controlling the process by checking the quality of work while it is being done). Process control plays a key role in reducing inventories, improving quality, and tightening leadtimes. The best way to carry out process control is to have workers do it themselves. This requires providing workers with basic statistical training so that they can track the performance of their processes, identify process variations, and act to remove the source of these variations. Identifying process variations is the first step in continuous improvement and leads to conscious efforts to modify existing processes to make them better.

Extensive process development is the key to eliminating variability and to reducing set-up times enough to make short production runs practical. The ingredients of process development are in-house technical expertise and appropriate investment in process technology. A classic example involved Toyota's modification of a heavy press used in stamping hoods and fenders – changeover time was reduced from four hours to 12 minutes. Toyota continues to improve its operations and has built a series of time buffers that allow process engineers to try new approaches in its assembly process. These buffers serve as active learning centers or assembly laboratories. The key is to proactively use process development to build better processes.

Workforce training and participation – JIT organizations view the worker as an integral part of the value-added system. The Japanese khangi for the word jidoka, which is the JIT practice of allowing workers to stop the entire production line when a quality problem is encountered, literally translates into "man and machine system." In a time-sensitive environment, a problem anywhere in the value-added process threatens to bring production to a halt. To achieve success in a system that depends heavily on its workers, organizations need to invest in the problem-solving skills of individual workers. Further, worker participation in every facet of the value-added process must become the social norm. In JIT, the workforce becomes a vital value-added asset as every member of the workforce is trained; each and every individual takes responsibility for action;

and workers are effectively integrated into all aspects of the process. Organizations that understand the importance of workforce empowerment tend to win the competitive battles where time is the essence of success.

Managerial responsibility – In a setting where workers take responsibility for their own work and actively participate in problem solving, managers take on the role of teacher, team facilitator, and motivator. The worker-manager relationship is more important than the position of authority the manager holds and mutual respect develops between workers and managers. Also, communication is enhanced and management is in a more credible position to convince workers of its commitment to excellence. An adversarial attitude is replaced by a spirit of cooperation with both sides working toward the goal of continual improvement. The ability to integrate workers more fully into the value-added process depends on this management/workforce relationship. In many organizations, efforts to adopt a JIT strategy are thwarted by skeptical managers who hesitate to give up their authority or change their view of the workers' ability to provide the organization a competitive edge.

Network orientation – The concepts of tight inventory control, exceptional quality, and cycle time reduction extend back to an organization's supplier network. JIT purchasing arrangements are characterized by the integration of purchaser/supplier activities. The degree of integration is dictated by the strength of the relationship. Three common characteristics are: establishment of long-term contracts; consolidation of purchasing requirements with preferred suppliers; and co-location of facilities. In effect, the supplier becomes a virtual extension of the organization. The goal is to maximize leverage, increase stability, and share resources to create greater value than would be possible through arm's length purchasing arrangements. Leading automakers have long relied on suppliers for a much higher percentage of the value-added component of each vehicle. For example, DaimlerChrysler relies on suppliers for approximately 70 percent of each vehicle's cost of goods sold and Honda outsources close to 80 percent of its vehicles to suppliers. Toyota's dependence on its key suppliers is evidenced by its willingness to increase its ownership stake in select suppliers to prevent competitors from gaining access to them.[4]

Synchronization – Coordination and discipline within the organization and throughout the supply network are critical to JIT success. The JIT ideal is to receive materials just-in-time to be used in production, to produce sub-assemblies just-in-time to be used in the final assembly process, and to deliver finished goods just-in-time to be sold. Assuring a timely flow of materials is one of the great challenges of JIT. A pull system, often called a "kanban" system, is the key to JIT synchronization. A pull system is a visual system designed to produce only the parts needed "downstream" as they are needed. Using a pull system helps prevent possible production crises by carefully controlling the amount of inventory in the system and by eliminating expediting. Because complexity makes synchronization difficult, JIT organizations carefully manage the active number of SKUs, simplify product design, streamline production flows, work with fewer suppliers, outsource complete modules, and aggressively pursue the development of excellent information systems. Simplification is the key to synchronization.

Competitive Implications of a Time-Compressed World

Because managers believe that "JIT lean" translates into competitive success, lean supply management strategies abound. Rockwell Collins, a leading manufacturer of avionics and communications equipment, adopted a lean purchasing program as a centerpiece of its competitive strategy. To achieve lasting success with these lean, time-based strategies, purchasers need to understand the following implications of a time-compressed supply environment.

Integration of key resources – Perhaps the two greatest potential strengths of any organization are its human and technological resources. Few organizations do a good job of developing these two resources. Even fewer effectively integrate them to achieve a competitive advantage. The propensity of many organizations is to purchase the latest and most popular technology available and then hope that it can be implemented successfully. Recent efforts to implement enterprise resource planning (ERP) systems illustrate the challenge that accompanies this strategy, many organizations have taken twice as long and spent twice as much as initially budgeted. In fact, a two-year study conducted by the Supply Chain Council in the mid 1990s failed to find a single successful ERP implementation. The ERP challenge was foreshadowed by similar difficulties in implementing electronic data interchange, robotics, flexible manufacturing systems, and other technological advances.

While many organizations embrace technology, efforts to develop human resources are often meager by comparison and poorly structured. Indeed, Peter Senge has noted, "We know how to invest in technology and machinery, but we're at a loss when it comes to investing in people." [5] Few training budgets equal those designated for technology despite estimates that systematic and structured investments in training can provide up to twice the return as investments in technology.[6] Further, the answer to the question, "what makes factories flexible?" has been found to be a cross-trained workforce, not technological investment.[7] Jack Welch, General Electric's Chief Executive, has consistently noted that one of the most vital jobs of senior management is to develop the people within the organization. Deere & Company, has put in place a comprehensive training program that helps current managers upgrade skills, new mangers build skills, and suppliers expand skills. Organizations that make such efforts, however, remain in the minority.

Transforming technological and human resources into a formidable competitive advantage requires a change in attitude regarding their development and use followed by their strategic integration. The following points should be kept in mind as managers invest in and develop these resources.

- The organization's needs must be matched with the technology's capabilities. As a general rule, the simplest technology that meets product and process needs should be given priority. Such technologies generally cost less and are easier to implement.
- The organization's technology strategy should support the organization's long-term approach to building world-class, value-added processes. This rule requires early thinking about how technology and human systems will interact to create value.
- The following technology pitfalls should be avoided: the "follow-the-leader" mentality, the "shiny-hardware" syndrome, and the "island of automation." Every technology investment should be carefully justified and closely tied to a real capability that is needed and that can be achieved.
- The organization must view its workforce as a critical resource and commit the necessary capital to training programs. Once manage-

ment starts investing in workers, it must also give the workers the responsibility and opportunity to use their increasing skills.

- Managers, including purchasers, must develop a greater familiarity with the organization's value-added processes and key technologies. Appreciating and understanding of the abilities of line workers and managers in other disciplines is needed to coordinate and integrate competitive efforts.
- Adequate organizational support must be in place to implement and support new technologies.
- Appropriate performance should also be adopted.

The final step in leveraging human and technological resources is to integrate them. If adequate work force training is coupled with the adoption of the appropriate process technologies, all that remains is for the organization to make the integration of the two a priority. A classic example involved the GM/Toyota Nummi joint venture. Under Toyota's direction, NUMMI integrated people and technology systems and quickly became GM's most productive assembly facility. Over the years, Toyota has continued to emphasize the development of world-class capabilities through the integration of people and machines. For example, a tour of one of Toyota's assembly lines, Toyota City, reveals that workers are never idle, they are constantly moving with purpose, and seemingly without wasted effort. Moreover, the workers move in synch with the machines on the assembly line in a carefully choreographed display of precision and efficiency. The payoff is clear. Toyota is the world's most productive carmaker, consistently achieves among the highest quality ratings, and is able to bring new cars from concept to market faster than its competitors.

A cross-functional approach – Cross-functional integration is fundamental to almost every time-oriented, value-added process, including new product development, cycle time reduction, and JIT purchasing. Focusing specifically on rapid new product innovation demonstrates the value of coordinating activities. Marketing provides a link to the consumer, sharing information on customer expectations and attractive product characteristics. Engineering provides a link to technology. Manufacturing communicates what is possible in terms of manufacturability. Purchasing is the link to all of the process and product knowledge that resides in the supply base. By coordinating activities across these functional areas, more attractive, technologically advanced products can be brought to market more quickly. Some organizations in the automobile and electronics industries have cut new product development times by 30 to 50 percent. Without coordination across functions and throughout the supply chain, the smooth flow of information and materials that is needed for JIT success simply cannot happen.

Continual, incremental improvement – Success today depends more on incremental productivity gains and consistent innovation than it does on occasional, dramatic process or product breakthroughs. The reality is that competitors can rapidly replicate most innovations. New products are often copied within a year with the imitators bringing enhanced products to market. Process gains are susceptible to the same challenge. Imitation is frequently less costly than innovation and avoids the risks. Organizations that master the kaizen philosophy of continuous improvement are certain to become the industry target. Fortunately, such a target is constantly moving. Organizations that emphasize continual improvement cultivate two attributes, a high level of workforce training and an organizational attitude that everyone is responsible for the organization's success. Continuous improvement in process and product develops a high level of organizational flexibility, which is critical to sustained competitiveness in today's supply environment.

A long-term perspective – By nature, JIT Implementation requires a long-term perspective. Competing as a JIT organization is inherently difficult. Sustained effort by top management and worker alike is a requirement. Inventory cannot be reduced without reducing set up times. A long-term commitment and proper reward systems are equally important in developing the human resource base that is so vital to JIT success.

Time-based strategies cannot be implemented without the redesign of an organization's value-added systems coupled with the redefinition of internal relationships. Managers who recognize this fact understand that time-based competition precludes business as usual. The benefits of lean operations and a rapid response capability are only realized through persistence and commitment. For many organizations, this is a high a price to pay for JIT success.

The Affect on the Purchasing and Supply Manager

Compressing replenishment leadtimes creates a real challenge for the purchasing and supply manager. Delay or disruption in the acquisition process can easily create havoc with downstream value-added processes because there is no time to compensate. In a lean inventory environment, a late delivery quickly translates into a value-added process that is no longer running. For one major U.S. manufacturer, a one-minute work stoppage on its main production line is equal to $400,000 lost production. Purchasing managers are very sensitive to the demands created by the emergence of time as a competitive weapon. Three facts delineate purchasing's new role in a time-centric world.

- Time-compression is a popular and widely used strategy. Purchasing often finds itself at the implementation crossroads of time-compression strategies.
- Functional shiftability, especially across the purchaser/supplier boundary, is becoming an everyday practice. Answering the question, "Who should do what?" is critical to purchasers.
- Continuous improvement in purchasing requires a constant effort to cultivate outstanding relationships with the very best suppliers.

Time Compression Everywhere

JIT initially emerged in the late 1970s as a production control system with application in the large-scale, repetitive manufacturing arena. However, by the 1990s JIT's short-cycle emphasis was being adopted in a variety of settings including small-organization manufacturers, purchasing, and transportation. Rapid replenishment philosophies quickly made the leap into fashion retailing under the name of Quick Response (QR). Organizations like Benetton, The Gap, and The Limited implemented QR strategies to "crunch" the replenishment cycle time between the manufacturer and the retail outlet. In fashion apparel, short cycle delivery allows a retailer to match colors and styles to quickly changing customer preferences. Better information systems, supplier management, and rapid-response logistics are the keys to QR success. Shortly after QR emerged as a viable competitive strategy, a study in the grocery retail sector found over 100 days of inventory in the entire supply chain. For an industry that gets by on meager margins, this huge capital investment in inventory represented an unacceptable cost. The Efficient Consumer Response (ECR) program was initiated by leading grocers to take the inventory out of the system. Better information sharing throughout the supply chain was the basis of ECR success. Most recently, Continuous Replenishment Programs (CRP) and Collaborative Forecasting and Replenishment (CFAR) have come into vogue and been implemented by leading retailers like Ikea and Best Buy. In both of these initiatives, information, better supply-base relationships, and efficient logistics are substituted for inventory. Wal-Mart, the largest retailer in the world, traces much of its success directly to its information systems, its tight purchaser/supplier relationships, and its logistics infrastructure. Wal-Mart can replenish its supercenters twice as often as its major competitors at a fraction of the cost.[8] The absolutely critical role suppliers play in these rapid replenishment models perfectly positions purchasing to help the organization simultaneously increase customer responsiveness and productivity. The purchasing manager's ability to build the right purchaser/supplier relationships, facilitated with the appropriate information sharing, and supported by efficient logistics determines whether or not these time-driven strategies truly deliver a competitive edge. Many organizations have tried to imitate Wal-Mart without achieving the same high-performance levels.

Functional Shiftability Across the Supply Chain

Functional shiftability is the term academics use to describe the shifting of value-added activities to the supply-chain member that is best positioned to perform them. The essence of role shifting is to aggressively evaluate the value-added roles of different supply-chain members. This evaluation can be perceived by less powerful supply-chain members as asking the question, "is there someone in the supply chain who can perform your job more efficiently or quickly than you can?". This line of questioning is often perceived as a serious threat and can reduce the willingness of supply-chain participants to reconsider who should perform what roles.

However, in a time-sensitive world, where competition is intense and alternative channels are emerging, the need to shift roles can no longer be viewed in the abstract. Supply chains that fail to compete at the highest levels can become irrelevant. Likewise, individual organizations that refuse to evaluate their value-added contribution risk being shifted right out of the supply chain. This reality has led both purchasers and suppliers to be more creative and flexible in defining their value-added relationship. Role shifting in the purchaser/supplier relationship has actually become quite common, especially in the areas of quality control, new product development, and supplier-managed inventory.

- **Quality control** – Historically, the purchasing organization has inspected the quality of purchased inputs upon receipt; however, a total quality emphasis has led to increased supplier certification, shifting the responsibility for quality to the supplier. Qualified suppliers now assure acceptable quality performance, eliminating the need for incoming inspection and making dock-to-stock practices possible. Suppliers that cannot meet this quality expectation are eliminated from the supply base.
- **Integrated product development** – A desire to shrink concept-to-market cycle times has led to the use of multi-functional product-development teams, consisting of managers from marketing, R & D, manufacturing, purchasing, and logistics as well as representatives from key suppliers. The inclusion of suppliers on the team is a dramatic shift from traditional purchaser/supplier roles. Instead of reacting to the purchaser's new product needs after the product design has been set, suppliers bring both process and product technology expertise to the team from the very beginning of the design process. The payoff of changing roles and relationships is higher quality products that are brought to market with dramatically shorter development leadtimes.
- **Supplier managed inventory** – Bose Corporation initiated the practice of placing the responsibility for managing the purchaser's inventory in the supplier's hands. Key suppliers locate their personnel on site at Bose' operations and work closely with the Bose' personnel to obtain better forecast information. They also monitor inventory levels for their products, place orders, and

handle all of the expediting and other issues involved in assuring timely product arrival. In many soft-goods retail settings, suppliers take responsibility for inventory as well as the floor display and promotion of their product. An automated approach involves a supplier that has constructed specialized racks fitted with computerized sensors. These racks are located at the customer's facility. As product is withdrawn from the rack, the sensors measure inventory levels and automatically place an order when the reorder point is reached.

- **Supplier integrated manufacturing** – Turning responsibility for assembly over to the supplier represents the most aggressive effort yet to shift roles in order to reduce costs and shorten cycle times. Dell's use of contract manufacturers and Volkswagon's truck assembly facility in Brazil that relies almost exclusively on suppliers for the assembly of the entire vehicle are advanced examples of role shifting.

In each of these examples, suppliers are more fully integrated into the purchasing organization's efforts to create value. For functional shiftability to deliver as promised, today's purchasing managers need to gain a more complete knowledge of the nature of their own organization's value-added processes as well as the capabilities of key suppliers. This knowledge is the foundation for determining who should do what in the purchaser/supplier relationship. Purchasers also need to redefine the purchaser/supplier relationship to facilitate supplier integration into key processes. Value-added relationships are built on open information exchange, cooperation, and shared resources. Knowing when to shift roles and responsibilities, how to design the integrated processes, and how to manage redefined relationships will make purchasing a more vital force in winning supply chains.

Continuous Improvement Always

The never-ending drive for improvement, especially in the area of customer responsiveness, is placing tremendous pressure on purchasing to take performance to a new level. As is the case with both time compression and functional shiftability, purchasing's ability to meet this challenge depends on how efficiently and effectively purchasing managers can build a world-class, globally competitive supply base. Monczka and Trent[9] quantified the required performance enhancements purchasers would need to coax out of their supply relationships. They noted that purchasing systems would need to achieve across-the-board improvements as follows:

- Year-to-year cost reduction of 5 percent
- Year-to-year quality improvement of 10 to 15 percent (from a base of less than 250 PPM defective)
- A 40 to 60 percent reduction in concept-to-market time
- Improvement in customer responsiveness of 30 to 80 percent from established levels

Very few organizations have consistently met the improvement challenge in these key performance areas. While improvements in innovation cycle times and customer responsiveness have lagged, the greatest improvements have occurred in the areas of cost and quality. Leading organizations include continuous improvement clauses in their contracts to target cost, quality, and innovation enhancements.

While the challenge of continuous improvement is daunting, the fact remains that the global competitive threat has amplified in recent years. Being able to compete with the world's best organizations is getting more and more difficult. For example, Toyota shocked the automobile industry in 1999 when it announced that it had developed a way to produce a custom car within five days of receiving the order (this compares to 17 to 18 days for General Motors and 10 to 12 days for DaimlerChrysler). The key to Toyota's five-day cycle is a virtual production line that integrates supplier production schedules. Incredible flexibility is achieved using a precise schedule of parts pickups and a standard transportation milk run among a fixed set of suppliers. Deliveries are made to the assembly operation 24 times each day.[10] New competitive standards, many of which rely on purchaser/supplier integration will continue to appear. Purchasers can help their organizations compete in this environment by cultivating a continuous improvement mentality within the purchasing organization and with every key supply relationship.

The Evolution of Time-Based Purchasing

Time-based purchasing requires cooperation and communication between the purchaser and the supplier and is characterized by the integration of value-added activities. The degree of integration and the specific arrangements depend on a number of factors including the importance of the parts and services being acquired; the degree to which the purchaser has focused on its own core competencies; the length of the purchaser/supplier relationship; and the overall strength of the purchaser/supplier relationship. Specific relationships vary, however, the following characteristics are common in JIT purchasing:

- The purchaser represents a large portion of the supplier's business. This assures a high level of service responsiveness.
- The purchaser reduces its supply base using sole sourcing from certified suppliers whenever possible. Some organizations source similar parts for different models from a second supplier to provide some backup capacity.
- Long-term relationships are established allowing for an increased use of blanket contracts and the sharing of technology plans, production schedules and other vital information.
- Performance specifications replace specific design specifications allowing the supplier to better use its expertise. Sometimes this means that purchasers need to trust that their suppliers have capable and talented engineers and managers.
- Joint problem solving efforts are undertaken to improve product quality and supply dependability. The purchaser works closely with the supplier, providing quality control and process engineering support.
- Critical performance criteria are focused on product quality and delivery dependability. Lowest total cost of ownership is emphasized over low price.

Clearly, time-based purchasing requires the rethinking and redesign of purchaser/supplier relationships. To support the development of these relationships as well as to assure the reliable, on-time delivery of purchased parts in a lean inventory setting, a unique set of practices must be implemented. These purchasing practices, along with an indication of their general implementation status, are listed in Table 3.1. It is quite remarkable that five of the six widely implemented practices are related to relationship building, partnership relationships, blanket orders, supplier qualification, supplier development, and supply base reduction. The purchaser/supplier relationship is the single most important feature of time-based purchasing. Long-term contracts provide the confidence and the motivation to invest in the relationship and each other's success. They also support the development of stronger, more focused capabilities. For example, Volvo offered a third-party service provider a 10-year contract to develop a proprietary rack system for use in shipping cars around the world.

TABLE 3.1
Time-based Purchasing Practices

Purchasing Practice	Usage Status
Long-term partnerships/contracts	Widespread Use
Blanket orders/minimal release paperwork	Widespread Use
Supplier qualification/certification	Widespread Use
Use of delivery time window	Widespread Use
Supplier development	Widespread Use
Supply base reduction	Widespread Use
Use of local, nearby suppliers	Frequent Use
Small, frequent deliveries to point of use	Frequent Use
Organization schedule/steady production rate	Frequent Use
Purchaser controlled transportation system	Frequent Use
Minimal purchasing specifications	Frequent Use
Value analysis	Frequent Use
Exact quantities/standardized containers	Frequent Use
EDI interface with suppliers	Limited Use
Extranet interface with suppliers	Increasing Use

Because partnership relationships are inherently more resource intensive than transaction-oriented relationships, the overall supply base must be reduced. Eighty to 90 percent reductions in the number of active suppliers are not uncommon. For example, Xerox reduced its supply base from about 5,000 to under 500 active suppliers. In a reduced supply base scenario, the purchasing organization can get to know its key suppliers intimately and can invest in their important skill building. Supplier quality certification is prevalent. Some organizations go much further in their supplier development strategies. Honda of America has been known to send a team of process engineers to important suppliers for up to three months at a time in order to help them improve their process capabilities.

Most organizations implement JIT purchasing practices incrementally. After key purchaser/supplier relationships are identified and developed, day-to-day practices associated with coordinating the flow of materials are addressed. For instance, using exact quantities/standardized containers and delivering small quantities of purchased items directly to the point of use is impossible before sound relationships have been built and suppliers are certified. The practice most organizations have struggled with is electronic communication with suppliers and carriers. Establishing EDI linkages with all suppliers and carriers is cost prohibitive. Only after desirable long-term relationships have been cemented does it make sense to invest in EDI, and then only if a common industry standard is in place. In many industries, competing EDI standards and the cost of using third-party networks has limited EDI implementation. Fortunately, extranets are beginning to fill the communication void for many organizations that have struggled with EDI. Many purchasers believe that extranets will entirely replace EDI within the next decade. Finally, delivery time windows are almost universally implemented in time-based purchasing strategies. Time windows are a type of insurance against non-performance.

As organizations consider whether or not to implement time-based purchasing, they need to evaluate the benefits and requirements of such strategies. Table 3.2 identifies some of the issues that purchasers should analyze as they gauge their organization's readiness to pursue time-based sourcing.

TABLE 3.2

Benefits, Barriers, and Bridges to Successful Time-based Sourcing

Benefits	Barriers	Bridges
Reduced inventories	Lack of top management support	Top management support
Reduced costs	Supplier reticence	Supply base reduction
Improved quality	Employee reticence	Supplier development programs
Increased productivity	Inadequate engineering support	Quality at the source
Improved supplier relations	View JIT as a panacea	Purchaser training programs
Shorter leadtimes	Poor product quality	Performance-based specifications
Enhanced responsiveness	Poor communication	Blanket orders
Better management focus	Poor purchaser/supplier relationships	Minimize variability of receipt quantity
Enhanced production scheduling	Logistics support	Minimize administrative paper work
Greater design innovativeness	Production schedule stability	Management of inbound freight

Benefits of Time-based Purchasing

Cooperative relationships have the potential to provide higher-quality, more innovative inputs, and the delivery of these inputs just-in-time to be used in the value-added process yields tremendous competitive benefits. These benefits can be categorized into two groups: cost-related benefits and non-cost benefits. The greatest cost benefits come from reductions in inventory. In Toyota's mass customization system, materials storage requirements are expected to decrease by 37 percent from already lean levels. Rework/scrap costs are also reduced dramatically. Other cost categories positively affected by time-based sourcing include unit costs, administrative costs, and inspection costs. When implemented correctly, time-based purchasing can enhance an organization's cost competitiveness.

The non-cost benefits of JIT begin with productivity improvements, product quality, and supplier response time. Each of these benefits by itself would be reason to consider time-based purchasing. When combined and focused via an aggressive materials strategy, the purchasing organization is in a much better position to provide superior value to its own customers. Two other benefits of time-based purchasing are smoother production scheduling and better product design. All of these benefits result from the changed nature of the purchaser/supplier relationship. By leveraging the volume aspects of the relationship, establishing high levels of trust, and investing in each other's success, the purchaser and supplier are able to effectively share information, coordinate operations, and work together to jointly solve problems. With time-based sourcing, synergies are created and competitiveness improved.

Barriers to Time-based Purchasing

Inertia created by traditional adversarial purchaser/supplier relationships as well as the philosophy of multiple sourcing creates the fundamental barrier to the implementation of time-based sourcing. Transitioning from a mindset that pits suppliers against each other in order to obtain the lowest possible price to a strategy that calls on suppliers to become a pivotal part of the competitive team is a major undertaking. Moving to a collaborative relationship requires that purchasers give up the sense of power that comes from leverage and that suppliers come to view purchasers as partners instead of opportunists. A comparison of two U.S. automakers illustrates the challenge and the value of developing more cooperative supply relationships. Chrysler's ability to make this transition created a reputation for having the most advanced and cooperative relationships with key suppliers of any U.S. automaker. This reputation was a major factor prompting Daimler's merger interest. Even as Chrysler was changing its approach to buyer/supplier relations, cross-town rival, General Motors, maintained a reputation as a brutal negotiator. J. Ignacio Lopez' willingness in the early 1990s to open up existing contracts to new bids from rival suppliers set a precedent for very aggressive supplier management.

Beyond the attitudinal and relational barriers that confront JIT implementation, a whole set of logistical barriers must be overcome. The first of these barriers is a fluctuating production schedule. It is very difficult for suppliers to plan their own production when the purchaser's requirements vary substantially. Likewise, standardized transportation milk runs cannot be established until manufacturing processes are flexible and stable. The entire logistics support system relies on schedule stability. Weak process engineering, poor forecasts, and a lack of supply chain communication represent legitimate and persistent barriers to successful time-based purchasing. Assuring the delivery of quality inputs in a timely manner is another major challenge. Selective supplier and carrier development improve "quality at the source" as well as the timeliness of materials delivery.

Bridges to Successful Time-based Purchasing

Developing high-level, broad-based managerial support for time-based sourcing and garnering external supplier support are prerequisites for success. These are the twin pillars of implementation success simply because the purchaser/supplier relationship is the key to success. Without top management support, purchasing professionals find it very difficult to take the risks associated with supply-base rationalization. Also, only top management can allocate the resources needed to sustain the development of a world-class supply base. From the supplier perspective, support is needed to commit to a long-term contract and the high levels of performance typically associated with today's relationships. While fostering this organizational support on both sides of the purchaser/supplier relationship can be difficult, most reticence can be overcome via education and training.

It is also critical to modify performance measures and reward systems to promote skill-building efforts, information sharing, cooperative decisionmaking, and time-based capabilities. As the purchaser/supplier relationship changes, supportive logistics systems must be established. In most instances it is best for the purchasing organization to control inbound freight. Purchasing organizations often enter into carrier-base reduction strategies that emphasize a few close relationships with dedicated and reliable carriers. These relationships are generally governed by longer-term contracts. Contract carriage has exploded with the advent of time-based purchasing strategies. In 1980, only 5 percent of all freight moved via contract carriage; by 2000 approximately 90 percent of freight moved under contract relationships.[11] These contract purchaser/carrier relationships often involve the use of delivery windows, guaranteed turnaround times, and streamlined receiving and inspection. While many time-based purchaser/supplier relationships still rely on fax, phone, and/or face-to-face meetings for a majority of the information exchange, Web-based extranets provide an increasingly viable linkage among purchasers, suppliers, and carriers.

Time-based Purchasing with a Global Supply Base

For many years, purchasers viewed time-based and global sourcing as incompatible. The most basic conflict is that of purchaser/supplier proximity. Frequent delivery of small quantities suggests the use of local suppliers. Such proximity is seldom attainable in global sourcing, which is characterized by longer, less-reliable international supply lines. Further, global sourcing strategies often emphasize the search for the "lowest-price" sourcing alternative, creating concern about the appropriate intensity of purchaser/supplier relationships. Two challenges thus complicate efforts to reconcile and integrate global and time-based strategies: assuring frequent, on-time delivery of smaller quantities across longer, cross-border supply lines and defining and developing intimate purchaser/supplier relationships across physical distances, languages, and cultures.

Supportive logistics is an important success factor (see Table 3.3) and is also the key to overcoming the challenge of obtaining on-time arrival of small lot sizes from worldwide suppliers. Thus, it is logical that organizations turn to innovative logistics systems. Only in the past few years have infrastructural improvements and technological advancements come together to make truly innovative logistics services possible. For example, doublestack rail service is now available from Chicago to Mexico City. Because product is shipped in-bond, there are no delays at the border. Transit time is a fairly consistent 96 hours, and documentation is electronically filed so that clearance occurs before the product physically arrives. Daily JIT delivery requires a manageable four to five days of pipeline inventory.

TABLE 3.3
Logistics Techniques Used to Facilitate Combined Use of Global and Time-based Sourcing

Facilitating Practices	Usage Status
Purchasing and shipping in container-sized lots	Widespread Use
Developing partnership relationships with transportation service providers	Widespread Use
Pre-clearance of customs	Widespread Use
Use of electronic tracking and expediting	Widespread Use
Collaborative Forecasting	Moderate Use
Use of local third-party warehousing to buffer global and JIT sourcing	Moderate Use
Reliance on air freight for regular shipments	Moderate Use
Outsourcing logistics to third-party providers	Moderate Use
Use of intermodal transportation	Moderate Use

A global logistical solution used by Texas Instruments and other organizations that ship high-value, low-weight products as well as some fashion retailers that ship high-value, time-sensitive products involves air freight and electronic information exchange. Air freight makes on-time, two- or three-day delivery of items sourced in Europe or the Pacific Basin possible. Combining containership and doublestack unit trains provides a lower-cost alternative. Transit time from Japan to Chicago using a single through bill of lading with pre-clearance of customs is a consistent 12 to 14 days. The turnaround (from ship to train) at the port of Seattle is a short 12 hours. By coupling the right business policies with the right logistical solutions, and the right relationships, it is now realistic to schedule daily JIT deliveries from suppliers located around the world and expect high levels of on-time performance. A brief description of the logistics practices at the core of today's innovative solutions follows below:

- **Small lot size shipments** – Purchasers often enter into volume contracts with global suppliers that call for frequent shipment of small lot sizes (from small parcels to entire containers). Shipments can be based on a schedule or on an electronic materials release. Frequent shipments work well when multiple parts from a single supplier or several items from various suppliers can be consolidated.
- **Transportation service partnerships** – Appropriate strategic alliances with logistics service providers can improve transportation reliability while reducing shipment leadtimes and total logistics costs.
- **Pre-clearance of customs** – Pre-clearance of customs has a positive affect on the organization's ability to manage pipeline inventories; reduce buffer stocks; and assure on-time delivery. Some transportation organizations have established an EDI linkage with U.S. customs to facilitate rapid, trouble-free customs clearance. A carrier's ability to provide a single, through bill of lading and to handle all of the documentation required for international shipments is vital.
- **Use of local warehousing as a buffer** – Local warehousing increases inventory and warehousing costs, but allows an organization to capture the other cost and competitive benefits of glob-

al sourcing, JIT delivery, and JIT production. Several transportation providers have established regional warehouses where they inventory items for important customers. This allows them to guarantee high levels of delivery performance even when unexpected problems occur in the global supply channel.

- **Use of intermodal transportation** – Intermodal transportation allows for a wide range of operating environments, provides long-haul economies, and enables high-quality, door-to-door service.

- **Order tracking and expediting** – Electronic information exchange helps purchasers track production and delivery schedules. Electronic linkages can help compensate for problems that occur in the supply channel by enabling firms to better track and expedite shipments. Today's satellite tracking can accurately pinpoint the location of a shipment almost anywhere in the world.

- **Reliance on air freight** – Despite its high cost, air freight can be used to enhance transportation reliability and delivery performance – especially among high-value added manufacturing organizations. A rigorous cost/benefit analysis often reveals that air freight is the best choice for global shipments.

- **Reliance on third-party logistics services** – Organizations that either do not possess in-house logistics services or lack the size and experience to develop strong relationships with logistics service providers often rely on third-party logistics organizations. Third parties can provide information and value-added services that shorten leadtimes, increase reliability, and enhance responsiveness.

- **Collaborative forecasting** – Accurate forecasts take the guesswork out of communication, making coordination much easier and reducing the need for expediting. One approach to reducing forecast error is to enhance collaboration so that more real information is shared.

Innovating a logistics system to support the concurrent use of global and JIT sourcing requires the adoption of a system's perspective, which incorporates channel mapping and a series of cost and performance tradeoff analyses. Such analysis empowers purchasers to know when integrating global and time-based strategies makes sense. Only a few leading organizations have these systems in place to map the supply chain and perform the total cost tradeoff analysis. Thus, a cautious, incremental approach that begins with non-critical items for which high levels of on-time delivery are not essential is suggested. A dual-source approach that uses local suppliers as back up might also be used. Further, while the logistics system is being established, local warehousing or buffer stocks can be employed. These practices help the organization gain experience with longer, international supply lines while it establishes partnerships with global suppliers and logistics service providers. The motivation to go to the effort to bridge the conflicts between global and time-based sourcing is simple – the opportunity to achieve a competitive edge unmatched by firms that rely on only one of the two strategies. Today's progressive purchasers have an opportunity to bring the world's best resources together just-in-time for success.

Time Counts

One reality of today's supply environment is that time counts. The old cliché that "time is money" still rings true, and organizations that can take time out of product development and order fulfillment cycles make more money than their competition. Time-centric organizations are more efficient and better satisfy customers' real needs. Such a combination is a powerful source of competitiveness. Imbuing purchasing with a time-centric mentality is vital to any organization's ability to compete on time. JIT purchasing and early supplier involvement in new product innovation are high-value-added practices at the core of time-based capabilities. Unfortunately, time-based purchasing strategies are not easy to design or implement. The pressure to eliminate waste and synchronize operations is present at every step in the purchasing process. Success depends on building cooperative relationships that span functional and organizational boundaries. Without cooperation, the seamless interaction needed to exchange information, share resources, and build integrative capabilities cannot take place. Despite their importance, long-standing "turf" issues and counterproductive reward systems hinder the development of cooperative relationships. Purchasing managers need to be outspoken advocates for stronger relationships. Assisting with the education process needed to break down existing functional barriers is an important role for managers. The journey toward integrative behavior and a fast-cycle capability is long and arduous, but relentless competition and demanding customers will push and pull the best organizations down this road.

Key Points

1. Time has become a valuable competitive attribute. Purchasers who can reduce cycle times and increase delivery dependability are able to help their organizations compete.
2. Modern time-based strategies emerged from the just-in-time revolution of the 1980s. Today, time-based strategies include integrated product development, collaborative planning and forecasting, and replenishment cycle-time reduction.
3. To achieve a time-based capability, purchasers must simplify the purchasing environment; develop a strong cross-functional capability; and adopt a long-term perspective complete with supportive performance measures.
4. Time-based capabilities require the integration of people and technology systems. Indeed, people and technology are the two primary sources of improvement in value-added processes.
5. Purchasers must constantly look for opportunities to shift roles in order to improve the organization's time-based capabilities. Examples of role shifting include quality certification (dock-to-stock), supplier managed inventory, early supplier involvement, and supplier directed assembly.
6. Global and time-based purchasing strategies can be integrated though the implementation of an innovative logistics system.
7. Cooperative purchaser/supplier relationships are the most important element of time-based purchasing.

Questions For Review

1. In what areas has time compression affected your organization's competitive ability? How have product development times changed over the past decade? Replenishment cycle times?

2. Evaluate your organization's current ability to compete on time? Is the value-added process transparent? Do managers and workers possess a cross-functional mindset? Are long-term investments that improve your organization's time-based capability supported?
3. Does your organization's performance measurement system promote time-based capabilities? What time-oriented measures does your organization use to evaluate supplier performance?
4. What efforts have been made to actively evaluate role-shifting opportunities? Are there any opportunities to shift roles and responsibilities and thereby improve competitiveness?
5. Evaluate your organization's continual improvement capabilities? What resources and training are needed to make improvements in this area?
6. What are the benefits, barriers, and bridges to successful time-based sourcing?

Endnotes

1. Salk, G. "Time – The Next Source of Competitive Advantage," *Harvard Business Review*, (66:4), 1988, pp. 41-51.
2. Schonberger, R.J. Japanese Manufacturing Techniques: Nine Hidden Lessons in Simplicity, *The Free Press*, New York, NY, 1982.
3. Naj, A. K. "Some Manufacturers Drop Efforts to Adopt Japanese Techniques," *Wall Street Journal,* May 7, 1993, p. A1.
4. Shirouzu, N. "Toyota Is Tightening Control of Key Suppliers In Bid to Block Encroachment by Foreign Firms," *Wall Street Journal*, August 3, 1999, p. A19.
5. Sherman, S. and A. Hadjian. "How Tomorrow's Leaders are Learning Their Stuff," *Fortune*, November 27, 1995, pp. 90-100.
6. Stewart, T.A. "How a Little Company Won Big by Betting on Brainpower," *Fortune*, September 4, 1995, pp. 121-122.
7. Upton, D.M. "What Really Makes Factories Flexible," *Harvard Business Review*, (73:4), 1995, pp. 74-84.
8. Taylor, J.C. and S.E. Fawcett. *"Retail In-Stock Performance on Promotional Items: An Assessment of Logistical Effectiveness,"* proceedings from Logistics Educators Conference.

9. Monczka, R.M. and R.J. Trent. "Global Sourcing: A Development Approach," *International Journal of Purchasing and Materials Management*, Spring, 1991, p. 27.
10. Simison, R.L. "Toyota Finds Way to Make a Custom Car in 5 Days," *Wall Street Journal*, August 6, 1999, p. A4.
11. *"Future Trends in Trucking,"* presented at the October 6, 1996 Round Table of the Council of Logistics Management, Salt Lake City, Utah.

CHAPTER 4

RISING EXPECTATIONS: MEETING THE QUALITY CHALLENGE

How can I help my organization meet demanding customer expectations?

Chapter Objectives

This chapter is designed to help the purchaser:

- Understand how information access has empowered customers and led to higher expectations.
- Develop a quality strategy for all purchased products and services.
- Gain the skills needed to help suppliers implement process control and problem solving techniques.
- Develop a supplier certification strategy.

Customer Power

Customers now have access to better information and are therefore more completely empowered in their purchase decisions than at any previous time. The ability to surf the Web, compile product specifications, and compare costs has greatly reduced the burden of the information acquisition process. In the auto industry today, a well-informed customer can enter the showroom with the invoice for a car in hand. Some car buyers skip the dealer negotiation process entirely and simply purchase the car over the Internet. This changing reality regarding customer empowerment holds true throughout the supply chain. In almost every industry, channel power has been shifting down the supply chain toward the end consumer. It is likely that this trend will continue, dramatically altering the way organizations must conduct business to survive.

The rule governing survival in a world filled with empowered customers is simple; organizations throughout the supply chain must increase their value-added capability. Shifting channel power together with information-based leverage is creating the "high-service sponge." High-service sponges are customers that use their market leverage to constantly demand higher levels of service. High-service sponges have a seemingly inexhaustible capacity to "soak up" more of their suppliers' resources. The emergence of service-hungry customers who possess tremendous channel power requires that purchasers understand how their organizations' customers define satisfaction and view value.

Customer Service, Satisfaction, and Success

Whenever a customer makes a purchase, what is bought is not simply a tangible product accompanied by some service. Rather, the customer is purchasing a set of "satisfactions." The customer's expectations and actual experience with the purchased product/service package determines whether or not "satisfaction" is achieved. This marketing-driven approach to delivering high levels of customer value is no longer adequate. The challenge is to use a set of limited resources to help preferred customers go beyond satisfaction to enhanced performance.[1] True value emerges when an organization helps its customers enhance their own competitive ability.

Organizations struggle in their quest to meet customers' real needs for two reasons. First, many possess a myopic view of what customer value really is.[2] Second, most organizations struggle with functional barriers that diminish their value creation and delivery capabilities.[3] Because purchasers have access to the resources and expertise of the entire supply base, they can help their organizations "do the right things efficiently." However, they need to understand the focus and critical issues associated with customer service, satisfaction, and success strategies (see Table 4.1).

Table 4.1
Critical Issues Associated with Different
Customer Fulfillment Strategies

Strategy	Focus	Issues
Customer Service	Meet internally defined standards.	• Fail to understand what customers value • Expend resources in wrong areas • Measure performance inappropriately • Fail to deliver more than mediocre service • Operational emphasis leads to service gaps
Customer Satisfaction	Meet customer-driven expectations.	• Ignore operating realities while overlooking operating innovations • Constant competitor benchmarking leads to product/service proliferation and inefficiency • Maintain unprofitable relationships • Vulnerable to new products and processes • Focus on historical needs of customer does not help customer meet new market exigencies
Customer Success	Help customers meet their customers' needs.	• Limited resources require that "customers of choice" be selected; that is, customer success is inherently a resource intensive strategy

- **Customer service** – Customer service initiatives focus on meeting internal standards that are believed to represent high levels of service. By performing well along the established metrics, organizations hope to meet customers' needs. Too often, the wrong activities are emphasized, dissipating resources on becoming excellent at something that is not valued by the customer.
- **Customer satisfaction** – Customer satisfaction initiatives recognize the threat of not knowing what customers really desire and focus on obtaining direct input from important customers regarding their service expectations. Achieving high marks in customer satisfaction requires that the organization learn to benchmark against customer requirements.

- **Customer success** – Customer success initiatives recognize that
  sustainable customer competitiveness is more important than
  maintaining a set of customers who are currently satisfied. The
  purchaser/supplier relationship must yield competitive advantage, or profit, to both organizations. Customer success strategies
  require a knowledge of the entire supply chain – that is, what do
  our customers' customers really want. Jack Kahl, CEO at Manco,
  has noted, "I have to know more about my customers than I know
  about myself."[4] Another CEO has summarized the essence of
  customer success as follows, "We turn our customers into win-
  ners. Their success is cash in our bank." [5]

One of the problems associated with a customer focus in a supply environment characterized by shifting channel power is verifiable
profit. In an effort to provide exceptional service to key customers,
many organizations have established policies and practices that
resulted in their losing money.[6] At one leading organization, the fact
that these key accounts were actually unprofitable was only discovered when more rigorous and accurate costing systems were implemented. Making the organization's production and delivery systems
efficient enough to guarantee profitability is difficult and requires
that the relevant value-added processes be simplified and made transparent. Because value-added processes span a variety of functional
areas, better information sharing coupled with a conscientious effort
to break down barriers among functional areas is needed to define
appropriate customer value and develop the processes that can profitably create and deliver it. Purchasing professionals increasingly find
that they hold the knowledge and manage the resources needed to
deliver profitable customer value in today's customer-centric world.
(See Table 4.2).

Table 4.2
Purchasing's Role in Creating Highly Valued,
Customer-centric Capabilities

Value Added	Activities/Processes	Functional Responsibilities
Possession Utility	• Recognize distinctive capabilities • Identify and evaluate customers • Understand supply chain imperatives • Define customer success factors • Communicate success factors • Select customers of choice • Build customer relationships	• Operations leads cross-functional effort • Marketing leads cross-functional effort • Marketing, operations, logistics, purchasing • Marketing takes lead • Top management • Marketing, operations, logistics • Marketing takes lead
Form Utility	• Balance market pull and technology push in developing distinctive capabilities • Focus on capabilities and processes • Convert inputs into finished goods/services	• Engineering provides technical expertise while marketing provides market awareness • Operations takes lead; purchasing supports • Operations creates the form and purchasing manages supplier capabilities
Time Utility	• Make products/services available to customers when they want them	• Purchasing provides materials on time; Operations meets production due-dates; Logistics stages and moves products; and Marketing interacts with customer
Place Utility	• Make products and services available where customers want them	• Logistics and marketing

Customers and Their Real Needs

Few organizations have the resources to please all customers, much less help them achieve higher levels of competitive success. Therefore, an organization must build value-added relationships with a select group of customers of choice. The process of selecting customers of choice occurs in two vital steps: the organization's distinctive capabilities are carefully defined and each customer's critical success factors are evaluated.

Distinctive capabilities – Distinctive capabilities derive from an organization's unique processes. Such capabilities emerge from cross-functional endeavors involving purchasing, engineering, production, logistics, marketing, and strategy working together to create value.[7] Because each function possesses different skills and perceptions, open discussion is needed to identify the organization's real distinctive capabilities. To build distinctive capabilities, key processes must be mapped to enhance their visibility; specific roles must be defined; inter-functional interactions must be understood; and greater cooperation must be established.

Customer success factors – Knowledge and understanding of supply chain imperatives enables managers to clearly and accurately define essential customer success factors, those factors that will help the customer meet its customers' needs. Most customer success factors fall into one of the following categories: quality, cost, responsiveness/flexibility, delivery/dependability, and innovation. It is important to note that once important customer success factors have been identified, they must be communicated throughout the organization to anyone and everyone.

Where alignment exists between the organization's distinctive capabilities and the customer's important success factors, opportunities to build strong and profitable purchaser/supplier relationships exist. Figure 4.1 matches customer success factors and the organization's distinctive capabilities, indicating what the likely outcomes are depending on the degree of alignment. The best situation occurs when customers need what the organization does well. The likely result in the other quadrants is diminished focus, wasted resources, and unprofitable customer relationships.

FIGURE 4.1
The Alignment Matrix

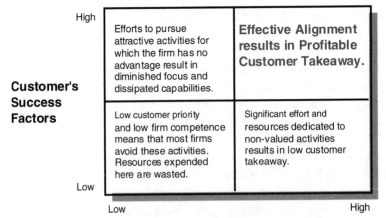

© Stanley E. Fawcett, Ph.D., C.P.M.

Today's Competitive Dimensions

In the early 1980s, Harvard professor Michael Porter noted that to be successful, firms had to develop a distinctive advantage.[8] The notion of distinctive, non-imitable advantage has since become the battle cry for leading organizations like Newell Corporation, Hewlett-Packard, VF Corporation, Nordstrom, and Disney. Distinctive advantage implies that an organization possesses some unique value-added capability that allows it to differentiate itself from key competitors in the mind of important customers. If an organization were to bring all of its managers together for a brainstorming session to identify the diverse opportunities where distinctive advantage might be enhanced, a long and unwieldy list would certainly be generated. However, a careful analysis would reveal that most of the opportunities could be classified into one of five basic areas: cost, quality, flexibility, delivery, and innovation.

Cost – To succeed, an organization must match the cost position of rivals from around the world who often possess lower cost structures stemming from low-cost labor or vital supply advantages. The three primary approaches to enhancing the organization's cost position have been to emphasize productivity; to locate operations in geographic regions that provide access to lower-cost inputs; and to source from the world's most efficient suppliers. Today, these approaches are often used in concert. Unfortunately, the cost challenge is much greater than pursuing productivity programs or simply following competitors around the world, building production facilities in countries with the lowest labor rates. As one manager in the consumer products industry has noted, the critical measure of cost performance today is "total landed cost to the customer's trunk." Thus, the organization's entire value-added network or system must be designed to be efficient. A total cost approach is required to design winning cost capabilities.

Quality – Quality is typically defined in terms of fitness for use or conformance to specifications. However, the ultimate measure of quality is whether or not the product or service lives up to customer expectations. The power of quality to influence perceptions and thereby purchasing behavior over a lengthy period of time has led some analysts to call quality the single most important factor for long-term competitive success. To achieve consistently high levels of quality, quality must be both designed and built into the product/service package. Juran[9] argued that over 80 percent of quality problems can be controlled by management. The performance affect of superi-or quality combined with the trend toward outsourcing has only increased the importance of outstanding purchasing practice in help-ing the organization achieve a differential quality advantage. Purchasing managers have a tremendous affect on overall quality simply because a finished product's quality can be no better than the quality of the individual parts that make up the product. Ultimately, a quality focus requires complete participation and support throughout the managerial ranks and functional areas of the organization.

Flexibility – Flexibility is defined as the "ready capability to adapt to new, different, or changing requirements." In today's com-petitive arena, flexibility is often characterized as "doing things fast" and "being responsive to the market."[10] A flexible organization oper-ates with short leadtimes, is responsive to special requests, and can adjust rapidly to unexpected events. By definition, flexibility is a cross-functional capability that depends on the adaptability of the organization's people. Flexibility also requires investments in infor-mation and automation technologies. The following steps are critical to making flexibility a part of the organizational fabric. They include the following:

- Making cycle time a priority throughout the organization
- Mapping/modeling the value-added process (i.e., make them vis-ible)
- Benchmarking against competition and customer requirements
- Identifying key time-related activities/decisions
- Cross-training workers and organize work in multifunctional teams
- Building learning loops into the organization
- Developing information systems to track value-added activities and disseminate vital information
- Designing performance measures to value fast-cycle capabilities

Organizations like Amazon.com, The Limited, and Wal-Mart have set the standard for flexibility. Wal-Mart combines cross-dock-ing, a satellite communications system, and a private trucking fleet to achieve superior operational flexibility and to assure that the right products are always on the shelf where the customer expects to find them – and at the low prices customers are willing to pay. At The Limited, the goal for responsiveness is to bring the desired product from the mind of the customer to the retail rack within 1,000 hours – about 60 percent faster than the competition. This speed allows The Limited to have the most popular styles and colors available in peak season – when the customer wants them. Amazon.com can trace much of its success to a "flexible" Web site that self customizes to each customer's purchasing habits and to a high level of rapid response to customer orders. The ability to leverage information, people, and processes to respond rapidly to customers' needs yields a tangible competitive advantage.

Delivery – A viable delivery capability must promise competitive delivery dates and deliver on time according to promise. Another way to look at delivery is to say that delivery performance means "doing things fast" - consistently. Developing a strong delivery capability requires the reduction of order cycle time and the elimination of variability throughout the order delivery system. By nature, delivery capability is cross functional. Any activity that increases the time or variability of the order cycle reduces the organization's ability to compete on delivery. For example, an incorrect order entry, a late supplier delivery, a machine breakdown, or a transportation delay can all adversely affect the organization's delivery performance. The materials management functions of purchasing, operations, and logistics play central roles in building a strong delivery capability. Operations and logistics typically represent 90 percent or more of the total order cycle time for most organizations. Purchasing supports both, providing the right materials on time, every time and managing important materials and service suppliers so that there are no delays in production or delivery. Efforts to achieve truly superior delivery performance should target all three functional areas. The following examples show that promising short leadtimes and then delivering on time can provide an important competitive edge.

- Motorola established itself as a world leader in pager manufacturing by reducing production time from 30 days to less than 30 minutes.
- National Semiconductor redesigned its global distribution network to enhance customer service through better delivery performance – a 47 percent reduction in delivery time delivered a 34 percent increase in sales.[11]
- Steelcase became a leading furniture manufacturer by promising set up of 80 percent of its custom design product line of office

furniture within 12 days from receipt of order to anywhere in North America.[12]

Innovation – Long-term success depends on the organization's innovation capabilities. Innovation helps create new market niches and change industry standards en route to improving market share and financial performance. Purchasing has taken on a more prominent and visible role in product innovation as suppliers have been included more and more in the early stages of product design. Indeed, early supplier involvement has been found to be a key element of leading organization's innovation strategies. For example, early and continued supplier involvement in the development process has been found to account for one-third of the reduction in man-hours and four to five months of the shorter leadtimes enjoyed by the leading innovators. Further, organization's that introduced products six months past the projected release date, but within budget, realized a 33 percent decrease in expected profits over the first five years. By contrast, introducing products on time, but 50 percent over budget, led to only a 4 percent reduction in profit.[13] Finally, new product innovation can open the door to successful market entry and dominance.

- When Yamaha publicly challenged Honda's dominance as the world's largest motorcycle producer, Honda responded to the challenge by introducing or replacing 113 models during the next year and a half. The technological sophistication of Honda's new designs made Yamaha's product line obsolete.[14]
- When Toyota's share of the Japanese market dipped below 40 percent, a new emphasis on bringing exciting new cars to market emerged. Several vehicles came to market in 18 months (the Ipsum actually went from concept to market in only 15 months).
- To achieve constant innovation, 3M gives its people time to work on pet innovation projects and expects 30 percent of all sales from products introduced in the last four years.[15]

Tradeoffs Versus Synergies

A challenge that has long faced purchasers has been to determine how much emphasis to place on each of the competitive dimensions discussed above. For many years, the generally accepted belief has been that implicit tradeoffs existed among the five dimensions. For example, quality was long believed to be inherently expensive.

Likewise, standardization and customization were believed to be at opposite ends of the spectrum. While there is some validity to the belief that tradeoffs prevail, an alternative perspective that suggests the existence of synergies among the different capabilities has emerged. Synergies arise from simplifying the operating environment and creating an organizational culture that is fluid and promotes excellence. Clearly communicated customer requirements, shared information, elimination of restrictive work rules, and proactive performance measures make it possible for cost, quality, flexibility, delivery, and innovation to work together to build competitive advantage (see Figure 4.2). Recent experience has shown that 40 percent of all quality problems can be traced back to inferior product design and 60 to 80 percent of a product's cost is determined during the design process. Further, the term "hidden plant" was coined to signify that 15 to 40 percent of an organization's capacity is used to find and fix poor-quality work.[16] The bottomline is that successful organizations now realize that they have to achieve excellence along multiple competitive dimensions simultaneously if they are going to win customer loyalty.

FIGURE 4.2

Tradeoffs or Synergies Among Competitive Dimensions

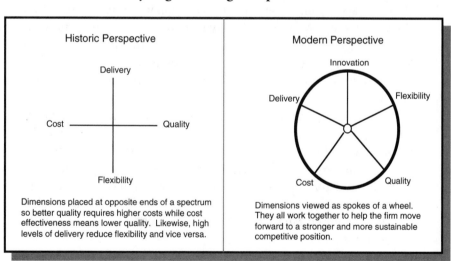

© Stanley E. Fawcett, Ph.D., C.P.M.

Quality — The Foundation of Customer Expectations

It is difficult to say that any one competitive dimension is more valuable or important than the others. The experience of the past 20 years clearly reveals that quality is the dimension foremost in the minds of consumers. Not only is quality highly sought after by the customer but the adverse affect of poor quality on cost, delivery, and flexible performance can be debilitating. In many respects, quality is the foundation for successfully developing the other capabilities. For these two reasons, quality is considered by many to be the single most influential factor in achieving a sustainable long-term advantage. As W. Edwards Deming noted, "You are not obliged to manage quality. You can also choose to go out of business." [17]

Quality, from a purchasing perspective, has primarily been defined as fitness for use; does the item conform to design specifications? Of course, this assumes that the design specifications are appropriate to the intended function and use of the product. Quality performance has long been measured in terms of percent defective. Best-in-class organizations now measure quality in parts per million (PPM) defective. Motorola's highly recognized "six sigma" program was launched to help Motorola make the leap from percent defective to parts-per-million performance. A few organizations have actually achieved this quality level of only three defects per million parts produced.

While this operational view is valuable from a measurement and control perspective, it fails to take customer expectations into full account. In a fiercely competitive market where rivals constantly seek to outperform each other, customers often find that they have multiple attractive options. This means that purchasers need to get into the minds of customers to understand how they define quality. Garvin[18] identified eight distinct factors that comprise quality in the minds of the end user.

- **Performance** – refers to the primary operating characteristics of the product.

- **Features** – are the "bells and whistles" or extras that distinguish a product from competitors' offerings.
- **Reliability** – represents the notion that a product can be counted on not to fail.
- **Conformance** – measures how well a product matches established specifications.
- **Durability** – refers to the product's mean time between failures and its overall life expectancy.
- **Serviceability** – refers to the speed of repair when quality problems arise.
- **Aesthetics** – deals with perceptions of fit and finish or artistic value.
- **Perceived quality** – deals with overall perceptions of a product or brand's quality reputation.

Organizations need to know how the customer defines quality as well as how the customer measures quality performance. Once this insight is gained, a "six sigma" caliber program can be executed to assure the highest performance in meeting customer expectations. Today, quality literally means doing the right things right the first time – every time.

Because purchasers work closely with suppliers to constantly improve supplier quality, they must be intimately familiar with the following quality concepts, statistical tools, and problem-solving methodologies. Many large suppliers have the necessary financial and managerial resources needed to successfully undertake a total quality program. For some, the major deficiency is a lack of motivation to actively move forward in the implementation of a world-class quality program. When this is the problem, the purchasing organization is often forced to use the leverage of supply-base reduction to animate their quest for quality. Many smaller suppliers possess neither the finances nor the knowledge to embark on a total quality expedition. These suppliers need the knowledge, experience, and at times, the financial resources of the purchasing organization. Proactive, quality-conscious purchasers often find themselves involved in a mentoring relationship, working to provide motivation and skills to valued suppliers.

The Evolution of Quality Philosophies

Following World War II, a "get the product out the door" mentality motivated managerial decisionmaking. Demand exceeded capacity and just about everything that was produced could be sold. In this productivity and cost-oriented environment, quality was relegated to the sidelines of the competitive battle. Quality experts like Deming, Juran, and Feigenbaum found little audience for their quality message. State-of-the art quality control consisted largely of in-process inspection and acceptance sampling. However, by the early 1980s, the quality gap had become apparent, and those organizations that had previously turned a deaf ear to the importance of quality began to see the need for it. Inspection could not yield the quality levels that customers demanded. Instead of simply controlling quality, it now needed to be managed proactively. Total Quality Management (TQM) quickly became the management mantra of the 1980s. More recently, the philosophical evolution took another twist. To take quality up to the next level and actually achieve parts-per-million performance, the quality effort had to begin before production. Only by focusing on quality from the initial product conceptualization could the highest levels of performance be attained. Of course, the notion that quality must be designed and then built into the product has not eliminated the need for inspection. The three approaches work in concert to deliver the highest levels of quality.

- **The inspection approach** – The intent of establishing a quality control (QC) department to monitor quality via inspection was to catch mistakes or defects so that they would not cause problems for downstream operations or customers. For purchasers, the inspection process for purchased parts took place once they arrived at the receiving dock. Inspection involved taking a sample to determine the overall shipment's fitness for use. When a sample failed the inspection because too many defective products were found, the shipment was either sent to a rework station or returned to the supplier. In either case, the supplier was expected to cover the costs associated with making the product fit for use. Unfortunately, inspection ignores the process where poor quality occurs. Without process improvement, an army of inspectors and 100 percent inspection is needed to verify that only quality products are shipped to customers. Such an effort is costly, and is never able to guarantee parts-per-million quality.

- **The build-it-in approach** – Total Quality Management – a complete organizational emphasis on improving quality everywhere (product, process, and mindset), underlies the build-it-in approach. TQM relies on personal responsibility coupled with relentless measurement. The responsibility for quality shifts from a QC department to each individual in the organization. When a defective part is found, instead of being sent to a rework station the part is returned to the worker who made the mistake. Immediate feedback and the responsibility to correct their own errors helps workers identify the root causes of quality problems and learn how to avoid making the same mistakes. By changing the nature of worker responsibility, providing workers with the appropriate quality training, and making quality visible, TQM focuses on process management so that the production of high-quality products becomes automatic. This makes constant improvement possible and moves the quality target of "zero defects" from rhetoric to reality. Of course, organizations that adopt a build-it-in approach expect their suppliers to do the same.

- **The design-it-in approach** – Genichi Taguchi claimed that "quality is a virtue of design. The robustness of products is more a function of good design than of online control of manufacturing processes." He noted that up 80 percent of all defects result from poor product design and argued that the costs of poor quality are usually six times greater than most organizations think.[19] Taguchi therefore advocated the use of controlled experiments to evaluate the average quality affect of different design factors. Insight gained from these experiments helps managers identify and eliminate the sources of variation that affect product consistency. The desire to design quality into the product has prompted a need to get suppliers involved in the product conceptualization and design process. By harnessing supplier insight, an organization can leverage the engineering, process, testing, tooling, and other capabilities that suppliers have developed. When suppliers are given the freedom to develop product designs based on their process capabilities, they often deliver higher-quality parts at lower costs.

Continuous Improvement Tools and Techniques

Continuous improvement is driven by the organization's ability to understand process capabilities and to consistently identify and remove the sources of process variability. Aggressive use of statistical tools combined with a team-oriented problem-solving methodology can help managers gain this understanding and promote a continuous improvement culture. It is important to note that statistical tools help monitor processes and assure that they are in control; they do not by themselves identify specific sources of variability. Statistical tools do, however, raise the red flag, warning managers that something is amiss by identifying when a process is no longer in control. Careful tracking of statistical "red flags" helps managers and workers alike identify specific problem areas. This insight becomes the starting point for rigorous problem solving.

Process capability analysis – Before quality can be built into a product, it is necessary to verify that the selected production process is capable of performing at the desired quality level. This process proving involves some form of trial run or pilot test. As the trial run takes place, managers must replicate as closely as possible the actual operating environment. Deviations from a realistic operating environment invalidate results. Therefore, the same equipment, the same procedures, the same workers, and the same suppliers should all be used in the test run. The output of the process should then be measured against the standard using rigorous statistical analysis to assess the overall process capability.

The process capability ratio helps assess the process' ability to achieve required quality levels. By comparing acceptable tolerances (set by engineering) with the process variation, this ratio indicates whether the process can consistently produce "good" quality parts. The ratio is calculated as follows:

$$C_p = \frac{|\,USL\text{-}LSL\,|}{6\sigma} \quad \text{where:} \quad \begin{aligned} USL &= \text{upper specification limit} \\ LSL &= \text{lower specification limit} \\ \sigma &= \text{standard deviation (process variability)} \end{aligned}$$

The process standard deviation is calculated using actual output from the trial run. A multiplier of six is used to establish the degree of confidence that the process' output will fall within the upper and lower limits. That is, using a standard normal distribution, 6s sets a standard of close to 100 percent confidence that the process can achieve the desired quality level. Because most processes do not yield a process mean that is exactly equal to the target mean, a correction factor k that reflects the difference between the actual process mean (μ) and the design target (D) must be introduced. The adjusted capability ratio is calculated using the following equations:

$$C_{pk} = Cp\,(1 - k) \quad \text{where:} \quad k = \frac{|D - m|}{(USL\text{-}LSL)/2}$$

A C_{pk} of 1.5 or higher suggests that the process can meet the desired or target quality levels. Working through an example can help clarify the methodology of the process capability ratio. Suppose that the design engineering team set the specifications for length of a stamped sheet-metal part at 10 inches (D) with acceptable tolerances of ±.05 inches (USL and LSL). The average length of the products produced by the actual stamping process is 9.99 inches (μ) with a standard deviation of .015 inches (σ). The calculations for the C_p and C_{pk} are as follows:

$$Cp = (10.05\text{-}9.95)/6(.015) = .10/.09 = 1.11$$
$$k = (10 - 9.99)/((10.05\text{-}9.95)/2) = .01/.05 = .20$$
$$Cpk = 1.11\,(1\text{-}.20) = 1.11(.8) = .88$$

In this example, the C_{pk} of .88 is well below the desired 1.5, indicating that the manufacturing process is not capable of consistently producing parts that will be 10 ± .05 inches in length. There is too much variability in the process to assure acceptable quality. Three options exist for improving the capability ratio. The numerator, which denotes the acceptable tolerance level, can be increased; the denominator, which is a function of process variability, can be decreased; or the process' ability to produce closer to target can be improved. If we assume that the tolerance limits are set based on real performance requirements, then the design specifications must not be arbitrarily altered simply to increase the process capability ratio. This reality leaves two options, both of which are dependent on improving the real performance of the process. Returning to the example above, management opts to bring in a process engineering team to modify the equipment. After making several adjustments, a trial run is held and the output is sampled. The average length of the sample is now 9.995 inches (μ) and the standard deviation has been reduced to .005

inches (σ). The new C_{pk} of 3.0 reveals that the process is now capable of producing to the required quality standards.

$$Cp = (10.05\text{-}9.95)/6(.005) = .10/.03 = 3.33$$
$$k = (10 - 9.995)/((10.05\text{-}9.95)/2) = .005/.05 = .10$$
$$Cpk = 3.33 \ (1\text{-}.10) = 3.33(.90) = 3.0$$

When working with new suppliers, new parts, or new processes, purchasers must take the time to verify that the process is capable of producing within acceptable tolerances. If the process is deficient, it makes no sense to try to control process quality. The root causes of the variability must be found and eliminated. Because design engineers often lack confidence in both the supplier's manufacturing capability and the purchaser's willingness or ability to verify supplier process capabilities they sometimes set the product specifications at levels that are much tighter than they really need to be in order to "design in" quality. Unfortunately, this practice, known as guard banding, almost always increases production costs and lengthens leadtimes while failing to improve quality substantially.

Statistical process control – Once process capability is established, the quality emphasis shifts to controlling the production process by checking quality while the work is being done. The best way to effectively carry out this quality effort is to train the workers in statistical process control techniques and have the workers do it themselves.

The most common process control tool is the control chart, which allows workers to periodically chart or plot a specific performance characteristic of a small sample of parts against a standard. The standard is expressed in terms of a target performance level with upper and lower limits. In a perfectly controlled setting, which never exists, every single item would measure exactly to specification. The existence of process variability, however, means that performance will vary above and below the ideal target level. As long as the variation remains within acceptable limits or tolerances, the process is considered to be in control. By periodically charting the performance of a process it is possible to identify the point at which a process is out of control and no longer producing quality parts. The process can then be stopped and the problem resolved, before too many defective parts are produced. While this is a key role of control charts, a more substantial benefit is the opportunity to spot trends and gain insight into the underlying sources of process variability. As this understanding is gained, the worker is empowered to begin to improve the process by removing the variability. It must be remembered that variability is quality's number one enemy.

The mechanics of SPC are quite simple once the statistics are understood (see Figure 4.3). To build the initial control chart, the product attribute to be controlled must be identified. Periodic samples, typically four or five parts, are then taken over a sustained time period. Each item in each sample is measured and the mean and range of each sample are calculated (most organizations use X bar and R bar charts concurrently). The process must be running according to specification – in control – during the entire sampling time. If it is out of control and producing defective parts, the control chart will be meaningless. To get a really good picture of the process, 25 to 30 samples are needed. Once all of the samples have been taken, an overall sample mean is calculated. The sample mean is the average of all of the individual sample means. This is the first piece of critical information, a measure of the target performance. If the operation has been in control, the average will be almost identical to the target performance level because the random variations will tend to cancel each other out. This mean becomes the center line for the control chart. Next, the upper and lower control limits are calculated. To do this, two pieces of information are needed – a measure of process variability and a measure of desired confidence. The measure of variability is the standard deviation of the process performance. The standard deviation of all of the items is then translated into a standard error by dividing by the square root of the number of items in each sample. The Z-score, the number of standard deviations away from the target, is the measure of confidence that the process is in or out of control. Remember, a ±3s represents approximately 100 percent confidence. The upper and lower control limits are calculated using the following equations and drawn on the control chart above and below the center line.

Upper Control Limit = Overall Mean + (measure of confidence)(measure of variability) = $X + Z\sigma_x$
Lower Control Limit = Overall Mean − (measure of confidence)(measure of variability) = $X - Z\sigma_x$

FIGURE 4.3
An Example of Statistical Process Control

Twenty samples of four items each were taken to set up the control chart.

Sample	Measures within the Sample				Sample Average	Key Information
1	2.81	2.79	2.78	2.80	2.795	Design process center = 2.80 cm
2	2.81	2.79	2.80	2.83	2.808	Measure of target performance = 2.799 cm
3	2.79	2.77	2.80	2.81	2.793	Measure of variability (σ) = 0.014
4	2.81	2.78	2.79	2.81	2.798	Number of items in each sample = 4
5	2.82	2.79	2.80	2.78	2.798	Standard error ($\sigma / \sqrt{4}$) = .007
6	2.78	2.79	2.82	2.80	2.798	Measure of desired confidence (Z) = 3
7	2.80	2.80	2.81	2.79	2.800	
8	2.79	2.80	2.80	2.82	2.803	
9	2.78	2.78	2.81	2.80	2.793	
10	2.81	2.79	2.80	2.81	2.803	Upper Control Limit= $\bar{X} + Z\sigma_{\bar{x}}$
11	2.78	2.82	2.79	2.80	2.798	= 2.799 + 3(.007)
12	2.80	2.82	2.81	2.79	2.805	= 2.820
13	2.78	2.79	2.78	2.81	2.790	
14	2.81	2.82	2.80	2.79	2.805	
15	2.78	2.82	2.81	2.79	2.800	Lower Control Limit= $\bar{X} - Z\sigma_{\bar{x}}$
16	2.79	2.80	2.79	2.82	2.800	= 2.799 - 3(.007)
17	2.80	2.81	2.80	2.78	2.798	= 2.778
18	2.80	2.80	2.79	2.82	2.803	
19	2.78	2.82	2.79	2.79	2.795	
20	2.77	2.81	2.82	2.80	2.800	
					2.799	

$\bar{X}$ Chart

After the control chart was established, daily sampling began as follows:

Time	Measurements in each Sample				Average
8:00	2.80	2.81	2.81	2.79	2.803
8:30	2.81	2.79	2.80	2.79	2.798
9:00	2.78	2.82	2.79	2.81	2.800
9:30	2.78	2.79	2.81	2.80	2.795
10:00	2.80	2.81	2.80	2.80	2.803
10:30	2.80	2.81	2.80	2.79	2.800

Do you see any trends? If there are no trends and the samples fall within the control limits, then the operation is in control.

Once the control chart is constructed, the process operator periodically samples the product, often every 30 minutes. The frequency depends on the process' proven ability to stay in control. The operator measures the attribute of importance, calculates the sample mean, and plots it on the control chart. Any sample mean that falls outside the control limits requires that the process be halted and the source of variance investigated. In addition to looking for samples that show the process to be out of control, the operator also looks for any trends in the plotted samples. A trend points to a non-random or systematic source of variation. Whenever systematic sources of variation can be identified and the source discovered and eliminated, the process can be improved.

A problem-solving methodology – Once a problem is detected, the real opportunity emerges. The source of the problem must be identified and corrective action taken. Leading organizations recognize that problem solving is the major part of a quality-improvement battle. These organizations endeavor to put in place a systematic problem-solving methodology that leverages the knowledge and experience of the entire workforce. Most formal problem-solving techniques have the following steps in common: identify problems, prioritize problems, select a resolvable problem, analyze the problem, generate possible solutions, perform a feasibility and payback analysis for likely solutions, select and plan the solution, implement, and evaluate. Deming was the first to widely introduce this approach to problem solving.[20] His approach consists of the following four steps, which create a cycle of continuous improvement:

- **Plan** – Define the problem and identify the root cause. Asking the question "Why?" five times can help get past the superficial symptoms and to the real root cause. An action plan can then be established.
- **Do** – Implement a corrective action to solve the problem.
- **Check** – Check to see if the corrective action really solved the problem. Without follow through, problem solving efforts quickly ring hollow.
- **Act** – If the solution worked, make it a formal part of the process. Cross fertilize wherever and whenever possible. Look for new quality problems and the underlying sources of variance so that the cycle can begin anew.

A formal methodology supported by appropriate performance measurement can help overcome many of the challenges associated with ineffective and sporadic problem solving efforts. Among the most prevalent problems are the following:

- The failure to bring the right people to the problem-solving team
- The failure to dedicate sufficient resources for a comprehensive solution
- The propensity to opt for quick and easy solutions
- The failure to follow through and then share knowledge throughout the organization

While most organizations know that a systematic problem-solving methodology is needed, recognizing the need and producing an effective methodology are distinct challenges. Generating and mobilizing the resources needed for effective problem solving can be particularly difficult for smaller suppliers. These suppliers often lack experience with formal methodologies like Deming's Plan-Do-Check-Act methodology. A purchasing organization that has practical and successful experience with an effective problem-solving technique is ideally positioned to share this expertise with important suppliers that have yet to develop problem-solving skills in house. Purchasers must make sure that key suppliers have rigorous problem-solving methodologies in place and should be prepared to provide the needed training and encouragement when they don't.

Problem-solving tools – One specific area where purchasing managers can enhance the quality performance of the supply base is to teach suppliers how to use some simple and proven problem-solving tools. Many of these tools can and should be used in the root-cause analysis and solution-generating steps found in the formal problem-solving methodology. For example, the Isikawa cause-and-effect diagram is a popular tool that requires the problem solvers to isolate and break down the major causes of variation according to what are known as the four M's – Man, Machine, Methods, and Materials (see Figure 4.4). The development of the cause-and-effect diagram is best done in a team setting so that diverse perspectives and knowledge sets are brought to the discussion table. A brainstorming session, in which team members jointly and rapidly generate ideas, is

an excellent approach to identifying a wide variety of possible causes. Brainstorming can help the problem-solving team get out of the
confining "same-old solution box."

FIGURE 4.4
The Ishikawa Cause-and-Effect (Fishbone) Diagram

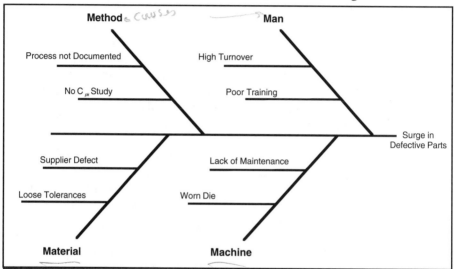

The Ishikawa Cause-and-effect (fishbone) diagram guides brainstorming sessions designed to get to the root
cause of a quality problem. As a possible cause is identified, a new path of investigation is begun. Each possible cause is explored until the root causes are determined. Because most of the variation that causes defects
can be traced to the Four M's, the typical cause-and-effect diagram focuses on these issues:

Man – variations that result from human error that results from poor training, fatigue, and lack of experience.
Machine – variations that result from poor maintenance, worn equipment, and use of wrong equipment.
Methods – variations that result from inappropriate processes, lack of process control, and poor documentation.
Materials – variations that result from the use of defective, damaged, or poorly specified materials.

© Stanley E. Fawcett, Ph.D., C.P.M.

After the potential causes are established, careful analysis is
required to verify the extent to which each is really a root cause of the
problem. A Pareto chart highlights the sources of variation that
should be attacked first. A Pareto chart is a graph that shows the frequency with which each cause occurs. Pareto charts rank orders
issues so that priorities can be set. By combining the frequency of
appearance with the associated cost impact, a manageable set of causes can be selected for eradication. The next step is to develop a set of
alternative solutions. Ideas for solving each problem can come from

a variety of places including past experience, documentation of the "what's", "how's", and "why's" of value-added processes, benchmarking, other best-in-class processes, and brainstorming. Once the complete solution set is on the board, open discussion that evaluates the pros and cons of each option can begin. Rigorous root-cause analysis followed by creative solution generation can lead to extremely effective problem solving. Purchasers should work to see that suppliers use these tools to improve their quality processes.

Facilitating concepts – A number of concepts that facilitate successful continuous quality improvement have been widely implemented. Most of the concepts focus on building continuous learning loops by engaging the creative energy of both managers and workers. Others emphasize making quality automatic. All of the concepts work to create a quality habit. Each of the concepts merits brief review.

- **Quality control as a facilitator** – When everyone takes responsibility for quality, the QC department's role is to train workers in quality control, work with suppliers, identify possible quality projects, monitor the overall process, and perform the tests that are too complex to be done by line workers.
- **Insistence on compliance** – Quality must come first and output second. "Close enough" is unacceptable. Management must communicate this priority and insist that it be followed.
- **Small lot sizes** – Reduced lot sizes remove clutter and make quality visible. Without excess inventory, defective products are quickly found and returned immediately to the responsible worker.
- **Correcting one's own errors** – When a mistake is made, the person who made the mistake makes the correction. Correcting mistakes at the source raises quality awareness and closes the learning loop.
- **Line stop** – When quality problems arise, a worker turns on a yellow or a red light to indicate a problem, and if the problem is serious (red light), the value-added process stops. Everyone then cooperates to solve the problem and get the process running again.
- **Purposeful removal of workers** – At some organizations, managers purposefully remove workers from a smooth running process until small problems start to occur. The objective of this practice is to identify problems that can then become the focus of quality projects.

- **Daily machine checking** – When workers take immaculate care of their machines, performing daily maintenance, downtime and equipment wear and tear are reduced.
- **Project-by-project improvement** – By promoting a constant succession of quality improvement projects in progress throughout the organization, continual improvement occurs year after year.
- **Housekeeping** – Maintaining a clean, well-organized workplace is essential to quality performance. Clearing the clutter is everyone's responsibility – workers must keep their own areas neat and clean.
- **Automatic checking devices** – Foolproof devices such as jigs can safeguard against poor quality. If a part does not fit in a specially shaped container, the worker automatically knows it is defective.

Statistical analysis working hand-in-hand with an engaging problem-solving methodology and supporting the concepts discussed above can dramatically improve an organization's quality performance. Of course, to truly compete on quality, an organization's supply base must catch the quality vision and develop commensurate quality capabilities. It is the purchaser's job to make this happen.

Managing Supplier Quality

Actively intervening in supplier operations is a strange concept for some organizations. Traditional arm's length transactions together with the philosophy of pitting suppliers against one another to get the best price has meant that cooperative improvement efforts have not been viewed as desirable or worth the time and expense. For those who continue to wonder why it is so important to invest in supplier quality, the answer is quite simple – without quality at the source, it is impossible to deliver quality to the customer. The fact that suppliers account for 55 percent of the typical manufacturer's sales dollar highlights the fact that up to half of an organization's quality outcome is in the hands of suppliers. Quality expert Philip Crosby estimated that suppliers account for 50 percent of product-related quality problems.[21] When it comes to managing quality, the "garbage-in-garbage-out" description fits perfectly.

Managing supplier quality has always meant that the purchaser has had a responsibility to clearly communicate expectations for the relationship and specifications for the product (see Figure 4.5). Keki Bhote, an expert on supplier quality has noted, "At least half or even more of the quality problems between customer (i.e., the purchaser) and supplier are caused by poor specifications, for which the purchasing organization is largely responsible."[22] Purchasers and suppliers need to be involved with engineering in the determination of mutually acceptable specifications that are feasible and clearly understood. Some purchasers feel that their quality job is done once the specifications are clearly communicated. Progressive purchasers know that their job has really just begun. They realize that there are many time-consuming activities that should be performed to elevate quality. Some of these activities are listed below:

- Developing a close relationship with key suppliers so that open dialogue is promoted. This often requires supply-base reduction so that more resources are available to devote to remaining suppliers.
- Providing quality improvement training programs for selected suppliers. Quality training usually focuses on quality motivation, total quality management, and statistical tools.
- Establishing a supplier certification program that encourages suppliers to assure the quality of their production processes.
- Working with suppliers to develop and enhance their quality capabilities.
- Measuring supplier performance rigorously and consistently and then sharing the findings with suppliers. Outstanding performance should be rewarded. Weak or deficient performance should be highlighted so that improvement efforts can be initiated.

The amount of effort and quantity of resources dedicated to improving supplier quality is tied to the strategic importance of the specific supplier. In most organizations, supplier development budgets are limited, therefore, scarce funds must be deployed carefully and their affect monitored closely to justify future investment. Critically important relationships receive the highest levels of resource commitment while some relationships receive little or no attention from the purchaser.

Certifying Suppliers

Supplier certification is the formal process through which purchasers work with selected suppliers to evaluate and improve supplier quality (see Figure 4.5). Suppliers typically pass through an intensive quality audit program designed by the purchaser to verify that the supplier's quality systems are capable of producing at the high-quality levels required by the purchaser. When a quality deficiency is discovered during the audit process, it is often resolved through a joint purchaser/supplier effort. In most instances, the purchaser's contribution to quality improvement is to provide expertise and, perhaps, engineering resources. The net result of supplier certification is that it shifts the responsibility for assuring quality back to the source — the supplier. When effectively carried out, supplier certification eliminates the need for incoming inspection of purchased parts. The actual product also goes through a rigorous quality evaluation before the supplier receives "dock-to-stock" status. Dock-to-stock simply means that incoming inspection is no longer performed and incoming shipments go straight from the dock to either inventory or the production floor. Many organizations, including Ford, have been able to streamline their receiving and supplier payment processes because of proactive supplier certification efforts.

When managed well, supplier certification is a win-win proposition and not a burden for either the purchaser or the supplier. The supplier gains access to knowledge and resources that it would not otherwise have. These resources are used to improve the supplier's internal quality performance. Certified suppliers typically receive preferred supplier status and become eligible for larger volumes and future contracts. Many suppliers use their certified status as a marketing tool. From the purchaser perspective, the return on investment begins with higher-quality purchased parts and extends to the confidence to rely on fewer suppliers as well as the cost and time saving that come from simplified receiving. Supplier certification often sets the stage for more intensive purchaser/supplier interaction in areas such as early supplier involvement in new product design, joint cycle-time reduction programs, and productivity enhancement programs.

FIGURE 4.5
The Supplier Certification Process

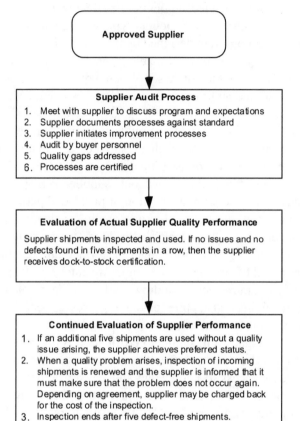

Approved Supplier

Supplier Audit Process
1. Meet with supplier to discuss program and expectations
2. Supplier documents processes against standard
3. Supplier initiates improvement processes
4. Audit by buyer personnel
5. Quality gaps addressed
6. Processes are certified

Evaluation of Actual Supplier Quality Performance

Supplier shipments inspected and used. If no issues and no defects found in five shipments in a row, then the supplier receives dock-to-stock certification.

Continued Evaluation of Supplier Performance
1. If an additional five shipments are used without a quality issue arising, the supplier achieves preferred status.
2. When a quality problem arises, inspection of incoming shipments is renewed and the supplier is informed that it must make sure that the problem does not occur again. Depending on agreement, supplier may be charged back for the cost of the inspection.
3. Inspection ends after five defect-free shipments.

Continuous Improvement Efforts Monitored and Supported

© Stanley E. Fawcett, Ph.D., C.P.M.

ISO certification – The fact that suppliers often have more than one important customer creates a dilemma because each customer develops its own certification standards (most organizations are reluctant to accept the standards established by their competitors). The result is that a supplier may have to go through multiple certification efforts, each of which is time and resource intensive. The duplication of effort can be draining and discouraging. To get around this certification challenge, some organizations are adopting the International Standards Organization 9000 registration program, commonly called ISO 9000. ISO 9000 was established in Europe in 1987 and has become widely accepted by European organizations as a prerequisite for awarding a purchase contract. As a result, many U.S. organizations are seriously looking at ISO 9000 so that they can sell to European customers. An outside certifying agency performs the quality audit and awards the registration. ISO 9000 is actually a series of quality standards (see Table 4.3) that focus on establishing

TABLE 4.3
ISO 9000 Standards

Elements	ISO 9001 (20 Reqts.)	ISO 9002 (18 Reqts.)	ISO 9003 (16 Reqts.)
4.1 Management responsibilities	√	√	√
4.2 Quality system requirements	√	√	√
4.3 Contract review requirements	√	√	√
4.4 Product design requirements	√		
4.5 Document and data control	√	√	√
4.6 Purchasing requirements	√	√	
4.7 Customer-supplied products	√	√	√
4.8 Product identification and tracing	√	√	√
4.9 Process control requirements	√	√	
4.10 Product inspection and testing	√	√	√
4.11 Control of inspection equipment	√	√	√
4.12 Inspection and test status of products	√	√	√
4.13 Control of nonconforming products	√	√	√
4.14 Corrective and preventive action	√	√	√
4.15 Handling, storage, and delivery	√	√	√
4.16 Control of quality records	√	√	√
4.17 Internal quality audit requirements	√	√	√
4.18 Training requirements	√	√	√
4.19 Servicing requirements	√	√	
4.20 Statistical techniques	√	√	√

and documenting appropriate quality processes. The least restrictive is ISO 9003, which focuses exclusively on final inspection and test standards. ISO 9002 builds on ISO 9003 by targeting installation, production, and purchasing capabilities. The most stringent standard is ISO 9001, which again builds on the other two by adding design and after sales service standards. As competition intensifies, more and more industries are moving toward the ISO 9001 standard. Of course, individual organizations must select the appropriate standard to implement based on an assessment of their current capabilities, their customer's current and future demands, and the direction their competitors are moving. ISO 9000 registration is a sign that a documented quality system in place, but it does not guarantee actual quality performance.

Baldrige award – The Malcolm Baldrige National Quality Award was originally introduced in 1987 as a national award for the achievement of world-class quality performance. The award was patterned after the highly regarded Deming Prize for Quality and sought to inculcate a superior-quality mentality among U.S. manufacturers (service organizations were later invited to compete for the award). The application and evaluation process is exacting and quite resource intensive, taking a full year; yet, for most organizations, the real work of putting a truly competitive quality system in place requires sustained dedication, time, and effort over many years. The Baldrige criteria promote both world-class process development and outstanding quality results that lead to customer satisfaction. Great emphasis is also placed on how the organization is going to achieve continual improvement on each important dimension. The seven areas of evaluation are leadership, information and analysis, strategic quality planning, human resources development, process management, product and service quality results, and customer satisfaction. Interestingly, 500 of the 1,000 points possible are allocated to the areas of quality results and customer satisfaction (see Table 4.4). A competitive score of 700 or more requires a broad-based and balanced approach to quality excellence The Baldrige award's criteria are now widely used as standards in the supplier certification process.

TABLE 4.4
Malcom Baldrige Award Criteria

2000 Categories/Items	Point Values
1 Leadership	125
1.1 Organizational leadership	85
1.2 Public responsibility and citizenship	40
2 Strategic Planning	85
2.1 Strategy development	40
2.2 Strategy deployment	45
3 Customer and Market Focus	85
3.1 Customer and market knowledge	40
3.2 Customer satisfaction and relationships	45
4 Information and Analysis	85
4.1 Measurement of organizational performance	40
4.2 Analysis of organizational performance	45
5 Human Resource Focus	85
5.1 Work systems	35
5.2 Employee education, training, and development	25
5.3 Employee well-being and satisfaction	25
6 Process Management	85
6.1 Product and service processes	55
6.2 Support processes	15
6.3 Supplier and partnering processes	15
7 Business Results	450
7.1 Customer focused results	115
7.2 Financial and market results	115
7.3 Human resource results	80
7.4 Supplier and partner results	25
7.5 Organizational effectiveness results	115
TOTAL POINTS	1000

Industry-specific certification standards – Another approach to reducing the duplicative efforts of multiple certification programs is for an overall industry to establish a common certification standard. Several examples of industry-specific quality standards exist. Interestingly, these common standards often incorporate the best elements of ISO 9000, the Baldrige award, and organization-specific programs. For example, the Semiconductor Industry Association developed the Standardized Supplier Quality Assessment (SSQA) as a tool to assist suppliers in developing a comprehensive quality-driven operating system. SSQA involves 114 distinct elements organized into three major modules:

- Module 1 is based on ISO 9000
- Module 2 is based on Malcolm Baldrige National Quality Award criteria
- Module 3 is based on Motorola Quality Software requirements.

A second example comes from the automotive industry, where the U.S. big three automakers jointly initiated the QS 9000 program. Its basic requirements incorporate all 20 ISO 9001 categories as well as components that are specific to automotive manufacturers. Common industry standards and certification processes promise to provide a unified voice in the call for enhanced quality performance and should make it easier for suppliers to focus their resources on making and delivering world-class products.

Developing Supplier Capabilities

For many suppliers, the ability to achieve the standards needed for quality certification depends on receiving assistance from the purchaser. Of course, not every supplier needs assistance; in fact, some suppliers have the resources and knowledge to provide valued assistance to their customers. Further, some suppliers are unwilling to engage in the close working relationship needed for effective supplier development. For relationships where development activities make sense, the most common form of assistance is to provide quality training for the supplier's personnel. Depending on the supplier's need and the purchaser's willingness to invest in the supplier's skills, several other development options exist. For example the purchaser can:

- Locate support personnel at the supplier's facility
- Share process engineering expertise via training and joint development projects
- Transfer technology or other proprietary knowledge
- Defray development costs through early payments, cost sharing, or longer-term contracts
- Provide capital or financing to upgrade the supplier's process and product technologies.

Supplier performance measurement – Purchasers have found that making resources available to suppliers is not always sufficient. Strong motivation for developing quality capabilities is sometimes needed to keep suppliers actively engaged in improvement efforts. The most frequently used motivator is performance measurement. Measurement not only lets the supplier know that the purchaser is serious about quality but also clearly communicates quality expectations. Measurement also identifies opportunities for improvement. However, this only happens when purchasers closely track specific measures over time and build in proactive feedback loops that make quality performance transparent at the supplier. A supplier scorecard communicates what is being measured, how it is measured, and the supplier's current grade as seen by the purchasing organization. Some leading organizations like Rockwell Collins now post scorecards on their extranet. Scorecards are updated at least every three months. A report card showing need for improvement can be a strong motivator, especially when the loss of business is the consequence for continued delinquent performance.

Quality improvement clauses – Quality improvement clauses are frequently included in purchase agreements to make very clear the expectation that improvement is a prerequisite to future business. Improvement clauses spell out the extent and type of quality improvement that is required. The typical improvement clause asks for incremental and fairly easy to obtain improvements. Some organizations, however, take a much more aggressive approach toward improvement. These organizations set tough, demanding goals for internal practice, and their external improvement clauses reflect a similar philosophy. Motorola is such a relentless, quality-driven organization. If a supplier wants to be a Motorola preferred supplier, it must be prepared to move constantly toward the attainment of perfect quality. Organizations like Motorola and Honeywell (formerly Allied Signal) rely on improvement clauses that target every major area of supplier performance including cost and delivery. Perhaps the most frequently used clause calls for a 3 to 5 percent year-to-year decrease in product price. Purchasing organizations must recognize that they have a responsibility to help suppliers achieve success in meeting the targeted improvements.

Reward sharing – Successful long-term relationships are founded on fairness and mutual support; therefore, purchasers need to acknowledge their suppliers' improvement in a tangible and meaningful way. The most profound approach is to share the fruits of performance improvement. Purchasers cannot hope to maintain a trust-based relationship if they consistently extract 100 percent of the value of every improvement. Those that attempt to do this quickly find that suppliers begin to act opportunistically and only report the most minimal of improvements as specified in the contractual improvement clause. A second counterproductive behavior can also result – the supplier can give up on continuous improvement. Why should the supplier invest time and resources to make the purchaser successful if the purchaser is not going to reciprocate? Many organizations share on a 50/50 basis the value of improvements that exceed the level called for in the improvement clause. Another practice is to increase the contract length or the total purchase volume with suppliers that make dramatic improvements. The bottomline is that both the purchaser and the supplier must share the benefits of improvement.

Resolving Quality Problems

Despite the best quality intentions and the most proactive quality practices, a quality failure can happen. When it does, the purchaser has several options, beginning with the return of the product to the supplier. When a product is returned, the supplier almost always bears the expense incurred in returning the product. When the defects are uncovered during receiving and inspection, these costs are generally limited to return transportation costs. In a dock-to-stock situation, the charge-back can be much more extreme because the problem is not likely to be discovered until the purchased parts are being used in production. Under this scenario, the cost of lost production, the cost of removing the parts from inbound storage, and the cost of return transportation can add up to a substantial charge-back. The most expensive situation occurs when the defective products come from a certified supplier for use in a JIT setting and therefore go straight to the production floor. Causing an entire production line to come to a halt can lead to a large penalty. Other potential resolutions to a quality problem include the following:

- The parts from the problem shipment can undergo a thorough, at times 100 percent, inspection with the acceptable parts being used in production. The inferior product is then either returned to the supplier or reworked by the purchasing organization. The supplier bears the costs created by the quality failure.
- The contract can be renegotiated to compensate for the delivery of inferior products that were still not usable in the production process. Such re-negotiation generally targets a price break based on having received a lessor-quality item.
- The disposal of the poor-quality parts. Sometimes, reworking or returning defective product costs more than the product is worth. The lowest-cost option might be to simply dispose of the product and then seek compensation for the costs incurred.

Whenever a quality problem arises, the purchaser has an obligation to provide quick, accurate, and specific feedback to the supplier. A supplier can only respond to a quality problem when the problem is clearly communicated. The proactive purchaser requires the supplier to take action to find and eliminate the root cause of the problem. As part of the resolution, the supplier is required to prepare a corrective action report that details the actions taken to assure that the problem does not occur again. The purchaser should carefully examine the corrective action report and, if necessary, the actual changes to the value-added process. Occasionally, the most appropriate response involves a joint problem-solving effort or the retraining of the supplier's personnel. It is also possible that the root cause for the quality problem lies in the product specifications, in which case the documentation needs to be reworked to more clearly and precisely describe the performance specifications. Finally, purchasers need to understand that the effort to resolve the problem and the communication regarding the resolution process needs to proactively include individuals from the user department. The user department probably has insight or resources that can bring the problem to closure more quickly.

Today's Rising Bar

A major challenge confronting organizations today is that customers are more demanding than ever. They have come to expect outstanding quality, rapid delivery, complete responsiveness, and the latest innovation for the lowest cost. One reason that customer expectations have risen is that a host of organizations from around the world vie for their attention and a larger share of their purchase dollar. This intense global competition has raised the competitive bar in almost all industries so that organizations now face the dual challenge of satisfying demanding world consumers while fending off tough global competition. Organizations that do not understand their customers' real needs as well as the reality that customers are increasingly information empowered cannot survive long in the new environment. Likewise, organizations that cannot deliver quality products will not survive. Progressive and proactive purchasers can help their organizations be among those that do most things right by helping them understand their customers' real needs and efficiently and effectively deliver the outstanding value that customers demand.

Key Points

1. Access to more and better market information has empowered customers. Performance expectations have increased and channel power has shifted downstream toward the end consumer.
2. Customer service strategies that focus on inward capabilities and customer satisfaction strategies that focus on understanding customer expectations are no longer adequate to create customer loyalty. Organizations need to focus more on helping customers improve their own competitive ability.
3. Customers expect a total product/service package. The dimensions of cost, quality, delivery, flexibility, and innovation are all important (most supplier scorecards include at least one measure

of each dimension). Proactive purchasing can often achieve simultaneous improvements along all five dimensions.

4. Quality has been identified as the single most important factor in determining long-term competitive success. Over time, the approach to quality has changed from inspection, to process control, to quality design. Today, elements of all three approaches can be found at leading organizations.

5. Purchasers must understand the basic statistical and problem solving methodologies and be able to use them to help suppliers improve their own quality levels.

6. Supplier certification is a valuable approach to improving the organization's overall quality performance. Certification often requires that the purchasing organization share expertise and resources to help important suppliers achieve processes capable of delivering consistent quality.

Questions for Review

1. Describe the differences between customer service, customer satisfaction, and customer success strategies.

2. What are your key customer's performance expectations? What factors are most important to their purchase decision? What factors are most important to their success?

3. Does management at your organization view the five competitive dimensions of quality, cost, delivery, flexibility, and innovation as mutually exclusive, somewhat opposed, complementary, or synergistic? Why?

4. Define quality. Why should purchasers be concerned with supplier quality performance?

5. Discuss different approaches to supplier certification such as organization-specific certification, ISO 9000 certification, and industry-wide certification. What are the pros and cons of each approach?

6. What are the benefits of quality certification programs? Be sure to consider both purchaser and supplier perspectives.

7. Do you understand process proving and statistical process control well enough to teach these concepts to your colleagues? To employees at key suppliers?

8. Do you understand quality problem-solving approaches well
    enough to lead a problem-solving team? What knowledge and
    experience do you need to be able to effectively use these tech-
    niques?

Endnotes

1. Drucker, P. F. "The Theory of the Business," *Harvard Business
    Review*, (72:5), 1994, pp. 95-104.
2. Blackwell, R.D. *From Mind to Market: Reinventing the Retail
    Supply Chain*, Harper Business, New York, NY, 1997.
3. Fawcett, S.E. and S.A. Fawcett. "The Firm as a Value-Added
    System: Integrating Logistics, Operations, and Purchasing,"
    *International Journal of Physical Distribution and Logistics
    Management*, (25:3), 1995, pp. 24-42.
4. Blackwell, 1997.
5. Ginsburg, L. and N. Miller. "Value-Driven Management,"
    Business Horizons, May-June 1992, pp. 23-27.
6. Bowersox, D. J., R.J. Calantone, S.R. Clinton, D.J. Closs, M.B.
    Cooper, C.L. Droge, S.E. Fawcett, R. Frankel, D.J. Frayer, E.A.
    Morash, L.M. Rinehart, and J.M. Schmitz. *World Class
    Logistics: The Challenge of Managing Continuous Change,
    Council of Logistics Management*, Oak Brook, IL, 1995;
    Fawcett, S. E. and M.B. Cooper. "Logistics Performance and
    Measurement and Customer Success," *Industrial Marketing
    Management*, (27:7), 1998, pp. 341-357.
7. Stalk, G., P. Evans, and L.E. Schulman. "Competing on
    Capabilities: The New Rules of Corporate Strategy," *Harvard
    Business Review*, (70:2), 1992, pp. 57-69; Ducker, 1994.
8. Porter, M. *Competitive Strategy*, The Free Press, New York, NY,
    1980.
9. Juran, J.M. and J.F.M. Gryna. *Quality Planning and Analysis*,
    McGraw-Hill, New York, NY, 1980.
10. Bower, J.L. and T.M. Hout. "Fast-Cycle Capability for
    Competitive Power," *Harvard Business Review*, (66:6), 1988, pp.
    110-118; Stalk, G. "Time-The Next Source of Competitive
    Advantage," *Harvard Business Review*, (66:4), 1988, pp. 41-51.

11. Henkoff, R. "Delivering the Goods," *Fortune*, November 28, 1994, pp. 64-78.
12. Bucklin, D., presented at the March 1996 Materials and Logistics Management Council, Michigan State University, East Lansing, MI.
13. Birou, L.M. and. S.E. Fawcett. "Supplier Involvement in Integrated Product Development Strategies: A Comparison of U.S. and European Practices," *International Journal of Physical Distribution and Logistics Management*, (24:5), 1994, pp. 4-14.
14. Stalk, Evans, and Schulman, 1992.
15. Loeb, M., "How's Business?: Ten Commandments for Managing Creative People," *Fortune*, January 16, 1995, pp. 135-142; Stewart, T.A. and M. Warner. "3M Fights Back," *Fortune*, February 5, 1996, pp. 94-101.
16. Feigenbaum, A.V. *Total Quality Control*, 3rd ed., McGraw-Hill, New York, NY, 1983.
17. Deming, W.E. *Out of the Crisis*, Massachusetts Institute of Technology, Center for Advanced Engineering Study, Cambridge, MA, 1986.
18. Garvin, D.A. "Quality on the Line," *Harvard Business Review*, (61:5), 1983, pp. 65-75.
19. Taguchi, G. and D. Clausing. "Robust Quality," *Harvard Business Review*, (68:1), 1990, pp. 65-75.
20. Deming, 1986.
21. Crosby, P.B. *Quality Without Tears*, McGraw-Hill, New York, NY, 1984.
22. Bhote, K. *How to Make the U.S. Suppliers Competitive*, American Management Society, McGraw Hill, New York, NY, 1987.

CHAPTER 5

What is my role in a reengineered world?

Chapter Objectives

This chapter is designed to help the purchaser:

- Understand how purchasing interacts with other areas of the organization to add value.
- Identify opportunities to participate in process reengineering efforts that increase collaboration.
- Be able to select the appropriate mechanism to increase cross-functional collaboration.
- Understand the nature of cross-functional teaming and identify the pros and cons of teams.
- Gain the understanding needed to be a more highly valued team member.

Purchasing's Role Within the Organization

For many years, purchasing's job was defined via the "seven rights" of purchasing: to obtain the "right" materials at the" right" time in the "right" quantity for delivery to the "right" place from the "right" supplier with the "right" service at the "right" price. Of these seven responsibilities, finding or developing the right supplier quickly emerged as the single most important goal of purchasing. Without the "best" suppliers, it was impossible to achieve the other six rights, especially given all of the performance tradeoffs that exist among

129

these purchasing objectives. While these seven rights are still relevant, they reflect only a part of the purchaser's job in today's intensely competitive global environment. The scope of responsibility has changed from simply purchasing the right materials from the right suppliers to the more challenging and dynamic role of supporting the organization's overall goals and objectives and acquiring access to and then managing the capabilities of suppliers. This reshaping of purchasing's role has been driven by several factors, many of which have been discussed in previous chapters:

- An intensely competitive global environment demands greater contribution from purchasing. The organization must have access to the best supplier capabilities available worldwide.
- The compression of product life cycles and the demand for instant response means that purchasing must be able to take time out of vital value-added processes.
- The emergence of empowered customers who "want it all" has forced organizations to rethink how they add value, bringing new attention to purchasing's quality and cost expertise.
- The drive for greater internal efficiency and effectiveness has highlighted a need to move from functional to process management.
- An increased focus on core capabilities has meant an increased reliance on outsourcing.

Purchasing cannot hope to support corporate goals and acquire the right supplier performance capability by itself – purchasing decisions cannot and should not be made in isolation. The fact that purchased inputs are used by almost every other area within the organization to carry out day-to-day activities means that purchasers must interact with an incredibly diverse set of managers from accounting to engineering to top management. Of course, purchasing managers work more closely with some areas than others (see Table 5.1). In most organizations, the majority of purchased inputs are used to produce a product or deliver a service. Therefore, purchasers work intensively with operations managers. Much of this work occurs in establishing appropriate specifications for required materials. Purchasing managers also work closely with logistics managers to ensure the proper coordination of materials into the production or service process. As noted elsewhere, today's purchasers work more closely with research and development to get suppliers involved earlier in the product design process. Purchasing also maintains a working relationship with accounting because suppliers must be paid in an accurate and timely manner. As a boundary spanning function, purchasing is a valuable source of insight for strategic planning purposes. The fact that purchasing must work with other functional areas to achieve its two primary objectives dictates the following:

- Purchasers must actively participate in the design of value-added processes and the day-to-day decisionmaking required for these processes to achieve world-class results.
- Purchasers will increasingly find that to make a meaningful contribution to the organization's success, they will have to work as part of a cross-functional team.

TABLE 5.1
Purchasing's Relationships with Other Areas of the Organization

Department or Area	Description of Role/Interaction with Purchasing
Top Management	Determines the organization's vision/strategy and allocates resources. Purchasing must understand strategic objectives and communicate clearly how it can support the organization's strategic objectives.
Engineering/Design	Develops technical specifications for a company's products and processes. Purchasing works with engineering to evaluate specifications and then ensure that sourced materials meet desired specifications. Purchasing also facilitates communication between engineering and suppliers in the new product development process.
Quality Control	Assesses materials and processes to determine their ability to produce quality products. Purchasing helps communicate suppliers' capabilities and works with quality control to provide supplier training, certification, and development.
Manufacturing	Schedules production, plans capacity, manages inventory, and designs facility layout. Purchasing and manufacturing are extremely closely related. Manufacturing is often purchasing's largest internal customer; therefore, the two departments coordinate their efforts extensively to ensure that the right materials are available when needed.
Accounting/Finance	Monitors cash flows/arranges future financing to achieve future plans of the company. Purchasing works with accounting to monitor/evaluate cost performance and to ensure timely payment of suppliers. Purchasing and finance work together to evaluate alternative sources of supply as well as to facilitate value analysis.

Department or Area	Description of Role/Interaction with Purchasing
Marketing	Helps create, promote, and deliver the best augmented product to meet customer needs. Purchasing must understand market needs and have access to the best possible forecasts so that it can purchase the right quantities of the best products and services to support the customer fulfillment strategy.
Facilities	Manages the location, layout, and upkeep of the firm's physical facilities. Purchasing needs early access to facilities plans to help select appropriate sources of service and materials, including capital equipment needed to establish and maintain world-class facilities.
Logistics	Plans and controls inbound and outbound movement of materials and finished products. Purchasing and logistics share information to ensure timely delivery of materials to support operations and distribution activities. Purchasing can also help logistics negotiate better contracts with service providers.
Information Systems	Designs and manages information technology to provide information for decisionmaking. Purchasing works with the IS department to ensure that the right information is captured, analyzed, and reported to facilitate excellent purchasing decisionmaking.
Legal	Protects organization against legal problems; reviews contracts and other legal documents. Purchasing activities are highly scrutinized because they typically involve contracts and relationships with external entities. Purchasing should have the legal department review all contracts before they are signed. The legal department can also provide education regarding regulations and laws that might affect purchasing.
Public Relations	Establishes a positive company image with the public, including customers and suppliers. Purchasing coordinates with public relations those activities that might have an affect on the outside public. Such activities might include minority supplier development programs and environmentally friendly sourcing efforts. Works closely with public relations when unexpected and potentially damaging events occur (i.e., chemical spills or kidnappings).
Merchandising	Manages the distribution and selling of goods at the retail level. Purchasing must work closely with merchandising to obtain sales plans that will affect the pattern of demand for purchased inputs. Immediate communication is needed to keep the hot items in stock and to kill the slow items before they become too much of a drain on company resources. Coordination can greatly reduce the dollar value of product markdowns.
Production Planning	Establishes production schedules and resource requirements. Purchasing's major responsibility is often to coordinate with production and obtain the materials needed for high-quality, low-cost production.
Research & Development	Manages basic and applied research related to products and processes. Purchasing works to ensure the best materials and equipment are available for use in the R & D effort. Purchasing also brings commodity expertise and supplier experience to the R & D process.

Department or Area	Description of Role/Interaction with Purchasing
Product Development	Designs new products and product modifications and sets product specifications. Purchasing should be involved early in the product development process to help establish the most appropriate specifications and determine the optimal materials. Purchasing can help bring the expertise of suppliers into the product development process.
Field Service	Supports the company's products after the sale has been made, installation and service. Purchasing must understand the product and service needs of the field service organization to help ensure that rapid and dependable service is always provided to customers.
Maintenance	Keep the facilities and equipment in good repair and reliable working order. Purchasing works with maintenance to coordinate purchases that are needed to keep production equipment up and running. At times, purchasing must expedite the acquisition of a part in order to get a broken piece of equipment back on line.
Other	Purchasing works with every area of the organization to make sure that the required materials and services are available when needed. Purchasing should establish strong working relationships with all internal customers and must learn to speak their language in order to expeditiously meet their needs.

The Nature of Process Management

For many years, "functional silos" have hindered communication and cooperation throughout most organizations and erected barriers to effective decisionmaking and value creation. The demands of today's supply environment make "functional silos" obsolete. Managers in world-class companies have adopted an integrative view, changing organizational structures from a functional to a process orientation. At GE Medical Systems, process integration has created some unique organizational units, including a unit headed by a vice president of global sourcing and order remittance.[1] One of the most talked about techniques for promoting process integration is Business Process Reengineering, which remains a popular strategic management initiative (see Table 5.2). However, reengineering results have been mixed with many organizations achieving "dramatic improvements in individual processes only to watch overall results decline." [2] Perhaps the greatest impediment to reengineering success is that too many reengineering efforts fail to fully take into account the challenge inherent in bridging functional boundaries.

TABLE 5.2
The Basic Steps Involved in Business Process Reengineering

In the early 1990s, the term reengineering was coined to describe the radical redesign of business processes made possible by improvements in modern information technology. Several ideas provide the foundation for reengineering business processes.

- New information technologies provided better capabilities for improving performance.

- Traditional restructuring efforts used technology simply to replace other resources — such as workers — without really changing the basic approach to getting a job done.

- Imagination and information technology needed to be combined to overcome outdated assumptions about how processes add value.

- Reengineering required that processes be redesigned from scratch, taking advantage of both new technologies and workers' increased skills and responsibilities.

The following principles guide reengineering efforts.

- Identify the desired outcomes of the process, why is the process performed in the first place? If the current outcomes are no longer important, eliminate the process. If they are still important, use them to direct the reengineering effort.

- Make the process visible. A correct understanding of how the process is done can provide insight into how it should be done and how technology can facilitate change.

- Organize around a value-added process by consolidating tasks. Each worker's job should involve performing as many of the tasks required to complete the process as possible. A process orientation often requires either cross-training workers or using a cross-functional team.

- Place responsibility for process reengineering where the work is done or the output needed. Getting individuals who do a job to be responsible for how it is performed takes advantage of their knowledge and provides greater motivation.

- Take advantage of today's information technologies to expand worker's processes to include related activities formerly performed by specialized departments. Also, use the new technologies like barcoding to relocate information processing to the point where the information is generated.

- Use information technology to bridge functional and geographic distance. Information technology allows for true coordination among dispersed activities. This coordination merges the efficiency benefits of centralization with the responsiveness benefits of decentralization.

Recognizing the importance of integrating value-added activities is relatively easy; actually moving from function to process is the challenge. Part of the difficulty comes from long-established attitudes and procedures. The organization's ability to add value does not arise from any single functional expertise or from the ownership of a unique technology. Competitiveness results from distinctive or core competencies that reside in a small number of key processes that are performed superbly.[3] Truly distinctive processes are cross-functional, relying on many skills that are housed in different functional areas. Value-added processes are a small part of many people's jobs, and those people are found in different areas that should cooperate, but often do not.

The reality is that most organizations can accurately be described as a system of processes, each of which consists of a set of identifiable activities and flows that work together to achieve a specific objective, to meet customers' real needs profitably. Competitive success depends on the organization's ability to select the right processes and then make these processes perform at world-class levels. As David Robinson, president of CSC Index, has noted, "It's a shift from [competing on] what we make to how we make it."[4] Unfortunately, few managers (purchasers included) possess a clear vision of what it means to manage integrated processes. Perhaps the best way to promote this understanding is to take a closer look at the anatomy of an integrated process, dissecting it down to its basic elements. Figure 5.1 depicts two value-added processes, new product development and materials acquisition – each of which is representative of the nature of integrated process management. While other processes such as the order fulfillment process can and should be managed for competitive advantage, the basic elements of process management do not change greatly from one process to another.

Activities and Flows Come Together

Every valued, hard-to-replicate process, such as the ability to bring new products from concept to market in 30 percent less time than the next fastest industry competitor, consists of two fundamental elements. First, processes consist of three distinct flows: an information flow, a physical flow, and a financial flow. Second, processes are made up of a set of value-added activities. These flows and activities are intricately and inseparably interconnected. Significant processes typically begin with an information flow, which almost always triggers a specific value-added activity. For example, the new product development process generally begins with an idea that is likely generated by either a customer or an engineering breakthrough. Once the idea is on the table, the activities of conceptualization and design move forward. In the materials acquisition process, the identification of a need initiates action via a request for a proposal (RFP) or a request for a quote (RFQ). Potential suppliers respond with a competitive bid. The bids are compared and a supplier is selected. The smooth and timely flow of information drives both new product/service design and materials acquisition processes.

FIGURE 5.1
Anatomy of a Value-added Process

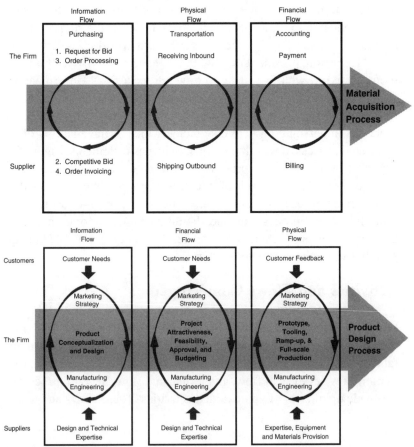

Physical flows vary greatly across different processes and consist of a variety of specific activities. In new product development, physical activities may include building a prototype, acquiring tooling, ramping-up production, and moving to full-scale manufacturing. For materials acquisition, the physical flow involves activities that take place in shipping, transportation, and receiving. The final flow is the financial flow. In the development scenario, the most important financial flow occurs as the project is approved and budgeting established. This financial flow precedes the physical flow. By contrast, the financial flow concludes the materials acquisition process. Once a product shipment has been delivered, inspected, and accepted, payment is processed. For some organizations, the entire payment process has been streamlined so that no inspection takes place and as soon as the shipment is matched to an outstanding order, payment occurs via electronic funds transfer. It is important to note that information, physical, and financial flows are difficult to disentangle. They are dependent on one another (see Figure 5.1). A clear understanding of the activities and flows that comprise a value-added process can help the organization increase its agility and respond more rapidly to customer demands.

Boundary Spanning at the Core

The examples of new product development and materials acquisition demonstrate that the typical value-added process involves multiple functional areas with individual activities dispersed throughout the organization. Specifically, the core activities performed in new product development take place in marketing, manufacturing, engineering, purchasing, and finance. For materials acquisition, the principal value-added activities occur in the areas of manufacturing, purchasing, transportation, and accounting.

The boundary-spanning nature of well-designed value-added processes extends beyond the organization's walls. Figure 5.1 shows that multiple supply chain members are often involved in key value-added processes. Looking first at the new product development example shows that some processes depend extensively on the expertise held by different supply chain participants. In this case, the organization and its customers and suppliers all play a major role. The customer provides knowledge about market attractiveness and the feasibility of the potential new product while the supplier brings technical expertise to the table. Turning to the materials acquisition example highlights the involvement of three supply chain members: the purchaser, the supplier, and a logistics service provider. Expertise, localized capabilities, and capital investment in specialized equipment make all three players valued members of the process team. The fact that knowledge resides throughout the organization and across organizational boundaries suggests a diverse composition for the well-designed process integration team.

Involvement of different functions and multiple supply chain members complicates the creation of hard-to-imitate processes. Each function or supply chain member contributes a unique set of skills and abilities to the value-added process, but also has distinct expectations and objectives. Because these objectives can conflict, sub optimization results in the absence of an integrative strategy. Managing diverse expectations requires that a process perspective be fully implemented. When relevant processes are managed as a system, greater customer value and competitive advantage result.

Barriers to Effective Process Integration

Many barriers to effective process integration exist, and they begin with understanding the needs of customers. Most organizations have weak mechanisms in place to understand customer needs and wants. Occasional and informal surveys or interviews with customers are often the primary source of customer-based information. As a result, managers are not sure which services customers value and often expend tremendous resources to improve performance in ways that customers do not fully appreciate. Several other barriers to effective process integration have been documented.

- **Inconsistent operating goals** – Local goals continue to drive decisionmaking. The challenge is to understand functional interrelationships and communicate organizational strategies and objectives. Only then can localized units revise their operating goals to support strategic initiatives.
- **Poorly coordinated performance measures** – Performance measurement provides understanding of key value-added processes and molds behavior, making inconsistency a serious

problem. The limited use of activity-based costing further limits the organization's ability to cost out important processes and perform segmental profitability analysis on important processes and valued customers.

- **Inadequate training** – Cross-functional and process-oriented skills are fundamental to integration. They must be built through consistent workforce training. Restructuring and reengineering are often viewed as thinly veiled approaches to workforce reduction. This perception can adversely affect employee attitudes and behaviors, making process integration more of a threat than an opportunity.

- **Inadequate information support** – A lack of connectivity is perhaps the greatest information system weakness. Information capabilities in different functional or geographic areas are developed, but not linked effectively for the sharing of information. Better information exchange, not just better information hardware, is required for true process integration.

Bridges to Effective Process Integration

While inadequate measurement, localized goals, poor employee buy-in, and a lack of accurate, relevant, and timely information can be a significant hurdle to successful process integration, some organizations have been able to clear the hurdle successfully (see Figure 5.2). These organizations realize that process integration mandates senior management support. Senior management must define the organization's mission and select customer-appropriate capabilities for development. Providing a clear vision and allocating the resources needed to accomplish it are vital to obtaining buy-in, generating early momentum, and achieving long-term success. Senior management support establishes the foundation on which the remaining bridges are built.

- **Define specific roles and relationships** – Getting managers in each area to understand and accept the roles that their areas must perform for the competitive strategy to be successfully implemented is a very important issue that only senior management can effectively address.

FIGURE 5.2
Flowchart of Steps that Bridge the Barriers to Process Integration

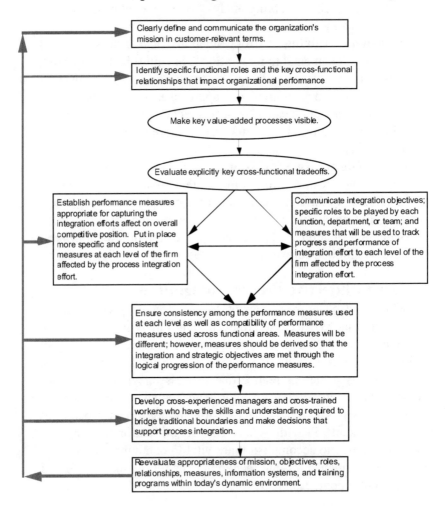

© Stanley E. Fawcett, Ph.D., C.P.M.

- **Make processes visible** – Mutually dependent activities often possess interrelationships that are not obvious but that affect process performance. Making "hidden" relationships visible is the objective of process mapping. Mapping involves a careful diagramming of product and information flows so that they can be understood and carefully analyzed. Mapping also provides a focal point for discussion, allowing managers from different areas to work through problems on a more realistic, factual basis.
- **Perform total cost analysis** – Total cost analysis makes the tradeoffs among decisions and activities explicit. Accurate and comprehensive total cost analysis is rare because of limited information availability.
- **Align performance measures** – An old saying suggests that "What gets measured, gets done." Measurement systems must therefore promote integrative behavior.
- **Communicate key objectives, roles, and measures** – Clear communication can help everyone within the organization, regardless of where they are housed, to work together in a systematic, targeted manner. A cascading waterfall of information conveys priorities to each successive level of the organization (see Figure 5.3).

FIGURE 5.3
The Integration Waterfall

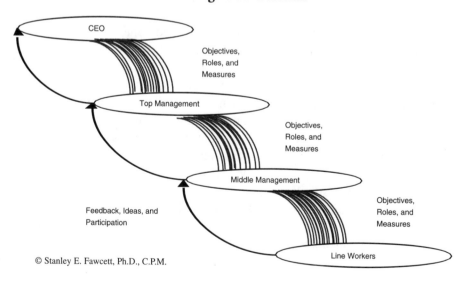

© Stanley E. Fawcett, Ph.D., C.P.M.

- **Develop a "cross-experienced" management team** – Organizations are implementing more extensive management trainee programs for new hires. A typical training program includes three to six months experience in a variety of functional areas. Periodic assignments to cross-functional task forces and project teams helps managers apply and retain their cross-functional experience.
- **Empower managers** – Managers are now more frequently empowered to make a broader range of operating decisions than in the past. This empowerment enables the cross-experienced manager and the cross-trained worker to take on greater responsibility to design and manage integrated processes.

Process integration is hard work because of resistance to change that stems from deeply entrenched operating procedures and performance measures. Despite the magnitude of the challenge, many managers believe they have no choice but to seek more seamless process integration. Seamless processes built on strong functional competence constitute the foundation for competitive success, either one in isolation offers only limited and unsustainable competitive advantage.

Achieving Process Excellence

Almost everything purchasing does to add value involves other functions and departments. Purchasing must therefore work actively and effectively to bridge emotional, informational, and physical distances. The boundary spanning effort begins with fully understanding the needs of other groups. At the same time, purchasing must educate other functions to help them understand purchasing's constraints and its need for accurate and timely information. Mutual understanding of roles and responsibilities as well as how the different areas and purchasing can work together is the foundation on which collaborative decisionmaking is built.

The mechanisms used to engender collaboration are varied and require different levels of effort and investment. For some organizations, communication efforts simply involve publishing a directory that contains telephone/fax numbers and e-mail addresses so that people can contact each other without wasting time trying to track down a number. Some organizations have set up an intranet that contains names and contact data along with information about areas of expertise and current "pet projects." Leading organizations make it a part of each person's job to act as a consultant to other areas of the organization when the need arises. This consulting role helps specialists share their knowledge and promotes a learning organization. An informal approach works best when workers and managers have participated in cross-training programs and/or worked on cross-functional teams. These activities help people get to know one another and establish relationships that reduce the transaction costs of collaboration.

For other organizations, the major effort to create more frequent and open communication begins and ends with regularly scheduled meetings where different groups can share information and report on items of mutual concern. While these meetings can be informative, the burden of too many meetings can diminish their integrative value. Likewise, key people can be involved in so many meetings that it is difficult to bring all of the right people together. Productive meetings are driven by tight agendas that are disseminated prior to the meeting. Other specialized mechanisms are used when two groups such as purchasing and engineering must interact frequently and intensively. A liaison can be used to coordinate interdepartmental communication. An ideal liaison is a person who possesses experience and relationships with purchasing and engineering. A challenge with the liaison approach is that a "guru" mentality can emerge with members of each group offloading the responsibility for integration onto the shoulders of the liaison. Co-locating departments to increase day-to-day interaction is another valuable approach. When people work next to each other, they develop relationships, trust, and appreciation for each other's jobs. Integrating departments is a more intense option. The drawback with co-location and integrated departments is that it can be impossible to physically co-locate all of the groups that need to work together. Some organizations have therefore co-located one or more purchasing managers in the engineering and other appropriate departments.

Building Successful Cross-Functional Teams

Teams have been used to make decisions from facility location to supplier selection. They have also been charged with carrying out initiatives like the implementation of ERP systems and supply base rationalization The popularity of cross-functional teams comes from their success in shortening decisionmaking and implementation cycles. Organizations can no longer afford to make decisions by sequentially handing decision responsibility from one functional group to another. This approach takes time and leads to inferior decisions as well as a lack of organizational synergy. Cross-functional teaming is vital to competitiveness because it can help bridge the "chasms" that prevent functional collaboration. In some organizations, the belief in the team experience is so firmly ingrained that a manager's progress up the leadership ladder is based in part on the capacity to contribute to team success. Purchasers participate on many teams because of their broad-based understanding of critical value-added processes.

Properly designed and managed teams can go a long way toward reducing the communication barriers that exist among functional areas. Better communication leads to greater cooperation, reduced turf protection, and better overall decisions. Decisionmaking shifts from seeking to optimize functional outcomes to emphasizing total organizational performance. Despite these benefits of cross-functional teams, they are not a universal answer. Nor are teams always easy to manage, even when they represent the best approach to problem-solving. Managers must carefully weigh the pros and cons of teaming before putting a team together to deal with an important managerial issue (see Table 5.3).

Advantages of teams – The greatest advantage of cross-functional teams is the opportunity to enhance communication and cooperation, bringing a diverse set of talents and expertise together to make decisions or solve a problem. More open communication allows for rapid and thorough decisionmaking. While speed and thoroughness are usually not considered to be companion characteristics, putting all of the right people in the same room and getting them to focus on a common goal changes the dynamics of decisionmaking. The altered dynamics bring the following benefits:

TABLE 5.3
Factors that Affect Team Dynamics and Success

Availability of resources

Clarity of team objectives

Commitment of members to the team

Complexity of team assignment/task

Executive management support

Functional and technical knowledge and skills of team members

Open and honest team communication

Organizational experience with teams

Overall organizational support for team success

Performance feedback and information support

Performance measures used for team and individual team members

Supplier involvement

Team autonomy/mandate

Team cohesiveness

Team leadership

Team longevity

Team member personalities

Team process skills of team members

Team reward structure

Team size

- **Decision ownership** – Cross-functional teaming builds ownership in the solution of choice. Team members may be selected because they are well thought of in their own functional areas. Once a team comes to a consensus, each member goes back to his area and explains/sells the decision. The personal credibility of individual team members creates a natural tendency to buy off on the outcome of the team process. Even when additional time is needed to arrive at a consensus, the overall implementation is faster because of the ownership that has been created.
- **Leveraged diversity** – The dynamics of team decisionmaking creates an opportunity to leverage diversity of experience and opinion. Trust allows team members to challenge current practice

(or a proposed idea) without attacking other team members. The entire team can then dig a little deeper to understand what is done and why. The objective is to find a better way, and by bringing diversity and expertise together in an open environment, more creative decisions are brought to light.

- **Better organizational understanding** – As team members interact, they come to understand the requirements and constraints encountered by other team members. Looking at specific issues from the perspective of different functional areas is a constant learning experience that team members take back to their own areas and share. Slowly but surely, a more complete understanding of the complex and diverse interrelationships that exist among the functional areas is being disseminated throughout the company.
- **Faster task completion** – Teaming reduces the temporal and physical distance that information needs to travel, leading to significantly shorter times for task completion. As members build trust in one another, a greater willingness to compromise emerges. With turf and other counterproductive issues mitigated, the team can move forward to make integrative decisions and then implement the recommended plan of attack.
- **More effective problem solving** – A cross-functional team can often provide fresh insight that can help identify the root causes to troubling problems. Moving to a team approach not only brings in additional expertise but new perspective. Bouncing ideas off of one another in an active and challenging brainstorming session can help identify the real root cause of a problem faster than an individual might be able to work through all of the options. Brainstormed ideas and synergistic solutions are an important benefit of cross-functional teams.

Disadvantages of teams – While cross-functional teams can help bridge functional boundaries, unlock tremendous creative power, and facilitate the creation of distinctive competencies, they can be tough to manage. Almost everyone has participated on a dysfunctional team at least once. Teams are inherently difficult because most people do not have the needed experience in managing teams. Further, managers who possess a strong individualist mentality find it difficult to work on synergistic teams. Purchasing professionals need to understand that just as team dynamics can lead to better decisions, improper management of the team approach can lead to the following problems:

- **The never-ending debate** – When a team is composed of talented individuals who are dogmatic and unyielding, it can be hard for the team to come to a consensus. A dominant team member can forestall meaningful progress. Another possibility is that because the overall team is not held accountable for developing a clear action plan and no one is individually responsible, tough decisions are never made. Endless meetings that seem to "get little or nothing done" can become a drain on organizational resources and kill the momentum for the future successful use of the team approach.

- **Groupthink** – The team process is designed to generate better decisions than managers would arrive at individually; however, some teams settle on mediocre decisions as a result of groupthink. A strong desire to "go along to get along" can prevent teams from challenging weak ideas or analysis, even when the needed information is readily available. It is important to stress not only the quality of the team process but also the quality of the team outcome.

- **Social loafing** – A common team phenomenon is for one or more members of the team to settle back and let the rest of the team carry the load. This common occurrence is known as team process loss or social loafing and occurs most frequently in larger teams where individual accountability is harder to track. The ability to "hide out" allows some team members to never fully commit to the team process. Such individuals may be equally committed to the success of the organization as the rest of the team, but simply focus their efforts on other responsibilities.

- **Peer pressure** – Involvement in a team process can exert considerable pressure on team members to alter their normal decisionmaking behavior in order to belong to the group. This molding of behavior can be a positive occurrence that lends stability to the group. However, if team members lower their standards of performance or accept a group decision that they do not agree with and will only support half-heartedly, the team influence is negative. Going against deeply held ethical beliefs to support the team can create a sense of uneasiness that reduces a member's commitment to the organization.

Team composition – Team building and team management are not without cost. For example, team members almost always continue to fulfill normal responsibilities in their own functional areas. Participating on a team can be viewed as a distraction from everyday responsibilities. Too much team participation can lead to loss of focus and even burnout for individuals serving on teams. Thus, serious consideration must be given to who should participate on a given team. Team socialization provides another compelling reason to carefully select team members. Effective teams typically have a strong team leader who has good people skills, strong credibility with other team members, and significant team experience. Training in the team process can mitigate the negative affect of distinct personalities and conflicting styles and objectives. The careful selection of team members can help overcome socialization difficulties before they arise, contributing to team success. To help guide the team formation process, several questions should be answered:

- Is there a well-defined goal that can be clearly articulated and communicated?
- Is a variety of expertise and experience needed?
- What time commitment is required?
- Who are the best people – those with the right knowledge and experience – to serve on the team?
- What assignments do these individuals currently work on? Can they add more value by working on the team? Can their other responsibilities be effectively performed by other individuals?
- Who will lead the team? Does this individual have the skills and clout necessary to guide the team?
- Does the team composition take into account different personalities and working styles?

Team success depends on two fundamental issues: a well thought out and designed task that is fully supported throughout the organization and the composition of the team. If the team goal cannot be articulated and the organization is unwilling to put the needed resources behind the team effort, then an alternative implementation methodology should be considered. One leading manufacturer set the ideal example when it recently defined the team task in terms of scope and duration with specific goals. The CEO then brought the team together and announced unequivocally that the team's task was "the most important challenge that the organization had faced in the past 20 years." The fact that team members had been carefully selected based on their experience and credibility facilitated greater success.

Team formation typically focuses on functional expertise. Member credibility and influence is also taken into account in the design of many teams. The role of personalities and working styles is, however, often overlooked. Kathy Kolbe, a consultant in the area of team composition, has found that teams formed without looking at inherent working styles are often dysfunctional. She has identified four primary working styles:[5]

- **The Quick Starter** – highly energetic, sees an opportunity and quickly mobilizes energy.
- **The Fact Finder** – very meticulous and oriented toward detail and analysis.
- **The Follow Through** – determined and focused on carrying out a task to its completion.
- **The Implementer** – very task oriented, with a particular penchant for hands on work.

Effective teams typically include individuals who are oriented toward each working style. Several other instruments including the Meyers-Briggs personality profile and the Learning-Style Inventory developed by David Kolb have been used to help design more effective teams.

Purchasing's involvement on teams. Purchasing mangers are ideal participants on a variety of teams because they possess broad-based experience. Some common teams that involve purchasing are supplier selection, new product development, cycle-time reduction, and value analysis teams (see Table 5.4). Purchasing's role varies depending on the organization's strategic orientation, purchasing's position within the organization, and the team's objective. For teams that focus on selecting and managing suppliers such as commodity teams, supplier development teams, and supply-base rationalization teams, purchasing finds itself in a leadership position in which it must provide extensive information and guide the overall decisionmaking process. However, on most teams, purchasing plays a supporting role. For example, purchasing supports the value analysis/value engineering team by providing information regarding supplier's capabilities and alternative materials specifications. Likewise, purchasing plays a facilitating role on integrated product development teams by acting as a liaison between engineering and the supply base. From time to time, purchasing takes on a project management role when a new material is being sourced or a new prototype designed by a supplier. Regardless of purchasing's specific role on a given team, purchasing brings information, experience, and a knowledge of suppliers' capabilities to the team to help resolve problems and create greater value.

TABLE 5.4
Purchasing's Role in Key Cross-functional Teams

Type of Team	Team Objectives and Purchasing's Role on the Team
Cost Reduction	Cost reduction teams take on many forms and consist of many different players. The fact that purchased inputs represent 50 to 80 percent of the firm's cost of good sold suggests that purchasing be actively involved on cost reduction teams that are looking at materials, product, and/or process costs.
Value Analysis	Value analysis teams study a product or process and all of its components in order to determine ways of producing the product at a lower cost, with improved quality, or with a material that is more readily supplied. These teams often include representatives from engineering, marketing, operations, and purchasing. Purchasing brings materials expertise and access to suppliers' knowledge to the team.
Capital Equipment	Capital equipment teams focus on the acquisition of general-purpose and specific-purpose equipment. Some of the tasks necessary to successfully meet the objective are determine the necessary specifications of the equipment; select an adequate supplier; conduct negotiations. These teams should include representatives from engineering, purchasing, materials management, and any other area the equipment will greatly affect.
Sourcing	Sourcing teams focus on the investigation and selection of one or more sources for a given material. The majority of sourcing teams are only temporary, adjourning once the sourcing decision is made. These teams are often led by purchasing and consist of representatives from supply management, quality, and finance.
Product Development	Product development teams reduce the time needed to bring a product from concept to market. Purchasing helps establish design specifications and select the materials from which the product is made. These teams consist of representatives from marketing, production, purchasing, engineering, quality, and a representative from one or more suppliers.
Budgeting	Budgeting teams create future forecasts for materials and any other related purchases for the coming year. These teams consist of representatives from finance and purchasing.
Supplier Development	Supplier development teams help suppliers upgrade process engineering, manufacturing, and quality capabilities. This team consists of representatives from production, purchasing, quality assurance, and engineering. Purchasing identifies the suppliers that would benefit most from intensive development efforts and manages the relationship.
Information Systems	Information systems teams determine the information needs of the firm and then design the information systems to provide this information. Information system specialists basically run the team but they need the input from purchasing, finance, and other areas for the coordination and integration of the information handling activities.
Cycle-time Reduction	Cycle-time reduction teams are responsible for taking time out of key processes such as the order fulfillment process. The increased use of just-in-time delivery of purchasing parts and supplier-managed replenishment has made purchasing a key member of these teams.
Quality Improvement	Quality improvement teams work to improve quality of products and processes. The team consists of representatives from production, purchasing, and engineering. Purchasing's role is to ensure absolute quality of purchased parts and the process capability of suppliers.
Inventory Control	Inventory control teams seek to reduce inventory levels while providing an uninterrupted availability of materials. This team consists of representatives from production and purchasing. Purchasing's primary responsibility is to reduce levels of incoming and raw materials inventories by developing just-in-time systems and dock-to-stock systems.

Successful Teams

Successful teams get a group of individuals to work as a cohesive team instead of merely a group of specialists. Differences between a group and a real team extend beyond behavior to performance and are often dramatic. Moving from a group to a team is a challenge because organizational cultures have not been designed to promote and support team decisionmaking. The following points are basic requirements for transforming the group into a team:

- **Common goal** – Successful teams possess a common goal that motivates all team members.
- **Leadership** – Teams are led by well-respected managers who understand team dynamics.
- **Communication** – Open, constructive communication is fundamental to team success.
- **Cooperation** – Effective teams cooperate even when this means that someone must compromise.
- **Specific roles** – Team members understand their specific roles and responsibilities.
- **Measurement** – Clear and precise performance measurement facilitates team success.
- **Individual responsibility** – Each member is held accountable for individual and team performance.
- **Resources** – Adequate resources, including information, are made available to the team.
- **Time** – True "chemistry" emerges as team members spend quality time working together.

Steps in the team process – Some teams greatly outperform their counterparts. Great effort has been dedicated to understanding exactly what makes a team tick. As early as 1965,[6] the team development process was described as a four-stage process, which became widely known as forming, storming, norming, and performing. A fifth stage of adjourning has since been added.[7] By working through each stage of the team development process, team effectiveness can be enhanced.

- **Forming** – The process of deciding who should belong to the team is known as forming. For many teams, the process of forming continues over time as some members leave the team and new individuals join the team.
- **Storming** – The process of establishing common ground and identifying individual roles and responsibilities is called storming. Honest and open communication at this stage helps the team understand exactly where everyone is coming from and begin to move toward common ground. Effective storming enables the team to establish direction, purpose, roles, responsibilities, and rewards for both the overall team and each team member.
- **Norming** – After the team passes through the storm, it begins the process of becoming a truly cohesive team. This process is called norming – the establishment of team norms and procedures. In the sports world, the norming process is often referred to as building chemistry. At this stage, individual role players begin to work as a synchronized team.
- **Performing** – Teams are established to perform a task that is too complex to be handled effectively by a single individual. Once the team establishes its own uniquely collaborative rhythm, it must go to work and perform, identifying problems and opportunities, establishing a plan of attack, and then implementing the plan. A well-designed team that has successfully progressed through storming and norming finds that performing is perhaps the easiest part of the team process.
- **Adjourning** – From the very beginning, the team strategy should include key milestones and define the ending point in terms of objective outputs and an estimated completion date. Successful teams often define objectives, responsibilities, and milestones for each team member. Teams help handle complex and difficult tasks. Once a team completes its designated task, it should disband, freeing up resources for continuous improvement elsewhere.

The team dynamic is just that — dynamic. Those companies that know how to use teams know that some projects are more suited for teams than others; some people work better on teams than others; and time and resources must be dedicated to the team development process. Trying to use teams without investing in their development and integration often costs much more than taking the time up front to form, storm, and norm.

The role of measurement – Regardless of the number of team building activities used to develop team cohesiveness, effective performance measurement is essential to team efficacy. Most organizations now recognize the need for team members to bond, and provide team members an opportunity to participate in mountaineering or other activities that require real teamwork not just for success but also for survival. During these activities, important relationships begin to take shape; however, team members return to work to measures that promote individual, and/or functional, excellence. Therefore, companies like Honeywell (formerly Allied Signal) that use teams extensively modify performance measures to support the team process. Perhaps the biggest challenge is to find the right balance between team-based measures and individual measures. Too much emphasis on team outcomes can lead to the social loafing mentioned earlier and a loss of personal motivation. Not enough emphasis on team-oriented measures and the team process can be undermined. Interestingly, General Electric evaluates people on what it calls "boundarylessness" in order to identify and weed out individuals who are not well suited for teamwork. Such individuals obstruct the free flow of ideas and disrupt team cohesiveness and effectiveness.[8]

The role of education and training – Proper training is critical to establishing successful teams. At Motorola, all new materials managers go through a six-month rotation program that enables them to see how different, related functions actually work. The trainee also has an opportunity to build relationships that will reduce barriers to cross-functional cooperation. Another leading organization believes so strongly in cross-functional training that it has experimented with a two-year rotation program that gives management trainees an opportunity to experience first hand four to six different assignments in the following areas: the assembly line, production control, purchasing, logistics, marketing, accounting, and finance. These rotation programs help create the understanding and build the relationships that will enable managers to function more effectively on interdisciplinary teams throughout their careers. Cross-functional experience should continue throughout a talented manager's professional life.

Working on cross-functional teams and special assignments in other functional areas helps keep managers in touch with the needs, responsibilities, and constraints of different organizational units.

Experience should be accompanied by formal education and skill building. A leading aeronautics manufacturer requires that every manager go through a minimum of 40 hours of training every year. The fact that the 40-hour rule applies to the CEO is noteworthy. "Pay-for-knowledge" programs that base compensation on the employee's ability to build new skills promote professional development. Deere & Company believes so strongly that education builds competitiveness that it offers over 50 courses to not only Deere & Company employees but to the personnel of first-tier and selected second-tier suppliers.[9] In addition to helping employees gain specific job-related skills, professional development classes bring managers together in a learning environment where they can build and extend relationships. As managers get to know each other and have confidence in each other's competencies, the time required to make teams effective is reduced. Moreover, team members demonstrate less reticence toward team assignments and are more dedicated to team success when they work with managers from other areas that they already know and have confidence in.

Beyond training for team effectiveness, purchasing has a responsibility to help the rest of the organization understand what purchasing does to support strategic objectives and how purchasing can help individual functional areas achieve greater success. Training manuals, open-enrollment courses on the purchasing process, and active participation and sponsorship in rotation programs and cross-functional teams all help purchasing fulfill this responsibility. Training manuals that document highly effective decision processes help non-purchasers appreciate purchasing at a higher level and can be used to help less experienced purchasers perform more effectively earlier in their careers. For these reasons, purchasing should take the development of training materials very seriously. The future of a purchasing organization is easily gauged by looking at the education and training it pursues today.

The Promise of Integration

The fact that most distinctive processes are inherently interdisciplinary mandates greater functional collaboration and suggests that cross-functional teaming is likely to demonstrate incredible staying power. Recognizing this new reality, purchasing and supply managers should aggressively seek to identify teams and processes where purchasing can make a contribution. Because purchasing is familiar with most areas of the organization and manages a tremendous reservoir of expertise held by the supply base, it is at the crossroads where important product and process decisions are made. By leveraging experience and expertise, purchasing can simultaneously enhance its reputation as a strategic, value-added function and help deliver greater value to the customer. Process management may yet prove to be one of the greatest benefactors of strategic purchasing management and should be viewed as an opportunity and not a threat by today's purchasers.

Key Points

1. Purchasing cannot support corporate goals and acquire the right supplier performance capability by itself. Purchasing managers must work closely with managers from other functional areas. Purchasing success depends on building good relationships.
2. Efforts must be made to eliminate functional silos. Business process reengineering is one approach to increasing cross-functional collaboration. Purchasing plays a role in many value-added processes.
3. Numerous approaches to better integration exist and range from facilitating communication through published directories to co-locating managers from different functional areas. Cross-functional teams are one of today's most popular integrative mechanisms.
4. Advantages of cross-functional teaming include enhanced decision ownership, leveraged diversity, increased organizational understanding, faster task completion, and more effective problem solving. Disadvantages may include excessive meetings and debates, groupthink, social loafing, and negative peer pressure.

5. Two critical issues in designing effective teams are composition and socialization. Team members must be carefully selected, provided appropriate training, given a clear objective, assigned specific responsibilities, and given time to work together.

Questions for Review

1. Purchasing is a boundary-spanning function. Purchasers must work closely with a variety of other functions. Which linkages are most important? Describe the nature of these relationships.
2. What are some of the possible ways that purchasing can strengthen its communication linkages with production, engineering, finance, and top management?
3. Identify two distinct value-added processes. What activities and flows comprise these processes? What is purchasing's role in each process?
4. Identify four different integrative mechanisms. When is each appropriate?
5. When is cross-functional teaming most appropriate? What are the advantages of cross-functional teaming? What types of behavior lead to dysfunctional teams?
6. What are the keys to transforming a group of talented individuals into a cohesive cross-functional team? What is the role of the team leader? What are some important criteria for selecting team members?

Endnotes

1. Jacob, R., R.M. Rao, and V.J. Musi. "The Struggle to Create an Organization," *Fortune*, April 3, 1995, pp. 90-97.
2. Hall, G., J. Rosenthal, and J. Wade. "How to Make Reengineering Really Work," *Harvard Business Review*, (71:5), 1993, pp. 119-131.
3. Prahalad, C.K. and G. Hamel. "The Core Competence of the Corporation," *Harvard Business Review*, (68:3), 1990, pp. 79-91.
4. Jacob, 1995.
5. Kolbe, K. *Conative Connection - Acting on Instincts*, Addison Wesley Publishing, Reading, MA, 1989; Kolbe, K., *Pure*

Instinct: Business' Untapped Resource, Random House, New York, NY, 1993.

6. Tuckman, B. "Developmental Sequences in Small Groups," *Psychological Bulletin*, vol. 63, 1965, pp. 384-399.

7. Tuckman, B. and M. Jensen. "Stages of Small Group Development Revisited," *Group and Organizational Studies*, vol. 2, 1977, pp. 419-427; Lawson, J. and T. Bourner. "Developing Communication Within New Workgroups," *Journal of Applied Management Studies*, (6:2), 1997, pp. 149-167.

8. Sherman, S. and A. Hadjian. "How Tomorrow's Leaders are Learning Their Stuff," *Fortune*, November 27, 1995, pp. 90-100; Hymowitz, C. and M. Murray. "Raises and Praise or Out the Door," *Wall Street Journal*, June 21, 1999, pp. B1, B4.

9. Row, A. *Interview at Deere & Company*, August 4, 1999, Moline, IL.

CHAPTER 6

PURCHASING IN AN INTEGRATED SUPPLY CHAIN ENVIRONMENT

Where does my organization and position fit in an integrated supply chain?

Chapter Objectives

This chapter is designed to help the purchaser:

- Understand the nature of supply chain management initiatives.
- Recognize opportunities to build core competencies and shift roles among supply chain members.
- Understand the important steps in building purchaser/supplier alliances.
- Understand the keys to building good supplier relations with non-alliance partners.
- Recognize purchasing's responsibility to represent the organization to the outside world.

Supply Chain Integration

Beginning in the mid 1980s, supply relationships began to shift from what were often adversarial, transaction-oriented relationships to more cooperative and collaborative purchaser/supplier partnerships. Purchasing practices such as supplier certification, single sourcing, and supply-base reduction had become more common by the early 1990s. The term "supply chain management" began to capture the attention of industry analysts and managers. According to Harold Sirkin, a vice president of Boston Consulting Group, "As the economy changes, as competition becomes more global, it's no longer company versus company but supply chain versus supply chain."[1] Since the mid 1990s, supply chain integration has been known as the process of building strategic relationships across organizational boundaries to manage the flow of materials and information beginning with the first supplier and ending with the consumer.

Despite the popularity of the term "supply chain management" in today's purchasing and supply management environment, its application can vary substantially from organization to organization and even from manager to manager within the same organization. Only a small number of organizations have carefully mapped out their supply chains so that they know who their suppliers' suppliers or customers' customers really are. Many manufacturing and service organizations can tell you how many first-tier suppliers they have but can only guess about the number of second-tier and third-tier suppliers in their supply chains. The same is true regarding customers - first-tier customers are well known but customers further downstream cannot be as easily identified. Truly synergistic alliances represent a small number of total supply relationships, almost always fewer than 10 percent of the total.[2] Even assertive supply chain organizations recognize that not all purchaser/supplier relationships are equal. They focus the majority of their attention and investment on their most important suppliers.

For most organizations supply chain integration is new and therefore in a fluid state of evolution. We can expect continued evolution in the operationalization of supply chain strategies.

What is Supply Chain Management?

Operational definitions of Supply Chain Management (SCM) vary greatly and change rapidly as organizations gain experience. Supply chain leaders emphasize the following themes as part of their organizational cultures:

- Open communication
- Investment in people
- Investment in information technology
- Relentless pursuit of customer satisfaction
- Recognition of the importance of inter-organizational collaboration

Based on these common themes, "supply chain management" can be defined as:

> Supply Chain Management is the design and management of seamless, value-added processes across organizational boundaries to meet the real needs of the end customer. The development and integration of people and technological resources are critical to successful supply chain integration.[3]

Benefits of Effective Supply Chain Management

Organizations that have embraced supply chain management (SCM) treat it as more than just a management fad. Purchasers, logisticians, and other supply managers are taking a serious look at SCM because it promises to help their organizations:

- Respond quickly to customer demands with more competitive value propositions
- Reduce costs and increase profit margins
- Focus on core competencies while relying on supply chain partners to perform other activities
- Ally themselves with strong channel partners that will help ensure future competitive success
- Reduce risks

The convergence of these competitive opportunities has brought SCM to the forefront of many organizations' competitive strategies.

Organizations that have adopted supply chain integration have begun to enjoy the benefits of synergistic cooperation – shorter product development leadtimes, enhanced productivity, and improved quality. It is not uncommon to achieve 10 to 20 percent improvements in these areas. Some organizations have enjoyed reductions in order fulfillment cycle times of 50 percent and more while simultaneously increasing on-time delivery by a commensurate percentage.[4]

Barriers to Effective Supply Chain Management

Serious attempts to increase supply chain integration can create a sense of organizational vulnerability and require workers and managers to step out of traditional comfort zones. Inertia created by the need to change organizational cultures can make supply chain integration difficult to achieve. Even when this inertia is overcome, the challenge of meshing diverse organizational cultures, incompatible information systems, diverse worker attitudes, and different approaches to performance measurement can seem insurmountable. Because of the nature and number of barriers to success, many emotionally charged questions arise as an organization begins to consider supply chain integration:[5]

- Who is really in charge?
- Can we really trust the other supply chain members not to take advantage of us?
- What does supply chain management really mean for our bottomline performance?
- How is our role going to change in the new, integrated supply chain environment?
- How am I going to develop the skills needed for success in the new "team" environment?
- Who are the best partners to align our competitive efforts with?
- How are we going to measure what adds value?
- How many different supply chains can we work with effectively?

Many organizations do not initially know the answers to these questions, and as a result struggle with the very notion of supply chain management. For some, these questions are reason enough to avoid participating in integrated supply chains. For others, the failure to address the question, "Isn't supply chain management just another fad that will pass quickly and without substantive impact?" ensures that the SCM process will fail.

Purchasing managers who are serious about using supply chain integration to help improve bottomline performance and increase long-term customer loyalty need to be aware of the barriers that can impede successful integration. These barriers include:

- A lack of top management support
- Organizational structures that inhibit cooperation and collaboration
- Non-aligned goals and objectives within the organization and between organizations

- A lack of willingness or the inability (poor systems support) to share accurate and timely information
- Inconsistent performance measures within the organization and between organizations
- Poorly defined roles and responsibilities within the organization and between organizations
- Opportunistic behavior among channel members

Only top management can alter the culture and allocate resources in a way that supports supply chain management. Long-standing functional silos are difficult to break down, making it very difficult to engender the cooperative efforts that are absolutely vital to supply chain success. Barilla, the world's largest pasta maker, has experimented with a customer service organizational structure that merged sales and logistics departments in an effort to reduce friction between the two groups. This allowed Barilla to be more responsive to customer demand while simultaneously reducing inventory.[6] This organizational change followed six years of struggle between the two groups as Barilla had attempted to implement a JIT distribution system.

Beyond leadership and organization, successful supply chain management requires that each team member share similar philosophies and goals. Members must share information so their efforts become synchronized. Despite huge investments in information technology, many supply managers remain dissatisfied with their organization's information technology capabilities. The very expensive enterprise resource planning systems that have received much attention in recent years often prove difficult to implement and seldom deliver the flexible, real-time information organizations need for effective supply chain decisionmaking.[7] While organizations like Rockwell Collins and Wal-Mart have developed capable Web-based systems designed to share demand information with suppliers, most organizations are still striving to improve their information sharing capabilities. As organizations struggle to share information, they continue to use performance measurement systems that reward counterproductive decisions and limit cooperative behavior. Many measurement systems do not provide the information nor motivate the behavior needed for effective cross-functional and inter-organizational process integration.[8] While not insurmountable, these barriers hinder most organization's SCM efforts.

Bridges to Effective Supply Chain Management

Because supply chain management is about coordinating value-added activities across organizational boundaries, once the prerequisites of top management support and aligned goals are in place, success depends on four mechanisms used to integrate value-added activities: cross-boundary process integration; information systems support; performance measurement; and alliance management.

Inter-organizational process integration – Process integration is driven by the desire to optimize supply chain efficiency by having the right member of the supply chain perform each activity regardless of historic roles and responsibilities. To make this happen, organizations are developing process maps that highlight leadtimes, inventory levels, and responsibilities for key value-added activities. These maps guide the total cost and cycle time analysis that must be done to determine if traditional roles and responsibilities should be shifted among supply chain members. For example, some purchasing organizations have analyzed their total purchase requirements together with the critical purchase requirements of key suppliers and found that they could increase leverage by aggregating demand across the two tiers of the supply chain. By directly contracting with the second-tier supplier on behalf of first-tier suppliers, the purchasing organization can facilitate an increase in overall supply chain efficiencies. Second-tier purchasing agreements are straightforward examples of shifting roles among supply chain members. Volkswagon's truck assembly facility in Resende Brazil is 90 percent staffed with supplier personnel who operate all of the major modules in the assembly process.[9] Suppliers do not get paid for the parts and labor they provide until the vehicle passes the final inspection at the end of the production process.

Information systems support – Information exchange links the diverse and often geographically dispersed members of the supply chain. Two distinct issues are involved in the sharing of information. The first is willingness, which is based on relationship strength and trust. Many organizations struggle with the notion of sharing "proprietary" information regarding demand patterns with suppliers. Suppliers can likewise be adverse to sharing technology or cost structure data with customers. The second issue focuses on connectivity; that is, are the appropriate information system platforms in place to enable the sharing of timely, accurate, and relevant data? When information is shared properly, it can be substituted for inventory throughout the supply chain. Information sharing is also the key to compressing cycle times through postponement, continuous replenishment, and other time-based competitive strategies.[10] Some leading organizations have developed Web-based information systems that make complete order history and forecast demand patterns available to suppliers. One apparel manufacturer has developed a system that allows it to see the status of any order down to the number of units that have passed through each major step of the production process. The purchasing and merchandizing team can expedite or "kill" production runs based on early sales returns. This capability allows the organization to meet unexpectedly high sales demand and reduce markdowns, creating a true cost advantage.

Performance measurement – To establish the right strategic orientation, promote integration among channel members, and achieve continuous process renewal, appropriate and aligned performance measures must be adopted by supply chain members. Performance measurement provides insight into the real needs of key customers; yields understanding regarding the value-added capability of supply chain members; influences behavior throughout the supply chain; and provides information regarding the results of supply chain activities.[11] In recent years, purchasers have improved the capabilities of their supplier measurement systems. One popular tool among purchasing organizations is the supplier performance scorecard. Scorecards are used by organizations of every size and across every position of the supply chain. Many organizations post scorecard summaries on the Web so that suppliers can assess their relative performance. Total costing and activity-based costing have also become much more popular as integrative tools, enabling purchasers to evaluate and compare product, supplier, and channel profitability.

Alliance management – Alliance management is the final critical integrative mechanism. An alliance is a formal agreement between two organizations to work more closely in order to obtain mutual benefit. In supply chain management, the traditional dyadic purchaser/supplier alliance must be successfully extended throughout the entire supply chain. This extension requires the application of best alliance practice at each tier of the chain. Because purchaser/supplier alliances are so important to supply chain integration and to supply management strategies in general, the next section focuses on alliance management and discusses the following practices:

- The use of clear guidelines and procedures for selecting alliance partners
- The use of clear guidelines and procedures for monitoring alliances
- The sharing of expertise and resources between alliance partners to build stronger capabilities
- The sharing of risks and rewards
- The use of long-term written contracts

Managing Alliance Relationships for Success

One of the forces driving purchasing's strategic rise is the increased emphasis on more closely aligned purchaser/supplier relationships. Adversarial, transaction-based relationships have been replaced by more proactive, mutually beneficial relationships. The most important relationships have become collaborative, partnership relationships, with a focus on long-term value. These alliance relationships add value by enabling the partners to:

- Focus on their core capabilities/competencies
- Leverage their resources
- Learn from each other and other supply chain partners
- Offer unique product/service packages and one-of-a-kind satisfaction opportunities
- Better manage the supply chain as a value system
- Increase flexibility
- Spread risk across the value chain

Both sides of the alliance relationship receive specific and tangible benefits. For the purchasing organization, well-managed partnerships lower costs, improve product quality, enhance responsiveness, shorten order fulfillment times, speed innovation, and yield more productive use of purchasing resources. The supplier benefits from longer-term, larger-volume contracts, which increase production stability, lower costs, and helps justify investments in product and process technologies. Suppliers also often gain access to the purchaser's expertise in quality control and process engineering. Sometimes the purchaser even provides capital to upgrade the supplier's plant and equipment or finance the purchase of materials. Purchasers spend an increasing amount of their time managing these relationships.

Selecting Alliance Partners

Purchasing managers must develop the ability to accurately gauge the appropriate nature and intensity of individual supply relationships (see Figure 6.1). The most likely alliance partners are those that have the capacity to have a dramatic affect on organizational competitiveness. Some of the characteristics that suggest alliance formation include,

- A large dollar volume is purchased from the supplier
- The purchaser represents a significant share of the supplier's sales
- The supplier possess skills and technology that cannot be found elsewhere
- The item or service being purchased is a strategic component
- Intensive collaboration can dramatically reduce cycle times or lead to another significant advantage
- There is potential scarcity in the supply market for the item or service

FIGURE 6.1
The Alliance Relationship Continuum

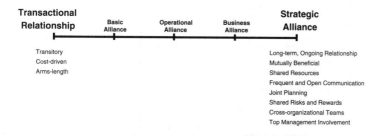

- **Transactional Relationship** -- No formalized relationship; rather, each purchase decision is made independently at arms length.
- **Basic Alliance** -- Tactical relationship designed to establish basic level of trust and honest, open communication.
- **Operational Alliance** -- More frequent communication regarding capacity and demand coupled with occasional joint problem solving.
- **Business Alliance** -- Greater mutual dependence coupled with specialized processes and unique products and services.
- **Strategic Alliance** -- Long-term relationship involving shared commitment/resources and dealing with strategically important products/services

Alliances tend to be long-term and resource intensive. They are also evolutionary, often transcending traditional roles and responsibilities. Clear guidelines and procedures for selecting suppliers are thus critical to alliance success (see Figure 6.2). These procedures emphasize a rigorous up-front analysis of the net affect of the potential alliance. Before the decision to pursue an alliance is reached, both the purchaser and the supplier should feel confident that specific benefits in the areas of quality, cost, order cycle times, product and process design, inventory reduction, and/or market responsiveness will be achieved. Because costs and benefits of alliance cut across

FIGURE 6.2
The Alliance Development Process

Alliances generally develop over time through a multi-stage process as follows:

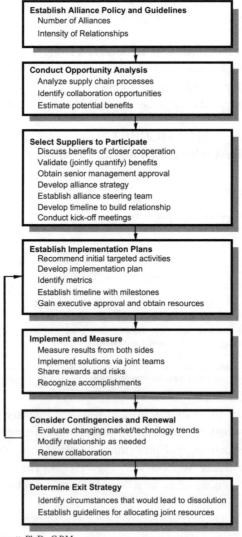

© Stanley E. Fawcett, Ph.D., C.P.M.

functional boundaries, supplier evaluation teams with members from purchasing, engineering, operations, quality control, finance, and, as appropriate, senior management analyze the long-term potential benefit of each alliance candidate. These teams bring together the expertise needed to verify that the benefits of collaboration are tangible, significant and attainable. After the benefits have been quantified, contract templates and resource sharing guidelines are also commonly employed to help standardize the alliance creation process.

Building the Relationship

Once the decision has been made to build an alliance, it is important that both sides understand the nature and intensity of the relationship. A set of clear alliance monitoring and management guidelines that are mutually agreed on by both sides can reduce ambiguity. A dedicated effort to establish behaviors conducive to alliance success should be pursued. Successful alliances typically include:

- Mutual trust between alliance partners
- Senior management involvement and support
- Frequent, open, and honest communication
- The sharing of information about demand, capacity, technology, and new products
- The sharing of expertise including quality training, and engineering support
- Joint development and problem solving
- Confidentiality agreements
- Collaborative continuous improvement efforts
- The sharing of risks and rewards
- Long-term contracts (defined between three to five years but can be up to 10 years)

Mutual trust – Next to ensuring that mutual benefits are attainable through collaboration, establishing a high level of trust is the most important alliance success factor. Strategic alliances usually require that organizations invest in each other's capabilities and go the extra mile to help each other achieve higher levels of success. Trust is established on the foundation of aligned goals and compatible competencies and is supported by frequent, open, and honest communication. Many organizations now provide rolling 18-month production plans to their key suppliers. Sharing information regarding new product, market entry, and other strategic planning issues can enhance the alliance's ability to achieve outstanding results.

Risks and rewards – Another behavior critical to building successful alliances is the willingness to share the risks and rewards created by the alliance. Leading organizations have established formal programs to facilitate mutually beneficial reward/risk sharing. For example, in addition to sharing production plans with its best suppliers, one catalogue-based apparel retailer expects suppliers to hold four weeks of inventory at the supplier's production facility. Shared demand forecasts combined with supplier-held inventory assures greater flexibility in meeting unexpected demand surges. In return, the retailer promises to purchase up to the four weeks of inventory should sales fail to materialize. When a sales forecast proves overly optimistic, the retailer assumes the risk of the inaccurate forecast. At the same time, this organization is always positioned to meet surges in demand. At Deere & Company, a program known as the Cost Reduction Opportunities Process (JDCROP) encourages selected suppliers to submit cost reduction suggestions to Deere & Company for evaluation by Deere & Company engineers, who respond to the supplier within 20 days. If the idea is approved, a joint supplier-Deere & Company team works to complete the project. Half of the first year's savings are shared with the supplier. Both partners in the alliance have a tangible reason to be creative and to strive for excellence.[12]

Collaborative improvement – Many outstanding supplier alliances share expertise and resources to build stronger capabilities. Philosophically, some organizations find it difficult to justify expending resources on external partners and limit resource sharing to training in specific value-added techniques such as quality control or cycle time reduction. Other organizations like Honda of America take a more resource intensive approach to supplier development. Honda sends teams of process engineers to work on-site with key partners for extended periods of time, often up to three months. The team's objective is to help the alliance partner establish world-class production processes and institute continuous learning loops. It is not uncommon for a team to begin its work by cleaning up workstations, installing new lighting, and enhancing basic ergonomics. These activities are performed to enhance efficiency and to gain the trust needed to successfully initiate continuous improvement suggestion programs and to redesign overall processes. Of course, resource sharing at successful alliances goes both ways. Suppliers often dedicate engineers to new product teams, manage the purchaser's inventory, and participate on joint problem solving teams.

Long-term contracts – Most alliance relationships are validated through the use of a long-term contract, which symbolizes the transition to a collaborative, on-going partnership. Typical alliance contracts are for one to three years and provide the benefits of cooperation while maintaining a degree of flexibility. These contracts incent supplier cooperation by guaranteeing a specific volume of purchases over the life of the contract. Some blanket contracts do not specify the exact timing of purchases but require the supplier to be flexible enough to meet the purchaser's fluctuating needs. The sharing of demand forecasts helps the supplier anticipate and plan for the demand fluctuations. Relationships that require greater resource commitments from one or both of the partners often extend beyond the standard one to three years. One European manufacturer sets the contract duration based on strict guidelines regarding supplier investment. In one instance, where a supplier undertook substantial research and development to build a unique racking system, the manufacturer entered into a 10-year contract.

Planning for Contingencies

Alliances that make competitive sense when they are formed may be hard to justify over time. Changing market and technology conditions should be monitored consistently and alliance structures modified accordingly. Joint planning and continuous improvement teams can provide new opportunities and thus the incentive to continue an alliance relationship. In all cases, alliance performance should be closely measured and benefits tracked. More and more organizations are adopting supplier recognition programs to generate additional good will. Some organizations use supplier conferences to create an opportunity to celebrate past achievements and plan for future success. Harley-Davidson brings its most important suppliers together for a supplier conference where it not only bestows its supplier-of-the-year awards but also shares design plans and lets suppliers ride its motorcycles.[13]

Despite efforts to maintain a productive alliance, changes in technology or market requirements can make a relationship obsolete. It is a good idea to plan for dissolution of the alliance when the alliance is being formed. Circumstances that might trigger the end of the alliance should be identified. Minimum performance standards should be specified so that the end of the alliance can be anticipated. Issues regarding ownership of shared resources or jointly developed technologies should be spelled out. An organization's reputation as a good partner depends on its ability to end an alliance amicably. Further, changes in the supply environment can make a former alliance partner a strong ally at a future date.

Alliances can help both partners achieve greater market share and profitability over the lifetime of the relationship. The following points can help purchasers design and manage effective alliances:

- View the arrangement as the implementation of a strategic plan
- Encourage the participants involved to consider their roles in terms of a value-added process
- Seek an arrangement that achieves scale-economy benefits while spreading risk
- Make sure that the information needed to succeed over the long run is shared among participants
- Build trust between the organizations by setting unambiguous goals, establishing clear roles, laying down clear and specific rules
- Measure performance rigorously
- Consider the contingencies and develop an exit strategy

Good Supplier Relations Without a Strategic Alliance

Most supply relationships do not merit the time and attention invested in strategic alliances; nevertheless, all relationships should be managed proactively and as part of an overall supply strategy. The goal for non-strategic relationships is to achieve good supplier relations a feeling held by suppliers that they are treated fairly. Good supplier relations can provide many returns, including lower overall product and administrative costs, better quality, more cooperation in providing technical support, and the delivery of special services. Of the many benefits, perhaps the most important is responsiveness to changes, such as the need to expedite an existing order, rush ship spare parts, or increase production to meet a sudden surge in demand.

Fair and friendly relations also help to keep negotiations simple, speed responses to inquiries, and facilitate the resolution of quality or other problems. Poor relations can take a solvable dispute to litigation, costing the purchaser time and money. Finally, good relations set the stage for more advanced relationships in the future, it can be difficult to forecast which relationships will be important over a five- or 10-year time period.

Good relations begin with an organizational philosophy that says that all suppliers should be treated fairly and in a way that supports a mutually satisfying arrangement. Organizations that are interested in beneficial relationships should establish a policy statement and a set of guidelines that promote good relations. The purchasing process should also be designed to be transparent and to remove obstacles, including inefficient payment procedures, obtuse quality policies, and poor feedback systems. Purchasers should be evaluated on their willingness to foster proactive relations and should receive training in methods that promote good relations. The purchasing organization should seek to become a "preferred customer." Some of the most important things a purchaser can do to engender good supplier relations are highlighted below. Each practice should be applied as appropriate, depending on the strength, duration, and importance of the purchaser/supplier relationship:

- **Top management interaction** – for critical relationships, senior management should meet to discuss long-term strategies and future relations. Senior managers can spend up to 20 percent of their time meeting with suppliers and customers.
- **Personal contact** – cultivating appropriate personal relationships between the purchaser and supplier can generate goodwill and reduce miscommunication.
- **Clear specifications** – product, process and contract fulfillment specifications should be clearly stated so that there is no confusion or ambiguity about expectations.
- **Timely payment** – suppliers should be paid as quickly and easily as possible for example some purchasing organizations have adopted 10-day payment cycles.

- **Equitable treatment** – policies should be applied equally. Each supplier must have an equal opportunity to supply each purchase order. Preferred supplier status should be based on real performance.
- **Supplier training** – it often makes sense to provide quality or other process related training to suppliers. Training is an investment in supplier skills and the relationship.
- **Open communication** – good electronic linkages and face-to-face communication skills are critical to good relations. Purchasers should communicate all needed information to the supplier as soon as the information is available.
- **Supplier feedback** – periodic supplier surveys coupled with face-to-face feedback can build trust while helping the purchaser improve its purchasing process. Some possible questions to ask include, "How knowledgeable are our purchasers?" "What aspects of our purchasing process are difficult?" "What can we do to make your job easier?" and "How could we work together to reduce your cost?"
- **Mutual consideration** – purchasers should not place unnecessary burdens on or make excessive requests of a supplier. Changes in product and service specifications should be communicated with as much notice as possible and differences in opinion should be discussed with an open mind.
- **Give and take** – changes in specifications that help the supplier without adversely affecting performance should be seriously considered. All suggestions should be evaluated quickly and feedback provided promptly.
- **Confidentiality** – all cost, technology, and performance information related to suppliers should remain strictly confidential. Confidentiality agreements are often appropriate.
- **Integrity** – purchasers should always exhibit a desire to fulfill all contract obligations without hassle or argument. Purchasers should model the integrity they expect from suppliers.

Managing External Relations

To maintain productive relationships with suppliers and other external constituencies, purchasers must acquire a wide range of knowledge and develop a variety of skills. For example, to build a world-class supply base, purchasers must become commodity experts, understand the economics of pricing, be aware of issues that affect product availability, know how to work with suppliers' sales people, and be able to effectively respond to supplier inquires and protests. At the same time, purchasers must have the skills of a coach and mentor, be able to develop small business/disadvantaged supplier programs, and be familiar with a myriad of legal and regulatory ramifications. Purchasing, like marketing, must deal extensively with external forces on a day-to-day basis. They must therefore acquire the skills that will help them successfully represent the purchasing organization in meetings with corporations, government agencies, professional associations, and the media. A high level of professional decorum combined with the ability to effectively communicate in meetings, presentations, and press conferences can help the professional purchaser advance the organization's strategic objectives.

Understanding Product Availability and Pricing

One of purchasing's primary goals is to provide the highest-quality and lowest-priced goods and services into the organization. Purchasers must therefore develop outstanding commodity knowledge with a particular focus on product availability and pricing. To assure adequate supply and to understand pricing issues and trends, a commodity team must examine both the industry structure of the target commodity and the potential affect of external events. Key questions to ask include:

- What are the critical market drivers for this commodity? Natural scarcity, capacity, government regulations, patent protection, supplier action, all affect product availability and price.
- What are current and future economic conditions and how will they affect availability and price?
- How much capacity do suppliers currently have? Do they have a policy that limits the level of sales to a specific customer? Are we close to the limit?
- Are we too dependent on any given supplier? Are alternative sources of supply available?
- If necessary, how much (and how quickly) could suppliers increase their capacity?

- How much worldwide capacity exists? How close is the industry to full capacity?
- What does the demand curve look like over the next several years? For our organization and for all industries that purchase this commodity?
- Are there any looming events such as a strike, economic sanctions, or political upheaval that could threaten our access to adequate supplies?
- Are imports of products that are subject to quotas approximating the maximum quantity? Are there any political issues that will change tariff or quota levels in the foreseeable future?
- What is our contingency plan in case of unexpected natural disaster?

Answering these questions will help the organization determine relative product availability and thereby enable the purchasing professional to establish appropriate sourcing and inventory policies. For example, if an organization is already purchasing 60 percent or more of its single-source supplier's capacity and it expects demand to increase, then the purchaser might want to identify and develop a second source of supply. If the three-to five-year demand forecast for a commodity shows that global capacity will be strained, then the purchaser might want to lock in long-term volume agreements with existing suppliers or work with an existing supplier to bring additional capacity online before the predicted shortage. If an industry approaches full capacity for example 90 percent factory usage, the purchaser should recognize that higher prices are likely to follow. If the purchaser sees signs of labor strife, then increasing inventories or establishing relations with an alternate supplier is reasonable. Some purchasing organizations single-source similar items for different models from different suppliers in order to develop relationships with multiple suppliers just in case an alternative source is needed. Natural disasters represent the most difficult supply disruption to manage because they are almost impossible to predict. A 1999 earthquake in the semiconductor manufacturing region of Taiwan created a shortage of semiconductors that slowed sales and increased prices of a number of popular computer models. It often makes sense to develop alternative sources in geographically dispersed regions to avoid a complete supply disruption caused by natural disaster or political upheaval. Rigorous environmental scans coupled with accurate demand forecasts and proactive contingency planning can help maintain an uninterrupted flow of materials.

The second half of the commodity analysis equation - pricing - is largely dependent on product availability because the laws of supply and demand are the primary determinant of price. Perhaps the single most important factor that affects price is market structure - the number of customers compared to the number of suppliers. In both monopolies and oligopolies, market power rests with the suppliers. The opposite is true in monopsonies and oligopsonies, where purchasing organizations have more negotiating strength (see Volume 1). Markets, however, tend to function efficiently, therefore, price is based largely on supply and demand. In markets where price is negotiable, purchasers focus on the cost of the product or service (by contrast, suppliers prefer to focus on value delivered). The goal is to acquire the desired product or service at the lowest possible fair price. Fair is usually defined as the price that allows the supplier to make enough of a profit to stay in business, developing and delivering outstanding products and services. Purchasers need to understand the following approaches used by suppliers to establish prices (price analysis techniques used by purchasers are discussed in Chapter 8).

- **Straight markup** – calculates the price by multiplying the unit cost by a markup percentage, which covers a contribution to overhead and profit Price = [Unit Cost + (Unit Cost)(Markup)]. From the purchaser's perspective, the key is to gauge an accurate product cost and to verify that the markup percentage is appropriate but not exorbitant.

- **Rate of return** – the price is based on the return required for the supplier to justify investments needed to make a product or deliver a service. To perform the calculations, the purchaser must estimate the unit cost of the item, the net new investment, the rate of return, and the potential sales quantity. The formula is as follows: Price = [(1 + ROR)(Investment)/Sales] + unit cost. From the purchaser's perspective, the key is to verify that the rate of return is reasonable, the level of investment appropriate, and the sales quantity is realistic. Separate quotes on the product cost and the tooling investment can clarify the costing analysis.

- **Variable pricing** – the supplier sets the price based on the need to cover variable costs. Suppliers resort to variable pricing in order to enter a new market, get customers "in the door" hoping they will buy other products, and maintain volume during economic downturns in order to retain skilled workers. Because variable pricing does not cover the entire cost of the product, purchasers can expect prices to rise in the future.
- **Value-based pricing** – the price is based on the perceived value delivered by the product or service rather than its cost. The goal of the supplier is to create a perception of value that shifts the discussion away from price. The purchaser must verify that any price above the normal cost plus reasonable profit is truly justified by tangible value. Some sources of value include a lack of substitutes, high switching costs, truly unique performance, outstanding service etc.

Dealing with Suppliers

The purchasing professional has many roles when it comes to day-to-day interactions with suppliers. Managing the purchase transaction is the most visible role of purchasing. Because both the sales representative and the purchasing manager seek to obtain the best possible deal for their respective organizations, the purchase/sales interaction can quickly become adversarial even when both sides want to cooperate. To manage this interaction well, the purchaser must understand the selling process, which can be quite complicated. The typical sales process consists of five phases:

1. **Prospecting** – is an effort by the sales person to evaluate the business potential. It involves identifying a need that the sales person's product or service can fulfill. The sales person is trying to create the perception that the products for sale will deliver value if purchased.
2. **The sales presentation** – focuses on illustrating need fulfillment of the product being offered. The sales manager is making a persuasive case that her product/service is the solution to one or more needs of the purchasing organization. The presentation is used to develop a feeling of mutual trust in the relationship. When selling to a purchasing team, the sales presentation must

help identify the source of decisionmaking power and resolve any conflict that arises among the purchasing team members.

3. **Responding to objections** – any concerns that the purchaser may have requires that the sales person know the facts and how to communicate them effectively. The sales person attempts to demonstrate why the purchaser should make an affirmative decision by showing how the product or service creates benefits that far outweigh the costs and that are superior to those available through competitors' products.

4. **Closing the deal** – involves getting the decisionmaker to say yes and to make the purchase. Sales representatives are trained to get to the point of commitment, to recognize purchasing signals, and to use effective closing techniques.

5. **Follow through** – involves resolving any unanswered concerns that may exist about a product or service as well as maintaining a positive relationship with key decisionmakers. It is vital that the purchased item be perceived as a real solution to a real need.

By understanding exactly what is going on at each stage of the sales process, the purchaser is well positioned to make sure that the purchasing organization's needs are met at the best possible price. Perhaps the single most important thing that a purchaser can do is to make sure that the sales person understands clearly the needs and objectives of the purchasing organization. Clear expectations and precise metrics should be communicated to the supplier and used to evaluate the ability of a supplier's product to deliver real value and meet the purchasing organization's needs. Also, because the sales team is generally active in the industry, many opportunities exist for the proactive purchaser to use the sales process as a source of competitive information and new ideas. When the purchase/sales transaction works well, the sales person can be a solid resource to help the purchaser understand better how to meet specific needs and build a stronger competitive advantage.

To ensure that the sales process is positive and helps build successful purchaser/supplier relations, most organizations have established policies to guide purchasers' behavior. Most of these policies touch on either ethics or professional courtesies. For example, most organizations discourage purchasers from requesting special favors or prices that would not be extended to other purchasers of like quality and quantity. Sharing sensitive pricing or technological information with a supplier or a competitor that should be held in confidence shows poor judgment and could violate various antitrust laws. Confidentiality must be guarded carefully. Regarding courtesy, purchasing professionals should learn to be prompt and polite, treating all suppliers equally and fairly. Suppliers need to have a fair and legitimate opportunity to win an order if they bring forth a competitive proposal. Further, purchasers should not take advantage of supplier mistakes (such as the misplacement of a comma in the price quoted in a bid). Clear communication that helps suppliers prepare more competitive bids by pointing out why previous bids have been rejected can be valuable to the supplier. Good customers help suppliers succeed by making it easy to do business with them. These behaviors are good business practice, costing the purchasing organization nothing but returning priceless goodwill. Ultimately, purchasers must remember everyday that they represent their organization and should behave in a manner that protects the organization's interests.

Responding to protests – It is courteous to respond quickly and accurately to inquiries and protests from suppliers. However, the fact that conflicts can escalate quickly elevates the need for rapid and clear response. All purchasing organizations should use a transparent dispute resolution mechanism. All suppliers should be educated about how these mechanisms work and should then have equal access to them. In the public sector, the dispute resolution process is typically specified by statute. Private sector organizations should take this issue seriously. Most dispute resolution methodologies begin with an attempt by the purchaser to solve the problem. If a mutually acceptable solution cannot be found, then the difficulty is passed to the Chief Purchasing Officer, an appeals board, and ultimately to arbitration or litigation. The closer to the source of the problem that the problem can be resolved the better. Every effort should be employed to avoid costly litigation. The Model Procurement Code was instituted by the American Bar Association in order to facilitate dispute resolution and minimize lengthy litigation. The Code suggests several alternative approaches to dispute resolution including the use of a written protest to the chief purchasing officer within 14 days as well as the establishment of an appeals board. Finally, public purchasers need to understand that the Freedom of Information Act establishes a basic standard of openness. Under this act, any information that is part of the public record and is not classified for security reasons must be made available to the general public on request. Suppliers whose bids are rejected can request information regarding the winning bid. When purchasers follow established guidelines, document each decision, act in good faith, and award bids based on merit, few problems will arise from making bidding information public. Decisions should be made as if the process were part of the public record.

Managing reciprocity – Reciprocity is the practice of giving preference to suppliers who are also customers. Reciprocity has long been an important practice in the global marketplace. Many government contracts are tied to the condition that local content or buyback requirements are met. In a supply chain environment, where more integrated relationships are sought and a serious effort to reduce total chain complexity drives decisions, reciprocity is also practiced more frequently. For example, one major food products organization now sources a significant portion of its domestic transportation needs from a customer. While the analysis has shown that this practice makes economic and logistical sense, it has at least one real drawback - when a shipment is late or otherwise mishandled, how do you tactfully chastise or fine one of your major customers? It is easy to lose objectivity in a reciprocal relationship. Two other potential problems limit the use of reciprocity. First, while reciprocity is generally legal, if its practice restricts competition, then the legal threshold has been crossed. In any questionable situation, the burden of proof rests with the purchasing organization. Second, reciprocity can have a negative affect on overall supplier performance. Suppliers who are also customers may relax their performance standards believing that the contract is secure despite inferior performance. Other suppliers may also be less enthusiastic about doing business with a purchaser who engages in reciprocity; after all, how can they "hope to win a contract when the competition is the customer's customer." The purchasing organization can thus find it difficult to find and develop new suppliers, losing out on opportunities to purchase the most advanced products. These potential limitations make it vital for purchasing organizations to have a published and visible policy that defines its position on reciprocity. For some organizations, the policy statement can read, "When important factors such as quality, price, and service are equal, we prefer to purchase from our customers." Strictly measuring supplier performance then becomes critical to success of reciprocal relationships.

Mentoring and developing suppliers – Today's purchaser must be a coach and mentor. Building a world-class supply base that is intimately familiar with the purchaser's technical and operating needs requires close cooperation and often necessitates that the purchaser provide training in quality control practices, just-in-time principles, or the implementation and use of unique information systems. In many cases, senior managers from suppliers are invited to visit the purchaser's operations for a two- or three-day supplier conference during which they become aware of materials requirements and operating procedures first hand. At Rockwell Collins, best practice seminars are taught to help suppliers catch the vision and gain the skills needed to become best in class. An important aspect of these seminars is that suppliers who have already mastered the best practice teach several of the seminars. By working closely with its key suppliers, Rockwell Collins has achieved 5 percent per year reductions in its purchased bills of materials cost since 1991. Over the same time, the consumer price index for the comparable basket of goods has increased by 3 percent per year. The difference between these two cost curves over a 10-year time period is huge.[14]

Mentoring requires that performance expectations be set at the highest levels. To motivate outstanding performance, many organizations now include continuous improvement clauses in long-term contracts. A typical improvement clause requires suppliers to reduce the purchaser's purchase costs by 3 to 5 percent each year or to reduce order fulfillment time by 10 percent annually. The improvement is expected to begin from world-class performance levels. Advantages of mentoring include higher levels of supplier performance, suppliers who are familiar with the organization's processes and procedures, and supplier's that network together and learn from each other. Creating a learning supply network is the best approach to achieving long-term competitive advantage.

Reverse marketing – On occasion, a purchasing need arises for which no suitable supplier can be found. The purchasing professional must then take on the role of creating a source by convincing an existing supplier to take responsibility for a new product or service. Persuading suppliers to enter new markets is often referred to as reverse marketing. Reverse marketing requires the use of assertive marketing-oriented techniques. The purchaser must answer the question, "What's in it for the supplier?" Volume business, better relationships, a relatively lucrative contract, and the promise of future business are all potential incentives. In reverse marketing, the purchaser and supplier work together to establish prices, terms, and conditions because no standard or comparison exists. Reverse marketing can lead to truly unique and competitive products.

Representing the Organization

No one has more contact with external constituents than the purchasing professional. This external contact carries with it both opportunities and responsibilities. The daily contacts of purchasing managers outside the organization can provide an opportunity to learn about the organization's competitive environment. Purchasing's competitive intelligence capability should be promoted through formal training and a culture that values gathering and sharing of useful information. Purchasing managers' external contacts allow them to help answer the following important questions:

- Who are the organization's major competitors and what are they doing to improve their competitive position?
- Are new product or process technologies being developed by competitors or by suppliers?
- What is the state of the overall economy?
- Will adequate supplies of resources (labor and materials) continue to exist?
- Are innovative marketing strategies being implemented by suppliers?

Purchasing's responsibility in working with external constituencies is to "carry the organization's banner," representing the organization to the outside world. At times, the primary (and perhaps only) contact an external party has with the purchaser's organization is through its association with the purchaser and the purchasing process. Because purchasing contributes extensively to the shaping of an organization's image, purchasing professionals must perform their responsibilities at the highest standard of professionalism. This means treating suppliers fairly and with courtesy, establishing sound and transparent policies that will guide supplier selection and management, and working to help suppliers and customers achieve higher levels of competitiveness. It also means participating in professional and trade associations in an effort to build both the organization and the profession. Purchasers must also adhere to the first standard listed in the NAPM Principles and Standards of Purchasing Practice, which is to "avoid the intent and appearance of unethical or compromising practice in relationships, actions, and communications." The fact that perceived wrongdoing often creates greater disruption than real violations suggests that purchasers shun any behavior that could be construed as inappropriate including the disclosure of confidential information or the discussion of topics that might violate anti-trust laws. Integrity of action is paramount to building a reputation as a great purchasing organization.

Developing a Disadvantaged Supplier Program

Participation in small-business and disadvantaged supplier development initiatives can contribute to an organization's image as a progressive and socially responsible member of the community. With over three million minority-owned businesses and more than nine million women-owned businesses in the U.S., it makes sense for organizations to make a concerted effort to include these businesses in the purchasing process. Purchasing from minority-owned or women-owned businesses can provide substantial benefits. Many government contracts include requirements that a percentage of the total contract be set aside for purchases from disadvantaged suppliers. In fact, in 1978, Public Law 95-507 mandated that bidders for federal contracts greater than $500,000 submit a plan that included a specific percentage of purchases from minority businesses. Executive Order 12432 later directed all federal agencies to develop specific goal-driven plans designed to increase sourcing from disadvantaged businesses. Today, organizations often set aside 5 percent of a contract for small disadvantaged businesses and women-owned businesses. Many non-governmental customers now make similar demands for the inclusion of small, disadvantaged, or women-owned suppliers. Further, it is not uncommon for these disadvantaged suppliers to offer world-class products and services. The proactive purchaser looks to minority- and women-owned suppliers as legitimate sources of supply. To qualify as a minority-owned or a woman-owned business, an organization must be at least 51 percent owned, controlled, and operated by an ethnic or racial minority or one or more women respectively.

Organizations that actively work to develop relationships with disadvantaged suppliers often codify their philosophies via a policy manual, which sets the parameters for the development initiative. The typical manual describes the purpose of the program, includes a definition of a disadvantaged supplier, sets goals for the program, discusses methods for execution and measurement, and establishes reporting procedures. It is vital for top management to emphasize the importance of the program and to assign responsibility for its success to a specific individual who is held accountable for consistent progress toward the goals. The designated program coordinator needs to be familiar with the primary impediments confronted and approaches used in developing disadvantaged supplier development programs (see Table 6.1). Education and training can then be put in place to help bridge the reticence and lack of specific skills. Every purchaser involved in working with disadvantaged suppliers should be aware of the following, well-established sources of information:

- **PRO-NET** – a computerized directory of over 75,000 small, minority, and women-owned business designed and maintained by the Small Business Administration (SBA). The Web page can be found at www.pro-net.sba.gov.
- **TRY US** – the best known and most widely used minority business directory. The 2000 edition provides information on over 8,000 certified minority sources by commodity and by state. The TRY US Web site can be found at www.tryusdir.com. Diversity Information Resources, Inc. (formerly TRY US Resources, Inc.) also publishes a National Women's Business Directory, which lists over 2,000 certified women-owned businesses.
- **Minority Business Information Resources Directory** – a listing of the major organizations established to promote minority business development. The list includes all 38 Minority Purchasing Councils, all five Minority Business Development Center Regional Offices, all 71 Minority Business Development Centers, all 10 SBA Regional Offices, the 87 SBA District Offices, and 56 Small Business Development Centers. Also included is a list of all minority business directories published in the U.S.
- **National Directory of Minority-Owned Business Organizations** – a directory of over 37,000 minority-owned businesses published by Business Research Services, Inc. (www.sba8a.com).
- **National Directory of Women-Owned Business Organizations** – a directory of over 19,000 women-owned businesses published by Business Research Services, Inc.

Table 6.1
Impediments and Approaches to Successful Disadvantaged Supplier Development Programs

Impediments to Success:

Corporate Purchasing Perspective
- MBEs are often undercapitalized
- MBEs are not available in specialized areas
- MBEs become disillusioned with corporate bureaucracy
- Finding contracts to bid is time consuming for MBEs
- It is hard to match the MBE organization with the corporation's need
- MBEs are clustered in a few industry areas
- MBEs don't expand their businesses to meet corporate needs
- Purchasers lack information on MBE capabilities
- MBEs sometimes act as a "front" for non-minority businesses
- Purchasers use MBEs just to satisfy statistics

Minority-Business Perspective
- MBEs are often undercapitalized
- Purchasers rely on their "old-boy networks" for suppliers
- It's hard for MBEs to get their foot in the door
- MBEs become disillusioned with corporate bureaucracy
- Purchasers use MBEs just to satisfy statistics
- Purchasers are inconsistent in implementing MBE programs
- Purchasers don't know much about minority-owned organizations
- Government doesn't enforce regulations on MBE purchasing
- Lack of corporate commitment to MBE purchasing programs
- Only small-volume orders are placed with MBEs

Approaches to Success:

Corporate Purchasing Perspective
- MBEs should continually improve their products/services
- MBEs should attend MBE trade fairs
- Corporations should identify long-term purchasing needs
- MBEs need to be aware of resources available to assist MBEs
- Corporations should attend MBE trade fairs
- Corporations should check references
- MBEs should be willing to introduce new products/services
- Corporations should perform credit checks
- Corporations should provide an MBE listing to all departments
- Corporations should hold quality assurance meetings

Minority-Business Perspective
- MBEs should continually improve their products/services
- Corporations should provide an MBE listing to all departments
- MBEs should attend MBE trade fairs
- MBEs need to be aware of resources available to assist them
- Corporations should list large volume opportunities
- Corporations should get top management involved in MBE programs
- Corporations should identify long-term purchasing needs
- Corporations should publish list of commodities sought
- MBEs need to be persistent in the pursuit of contracts
- MBEs need to develop multiple sources of financial assistance

- **National Association of Women Business Owners** – an advocacy organization that promotes women-owned businesses. The organization publishes a directory that is available only to its members.
- **Women's Business Enterprise National Council** – an organization that provides information on 1,600 certified women-owned businesses via an Internet database called WBENCLink. The Web page can be found at www.wbenc.org.
- **The National Minority Supplier Development Council** – operates 38 Minority Purchasing Councils throughout the U.S., which certify minority business suppliers, promote corporate minority purchasing programs, provide training and technical assistance, and refer corporate purchasers to minority suppliers. The Web site is at is at www.nmsdcus.org.
- **Local Minority Chambers of Commerce** – represent minority owned business of various ethnic and racial groups in cities with large minority populations across the country.

Relationships Matter

Establishing good relationships with current and potential suppliers as well as with other external entities is essential to the success of any organization's purchasing strategy. One of the most important responsibilities a purchasing organization has is to establish an optimal relationship with each supplier. The nature of human relations coupled with the dynamics of today's supply environment make the establishment of optimal relationships close to impossible. However, successful organizations realize that while the intensity of purchaser/supplier relationships varies, each relationship must be designed to treat the supplier in a fair and reasonable manner while helping the organization become more competitive.

In a world where supply chains compete against supply chains in a battle for global market share, assembling the best possible "team" is critical. A globally competitive supply chain – as with any championship team – must establish a certain chemistry that comes from mutual respect, hard work, and a sincere desire for each team member to be more competitive. This chemistry results only as great supply relationships are built throughout the supply chain. Moreover, it facilitates proactive role shifting and truly synergistic performance.

Today's purchasing professionals recognize that for their organizations to become an integral member of a world-class supply chain team, they must become world-class suppliers and world-class customers simultaneously.

Key Points

1. Supply chain management, which requires the building of the best supply team possible, has become an important competitive thrust that is likely to grow in the next decade.
2. Supply chain integration depends on the development of process integration, information sharing, performance measurement, and alliance management mechanisms.
3. Winning supply chains succeed because they actively evaluate core competencies and shift roles and responsibilities to leverage each supply chain team member's strategic and tactical advantages.
4. The important steps in alliance building are to carefully select compatible and complementary supply partners; establish relationships based on trust, clearly communicated goals and roles, open communication, expertise sharing, and measurement; and plan for contingencies and the ultimate dissolution of the relationship.
5. Building good, fair and mutually beneficial, relationships with all suppliers is important even when the relationship does not merit the time and expense dedicated to a strategic alliance. The general goal for the purchasing organization is to become a "preferred customer."
6. Purchasing managers represent their organization to the outside world. Professionalism and effective communication skills can help the professional purchaser advance strategic objectives.

Questions For Review

1. Discuss the rationale for understanding an entire supply chain from the suppliers' supplier to the customers' customer. What are some of the barriers that occur in supply chain integration?

2. What is your organization's competitive strength? What does this mean regarding your organization's position in the supply chain? Are there opportunities for role shifting? Threats?

3. What are the advantages of selecting a single supplier versus using multiple suppliers? What are the disadvantages of sole sourcing? Of multiple sourcing?

4. Why would a purchasing organization be interested in developing longer-term relationships with a supplier? Why would a supplier be interested in such a relationship?

5. Describe the profile of a supplier that is a likely candidate for partnership status with a purchasing organization.

6. What are the primary difficulties in achieving sound relationships with non-strategic suppliers? What are the most important steps in building proactive supplier relationships with non-alliance suppliers?

7. What possible challenges arise when an organization fails to establish a transparent and efficient process for responding to supplier inquiries and protests?

8. What skills would a purchasing manager want to develop to more effectively represent the organization in interactions with suppliers, government organizations, or professional associations?

Endnotes

1. Henkoff, R. "Delivering the Goods," *Fortune*, November 28, 1994, pp. 64-78.

2. Krause, D.R. and R.B. Handfield. "Developing a World Class Supply Base," Center for Advanced Purchasing Studies, Tempe, AZ, 1999.

3. Fawcett, S.E. and G.M. Magnan. "Achieving World-Class Supply Chain Alignment," *Purchasing Today* ®, November 1999, p. 58.

4. *Ibid.*

5. Elliff, S.A. "Supply Chain Management-New Frontier," *Traffic World*, October 21, 1996, p. 55.

6. Bowersox, D.J., R.J. Calantone, S.R. Clinton, D.J. Closs, M.B. Cooper, C.L. Droge, S.E. Fawcett, R. Frankel, D.J. Frayer, E.A. Morash, L.M. Rinehart, and J.M. Schmitz. *World Class*

Logistics: The Challenge of Managing Continuous Change, Council of Logistics Management, Oak Brook, IL, 1995.

7. Nelson, E. and E. Ramstad. "Hershey's Biggest Dud Has Turned Out to Be New Computer System," *Wall Street Journal*, October 29, 1999, pp. A1, A6.

8. Fawcett, S.E. and M.B. Cooper. "Logistics Performance and Measurement and Customer Success," *Industrial Marketing Management*, (27:7), 1998, pp. 341-357.

9. Siqueira, M. Conversation with author, Resende, May 6, 1999, Brazil.

10. Bleakley, F.R. "Strange Bedfellows," *Wall Street Journal*, January 13, 1995, pp. A1, A6.

11. Fawcett, 1998.

12. Row, A. Interview at Deere & Company, August 4, 1999, Moline, IL.

13. Murphree, J. "Building a Customer-Centered Supply Chain," *Purchasing Today* ®, (10:6), June 1999, pp. 34-43.

14. Robinson, D. "What Keeps Materials Managers Up Late at Night?", presented at the June 12, 1999 APICS – The Educational Society for Resource Management, Toronto, Canada.

CHAPTER 7

INFORMATION TECHNOLOGY IN PURCHASING

What is the role of information technology in purchasing?

Chapter Objectives

This chapter is designed to help the purchaser:

- Identify opportunities to use information technology to automate the purchasing process.
- Understand the role of various decision-support tools to improve purchasing decisionmaking.
- Identify opportunities to use the Internet as a communication and transaction tool.
- Recognize potential pitfalls associated with information technology (IT) initiatives.

The Technological Revolution

Technological advances are changing the world in which supply professionals operate. For example, technology has sped the transition to a global marketplace, facilitated time compression, increased competitive parity, made process redesign and integration possible, and enabled supply chain management. Nowhere is the affect of technology more potent and prevalent than in the area of information technology. Phil Condit, Chief Executive Officer at Boeing, has suggested that information technology is having as dramatic an impact on the today's economy as the industrial revolution had on the agrarian society.[1] He noted that one of the marvels of information technology as it is currently emerging is that it enables managers to be "in communication any where in the world that we want to be." Cellular phones, satellites, and the Internet are making globally seamless communication possible. This reality has implications across each organization and throughout the supply chain. Information technology's influence is particularly pervasive in purchasing and supply management. Today's purchasing information systems, provide numerous benefits to the purchaser, including

- **Alignment** – information can be shared in real time across the organization and supply chain despite geographic distance. It is thus easier to cultivate a shared vision and commitment to common goals.
- **Reduced uncertainty** – the ability to capture, store, analyze, and transmit data almost instantaneously greatly reduced the uncertainty that managers have to deal with.
- **Coordination** – information exchange allows organizations to coordinate value-added activities, making global time-based supply strategies possible. Information technology makes cross docking and continuous replenishment possible.
- **Substitute for inventory** – information is used as a substitute for inventory in today's purchasing and logistics systems.
- **Reduced cycle times** – the speed at which information can be shared has facilitated cycle-time reduction, enhancing the responsiveness of supply replenishment as well as delivery to the customer.
- **Greater productivity** – direct electronic information exchange and automation of day-to-day transaction management enables purchasers to dedicate their time to more productive and profitable responsibilities like the development of a world-class supply base.
- **Better decisionmaking** – getting accurate and relevant information to purchasing decisionmakers at the right time and in the right format allows them to make better decisions.

In purchasing, an ideal information system collects, stores, and manipulates information on suppliers, products, and internal needs and makes the information user-friendly and available to the right managers when it is needed. Such a system creates understanding and improves decisionmaking. To make this happen, purchasing must determine its information needs, such as what data is to be collected, how data must be analyzed, and the format in which to disseminate it. Purchasing must work closely with the information systems group to assure that these needs are met. An ideal information system also links purchasers throughout the organization while connecting purchasing to every other functional area within the organization and an ideal system enables accurate and timely communication with both customers and suppliers up and down the supply chain. Finally, an ideal information system supports decisionmaking in areas such as product design and specifications; supplier selection, evaluation, and management; inventory management; order creation and order tracking; transportation routing, tracking, and expediting; and receiving. A system such as this gives every manager within the organization and on the supply chain team access to relevant information to make the best decision possible.

No organization has achieved the ideal information system. Capturing and manipulating millions of data points, analyzing them, and disseminating information to everybody who needs it is a huge task. Despite the challenge, investment continues to be directed toward the goal of leading-edge information capabilities. To help in this effort, purchasers must be proactively involved in the information system design to ensure that the organization's IT strategy supports purchasing and materials initiatives. Without early and active involvement, it is not likely that purchasers will have the information they need to make good decisions. To have the greatest possible affect on system functionality, purchasers must learn to communicate effectively with the organization's information systems personnel. Every purchasing manager should become conversant with basic information technology/systems terminology. A glossary of information systems terminology has been appended to the end of this chapter to help purchasers gain this basic background. Purchasers should also be familiar with the hardware and software options on the market and understand their essential uses (see Table 7.1). An additional idea purchasing departments may want to consider is the designation of an information specialist from within purchasing. Such a specialist helps train other purchasing managers and interfaces closely with the information systems personnel. A purchaser who knows what can and cannot be done is an important asset in today's knowledge economy.

TABLE 7.1
Information Technology Basics

Common questions to ask in designing an effective information system:

- How many people will need access to the system?
- Where are they located?
- How will each individual connect into the system?
- What data input and output devises are really needed?
- How powerful does the system really need to be?
- How fast can the system process data?
- What is the total memory or storage requirement?
- How will people actually use the information technology?
- What applications will they run and what tasks will they use the system to perform?

Common Hardware:

Personal Computer (PC)	A stand-alone computer system that can be used separately or in a network with other computers. It consists of a CPU, an input device, and a display monitor.
Minicomputer	A midrange computer that functions as a server for multiple users. The DEC Vax and the IBM AS/400 are examples of minicomputers.
Mainframe	A very powerful computer that is used to run large scale applications and accommodate several hundred users on connected terminals.
Computer Workstations	The most common definition is a high performance microcomputer that is used for graphics, CAD/CAE, simulation or other intensive applications. A second definition is a personal computer in a networked system.
Client-server Configuration	A networked configuration in which a group of computers are physically connected to a file server. The network enables the sharing of software.

Common Software:

Systems Software	The systems software is the platform that enables other software to function. Examples include MS-DOS, OS/2, and MAC-OS.
Application Software	A program that processes data to produce information needed by users. Examples include word processing, databases, graphics, and spreadsheets.
Network Software	Software that supports networking capabilities for LANs and WANs.
Enterprise Software	An integrated information system that serves various organizational departments. Most ERP packages are modular and include modules for finance, accounting, manufacturing, logistics, human resources, warehousing, and purchasing.

Common Hardware/Software Uses:

Word Processing	The editing of text to create documents, reports, tables, forms, and graphics.
Desktop Publishing	Combines text and graphics to produce professional-quality publications
Spreadsheets	Enables the organization and analysis of numerical data.
Database Management	Enables the management and analysis of large quantities of data.
Forecasting/Modeling	Takes existing information and processes it to support decisionmaking.
Graphics	Enables the organization of information in visual form to enhance communication.
Electronic Mail	Allows the transmission of information over a network to one or more recipients.

Technology Applications in Purchasing

Numerous opportunities to use information technology that enhance purchasing performance exist. The first step in taking advantage of today's IT capabilities is to determine the role information technology should play in the management of purchasing's responsibilities. The most basic application of technology is to computerize forms and paperwork associated with managing a requisition and processing a purchase order. A decision to adopt this level of technology generally leads to the automation of fundamental purchasing transactions. Another use of technology is to capture and analyze information on the supply environment. A better understanding of both factors that influence performance and potential trends can help purchasers make better decisions. Two useful tools are purchasing databases and computer-based decision-support tools. Information technology can be used to enhance communication between the purchasing organization and its suppliers. As purchasers gain an understanding of the essential information technology applications, they are able to develop a purchasing IT strategy that will support superior purchasing performance.

The Computerized Purchasing Process

The most common application of computers in purchasing is to automate the purchasing process, which has greatly reduced the countless hours spent filling out requests for proposals, requests for quotes, purchase orders, and other documents associated with the purchasing process. The information contained on most paper purchase orders must eventually be transferred over to a computer system before the manufacturing or service delivery process can begin. This data entry process is a tedious task in which errors are often made. Illegible handwriting, poor transcriptions, and missed keystrokes all account for time spent trying to resolve problems tied to late, lost, or mistaken orders. By creating computer-based document templates, information for any order only needs to be entered a single time, eliminating significant duplication in the manual purchasing process. Many routine purchases can be handled entirely by the automated purchasing system. Such systems track inventory levels, place purchase orders, track delivery performance, issue status requests if necessary, and update the order file at each step of the purchasing process. The purchaser is involved on an exception-only basis. As routine orders are handled automatically, purchasing time is freed up to dedicate to strategic purchasing initiatives such as supplier selection, evaluation, and development. To achieve this level of automation, purchasing data bases must be built, technology-assisted materials management modules implemented, and end users and suppliers brought into the technology loop.

Purchasing databases – Automating the purchasing process begins with the creation of document templates and relies extensively on a purchasing database that captures and stores information used at various stages of the purchasing process. Standards that specify the format of computerized purchasing documents are often adopted. These standards make it easier for multiple customers and suppliers to communicate efficiently with each other. The actual database is an integrated collection of computer files that contains the basic information needed to make a decision or perform a specific transaction. The database organizes the data in ways that facilitate cross-referencing and allow easy access to authorized individuals.

Specific sets of information within the database are known as files. While purchasing must have access to the information contained in the database, the data stored in each file comes from different departments within the organization, including engineering, production, marketing, and forecasting. At least seven file types are common to most purchasing databases:[2]

- **Part file** – identifies each unique part or stock keeping unit (SKU) used by the organization. Part files typically specify the part name, number, and description and often provide information about the part's usage.
- **Engineering requirements file** – specifies the engineering and performance requirements of a part. Accurate, detailed part descriptions communicate needs and expectations to suppliers.
- **Supplier file** – contains the names and addresses of suppliers that an organization does business with. Preference status and historical performance is generally recorded in the supplier file.

- **Historical usage file** – tracks and stores the usage patterns for each part number by location so that order quantities and inventory levels can be more effectively managed. The historical data is a direct input into the creation of the organization's demand forecasting system.
- **Forecasted demand file** – uses historical demand information to estimate demand requirements for each part number found in the part file. Increasingly, organizations are providing suppliers direct access to the relevant information found in this file so that they can better anticipate and level their own internal operations. Accurate demand information is critical to efficient purchasing.
- **Bill of materials file** – breaks each part number down into its component elements, showing their relationship to each other and the final part. The bill of materials is a time-phased parts list that enables more accurate planning of purchasing and production activities. The bill of materials is one of the key inputs into a MRP/MRPII system and must be continuously updated to assure accuracy.
- **Open order file** – tracks the status of all orders that have been placed but not yet received. Orders not received by the stated due date are flagged as past due and purchasing is notified. A well-designed open order file is essential to successful management of the order fulfillment cycle.

Record keeping has always been an important purchasing responsibility. In an automated purchasing system, precise record keeping is even more important because routine purchases are processed automatically. Poor or inaccurate data can lead to excess inventory or stockouts. A tendency to give computer-generated data added credence makes accuracy even more important. (Managing by the numbers is dangerous when the numbers are wrong.) To be of value, each data file must contain accurate, up-to-date information. Because no single entity within the organization controls all of the data, maintaining data reliability can be difficult. At many organizations, specific departments or functions have independently developed their own information systems. The ability of these legacy systems to share data is often limited, and integrating each module into a single system is a serious challenge. Purchasers therefore need to work closely with the information systems group as well as the various departments responsible for providing data to help assure that the files not only contain the very best data available but also are able to exchange it as needed. Building good relationships also helps ensure user-friendly access to the information needed to make good purchasing decisions.

Materials management system modules – The purchasing transaction is particularly information dependent and is an ideal candidate for the application of information technology. The following two information cycles define most purchasing transactions. First, in the non-routine purchase scenario, recognition of a purchase need initiates the supplier selection process. This involves requests for quotes, comparison of alternatives, the identification of acceptable suppliers, and the issuance of a purchase order. The cycle is completed when materials are shipped and received or the service provided, the supplier's performance is measured, and the appropriate management reports are generated. The second cycle occurs when a blanket purchase order is used and the materials release process has been automated. When inventory drops below a certain level, a materials release is triggered. The supplier receives the release and then prepares and ships the order. Receiving, performance measurement, and management reporting completes the cycle. Each of these information exchanges is well suited for standardization and automation. Many organizations have developed computer-based modules to manage them. Some common purchasing and materials management modules are discussed below.

- **Inventory management** – this module tracks inventory levels for each item in the part file. When an item is received, the inventory status is adjusted upward. As parts are withdrawn from inventory for use, the recorded inventory status is updated. When the inventory level reaches the reorder point, an order is forwarded either to the purchaser for review or to another module in the automated purchasing system. Today's inventory management systems benefit from barcode and other input technologies that update the inventory status in real time. For example, the barcode scanner at the grocery store automatically adjusts inventory levels every time a product is sold. Inventory management modules help evaluate inventory performance on an item-by-item basis, helping managers make adjustments to reorder points and order quantities. Inventory turnover and flow through rates also guide SKU rationalization efforts.

- **Purchase order** – this module manages the issuance of purchase orders and tracks all outstanding orders. For blanket purchase orders, the module tracks total purchases and provides the purchaser feedback on actual versus planned purchases. Any serious deviation from plan results in a "red flag" being raised so that the purchaser can take appropriate action.

- **Materials release** – this module is typically driven by a signal from the inventory management module that indicates a need for an order to be placed. The materials release module verifies that an actual blanket order exists and then generates and forwards the materials release request to an approved supplier.

- **Supplier management** – this module monitors supplier performance. Some specific items that are frequently monitored include on-time delivery, percent defective, price variances, and over, short or damaged (OS&D). An important feature of this module is the ability to make the performance status of each open order visible. Is the order on track for on-time delivery? Is the order past due? If the order has arrived, is it acceptable or are there quality or other problems? Immediate notification of any potential problem gives the purchaser an opportunity to take action and minimize the negative consequences of the problem. Summary reports of supplier performance are made available on a periodic basis or as needed. These reports become a critical input to the supplier scorecard.

- **Receiving** – this module updates the appropriate database records once an order is received, processed, and transferred to the appropriate stocking location. The receiving module also transmits information to other modules including inventory management, supplier management, and payment.

- **Payment** – once an order is received and accepted, this module arranges for payment by sending the appropriate information to accounts payable so that a check can be prepared and sent. For amounts under a certain dollar value, the check-cutting process is often automated. More and more, organizations now use electronic funds transfer to reduce paperwork costs and increase payment responsiveness.

- **Management reporting** – this module generates the various reports needed to provide up-to-date visibility of the entire purchasing process. The number of reports generated as well as the timing of the report generation depends on the needs of the organization. Some common reports are supplier performance summaries, forecasted materials requirements, inventory status and performance, past-due orders, quality exception notices, and advance shipping notices. Purchasers need to clearly specify exactly what information is needed, how often the information needs to be updated, the correct reporting format, and whether or not the report should be printed or only available online.

Each materials systems module is activated when it receives information either from an input device such as a barcode scanner or computer keyboard or from another module in the computer-assisted purchasing system. For example, the materials release module is activated by communication from the inventory module. Individual modules receive information, access the appropriate data files, perform any needed analysis, and initiate the appropriate action needed to efficiently manage key transactions in the purchasing process. While each module increases the efficiency of a specific task, a well-integrated system enables the purchasing organization to become more productive and responsive.

Technology and Purchasing Decisionmaking

Beyond improving the efficiency of the standardized, structured tasks that comprise the purchasing transaction, today's information technologies are helping purchasing managers make better decisions in a more complex and dynamic supply environment. Technologies known as decision-support systems and resource-planning systems are now employed in almost all purchasing organizations to support a variety of decisions from budgeting to forecasting as well as from project management to product design. Decision-support systems are also being used to increase the effectiveness of purchasing training. These tools range from relatively simple spreadsheet-based applications to $100 million enterprise resource planning systems.

Data Warehousing and data mining – Greatly expanded computer storage capacities combined with faster search engines and data processing has led to the creation of vast data warehouses that managers "mine" for insight about business opportunities. Numerous examples exist.

- Wal-Mart uses a data warehouse to evaluate product placement and store layout. The key is to find out what items sell best in combinations and then to locate those items together to increase overall sales. Each store layout modification is monitored to identify its affect on the sell-through rate of individual items as well as overall store sales.[3]
- Staples has used store credit cards combined with data warehousing techniques to profile customers. Targeted advertisements and special promotions can then be directed to individual customers based on their personal purchase history.[4]
- A regional grocer examined the affect of its weekly advertising flyers and decided that they were encouraging "cherry picking" by bargain shoppers. By implementing a store credit card and data mining strategy, the grocer was able to replace its weekly promotions with personalized mailings to its best customers. Both sales and profits increased.[5]
- Some banks have even used data warehousing and mining approaches to determine the profitability of individual customers. High-maintenance, low-profit customers are assessed a fee for individual services that more highly profitable customers receive at no charge.[6]

Industrial applications also exist. Common manufacturing databases create SKU profiles that are kept on file. When a new product is designed, the database is searched to see if a similar product is used elsewhere in the organization. In one instance, a new product called for a special fastener. Rather than design the fastener from scratch, the database was searched and a similar, suitable item was found. In purchasing, the common parts database can be combined with a supplier performance database to help design the kind of hybrid organizational structure described in Chapter 2. Common purchase requirements can be aggregated and an overall purchase agreement established with the best available supplier worldwide. Items purchased by a single facility are managed by that facility. Without data warehousing and mining techniques, it is almost impossible to gain the visibility of purchase requirements needed to better manage a global supply base.

Decision-support tools – Spreadsheets are a basic decision-support tool that can be set up to analyze and compare alternative scenarios. Make-versus-buy and supplier selection decisions can be enhanced through the use of a well-designed spreadsheet. Once the decisionmaking procedure has been modeled via the spreadsheet, the purchasing manager can input data associated with a variety of alternative scenarios to see how the decision would change under different circumstances. Through this type of sensitivity analysis, a more robust decision can be made. More sophisticated decision-support tools are commercially available. For example, many project management packages exist that can be used to assess the impact of diverse resource allocations on the overall project completion time. Computer-support tools such as CAD/CAE (computer-aided design/computer-aided engineering) are also valuable in product design. The benefit of using CAD/CAE is that individual parts can be put together, doors can be opened and closed, and ergonomics analyzed virtually to see if everything works the way it should. These CAD/CAE systems also allow product designs to be exchanged between the purchaser and supplier electronically.

Expert systems are another decision-support tool that differs in basic approach from the tools discussed above. Decision-support applications rely on the knowledge and expertise of the purchaser to structure the analysis and to provide the basic data. The application processes the data and facilitates sensitivity analysis so that the decisionmaker is better informed. By contrast, expert systems do not follow a fixed algorithm, rather, they captures the knowledge and experience of the "expert." Expert systems model the process an expert would follow, incorporating alternative paths and short cuts depending on the specific situation being considered. Expert systems make the knowledge of the expert available to purchasers throughout the organization, enabling less-experienced purchasers to gain knowhow as they are "guided" by the expert, and create a reservoir of knowledge that can be used long after the expert is no longer with the organization.

Another benefit of expert systems is that they can be used as an excellent training tool. They make it possible to simulate a wide range of scenarios and provide immediate process and outcome feedback to the purchaser. Expert systems are also flexible and can be used anytime, anywhere as long as a personal computer is available. The negotiation support-system – a specific type of expert system – is particularly useful because it permits participants to test different negotiation tactics before the "real event." This practice can help the purchaser refine the overall negotiation strategy. Purchasing professionals must remember that decision-support systems are only tools that provide structure and insight, they are not a replacement for rigorous analysis and good managerial judgment.

Resource planning systems – A desire to manage materials requirements in an environment of constantly shifting priorities and unpredictable demand created a need for sophisticated inventory management throughout the production and purchasing processes. Materials Requirements Planning (MRP), a powerful computerized planning and control system, was developed to help meet this need. MRP recognized the distinction between dependent demand and independent demand. Independent-demand items include finished goods and spare parts, which are subject to market conditions. Dependent-demand items are goods and services that are used in the production and delivery of the independent-demand items. The logic of MRP is straight forward. If managers know the demand for the end item, the structure and acquisition leadtime of parts used to produce the end item, and the inventory status of these parts, then they can plan for the production or purchase of all dependent-demand items. Three information items are needed to use an MRP system: a master production schedule (demand for the end item); inventory status; and a bill of materials (product structure with leadtimes). It is vital that the inventory status and bill of material information sources provide as close to 100 percent accurate information as possible. The process of planning materials releases backward from end-item demand is often called "exploding" the master schedule. In essence, when forecast demand and orders exceed on-hand inventory, materials releases (purchase or shop orders) are triggered. The bill of materials determines the items released and the timing of their release. MRP is essentially an information system used to plan and control materials (see Figure 7.1). Second-generation materials requirements planning systems that verify available production capacity and provide a feedback loop to the master schedule are often called Manufacturing Resource Planning (MRPII) systems.

FIGURE 7.1
A Basic Materials Requirement Planning System

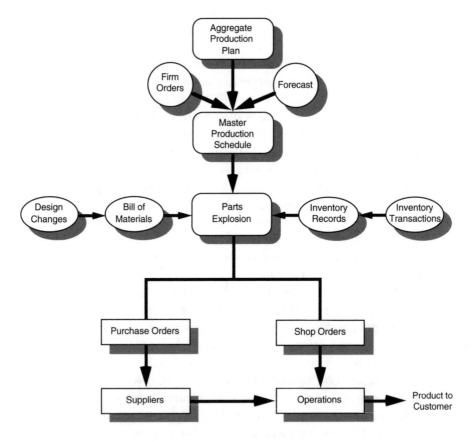

The basic MRP logic of time-phasing inventory replenishments has been extended to the distribution arena in the form of Distribution Requirements Planning (DRP). According to the Transportation-

Logistics Dictionary, DRP is "a system of determining demands for inventory at distribution centers, consolidating the demand information backwards, and acting as an input to the production and materials system." A DRP system translates the demand for each SKU at each distribution center into a time-phased replenishment plan. Another extension of resource planning has led to the notion of enterprise-wide information systems, which are used to manage all of the organizations resources, including inventory, capacity, capital, personnel, and facilities. These systems are commonly referred to as Enterprise Resource Planning (ERP) systems. The basic idea behind ERP systems is that all relevant information is communicated to and stored at a central database from which every member of the organization can access the information as needed to make good, coordinated decisions. Theoretically, if everyone is working with the same information, then it is possible to coordinate the entire organization's resources to add greater value and eliminate waste. Of course, to make this happen, all of the organization's information subsystems must be tied together into a single cohesive system. Bringing accounting systems, financial systems, human resource systems, logistics systems, manufacturing systems, purchasing systems, and sales and marketing systems together is a tremendously difficult proposition. Many organizations have invested hundreds of millions of dollars in ERP systems and several years in the implementation effort without attaining the sought after result of a fully integrated information system. The primary providers of ERP systems such as SAP and Bahn are developing Web-based versions of their ERP systems in an effort to streamline the implementation challenge.

Technology and Communication

Because the purchasing process requires an intensive exchange of detailed information, information technology has the potential to speed communication while reducing costs and eliminating human error in filling out and transmitting purchasing documents. The communication between the purchaser and supplier begins in the very early stages of supplier selection as the purchasing organization sends out a request for proposals that includes detailed product specifications. Potential suppliers then submit bids with the purchaser selecting a winning bid and transmitting a contract. During contract fulfillment, materials releases, advanced shipping notices, bills of lading, receiving documents, and invoices are among the documents that are exchanged. Efficiently and effectively managing all of this information is critical to the success of the purchasing process. To ease the information-exchange burden, organizations have implemented electronic data interchange (EDI) and Web-based purchasing systems. These computer-based communications systems can help organizations streamline the purchasing process and enable purchasing professionals to focus on high value-added initiatives.

Electronic data interchange – EDI is the inter-organizational, computer-to-computer exchange of common business documents and information. The adoption of EDI requires a great deal of cooperation between a purchasing organization and its suppliers. All parties to the EDI implementation need to adopt the same EDI protocol, standardize document formats, and invest in compatible systems software. The initial costs of developing a comprehensive EDI system can be substantial, especially for organizations with large supply bases. Further, many implementation efforts are complicated by the existence of competing EDI protocols. When major players in the same industry adopt different EDI standards, suppliers must adopt multiple standards in order to communicate with different customers. Rather than invest in multiple systems, many suppliers simply refuse to move into an EDI environment. Thus, many organizations continue to run parallel communication systems. The challenge of getting suppliers to implement a specific EDI standard has limited the adoption of EDI in many industries.

EDI standards establish the rules of EDI use. EDI standards determine which documents can be transferred electronically, the information that should be included in each document as well as its sequence and meaning. The American National Standards Institute (ANSI) has been particularly influential in promoting the standardization of EDI transactions and has produced a set of standards that are widely applicable to the various purchasing transactions. The ANSI X12 standard applies to purchase orders, invoices, shipping notices, freight bills, acknowledgements and other documents used in managing the purchasing transaction.

Once the standard has been established, translator software and a mail service are needed to get the system up and running. Good translation capability enables all organizations involved in the EDI linkage to speak the same language. The mail service is the vehicle by which information is transmitted. In relatively simple EDI relationships, exemplified by a single purchaser connected to a limited number of suppliers, a direct linkage is established (often via modem). For more complicated networks, a value-added network (VAN) is needed. A VAN is an electronic warehouse or "post office" that receives transmitted EDI documents and places them in a designated location that is unique to the recipient. When the purchasing organization transmits its purchase orders for the day, the VAN sorts them by supplier, placing each electronic document in the appropriate "mailbox." The EDI messages are held until a predetermined time (often at night) when they are either downloaded by the recipient or are transmitted to a virtual inbox. VANs are capable of receiving, sorting, and holding huge volumes of data. Because VANs are generally operated as third-party networks, a service fee is generally associated with their use. It has been estimated that third-party VANs cost approximately $150 per hour.[7] One manufacturer calculated its EDI cost at about eight cents per transmission or a little less than $80,000 per year.

EDI implementations are often difficult because they require cross-functional and inter-organizational coordination and support. To facilitate a successful EDI implementation, a structured approach similar to that shown in Figure 7.2 should be followed. A successful EDI program provides the following benefits:

- Creation of a near-paperless purchasing environment
- Reduction of the leadtime associated with the order cycle
- Increased order accuracy and the elimination of clerical errors
- Reduced safety stocks
- Diminished expediting (less need to use premium transportation)
- More rapid adoption of complimentary technologies such as bar coding and electronic funds transfer
- Better supplier relations

FIGURE 7.2
An EDI Implementation Model

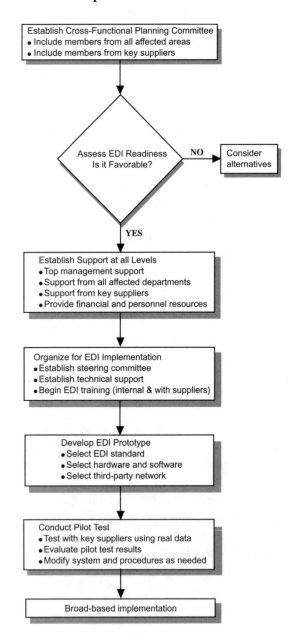

Web-based purchasing – The Internet has emerged as a valuable purchasing tool. The Internet is a system of connected computers that can be accessed from any linked computer around the world. Once connected to the Web, it is possible to use a search engine and a few key words to find vast amounts of information on almost any topic. If the information can be digitized, it can be transmitted over the Web. Pictures, text, graphics, and music are all available on the Web. Most of the information is located on home pages, which are designed by an organization or individual to contain information of interest. The National Association of Purchasing Management has created a home page at www.napm.org to provide information about NAPM's professional activities, the Certified Purchasing Manager (C.P.M.) program, the annual international conference, and general resources for purchasing professionals.

Most major organizations now maintain a home page. Basic home pages simply display information that is available to be browsed. Others are interactive, allowing users to perform a variety of tasks from downloading music to competing in an online auction. The most advanced home pages have been established by e-retailers. These pages act as online catalogues, enabling customers to order directly from their computers. Amazon.com set the standard for functionality, developing a Web site that allows users to shop with "point and click" ease. Once a customer inputs their address and other information into a secure database, the information is permanently stored so that future transactions are quick and easy. The database also creates a customer profile that tracks the likes and dislikes of individual customers based on past purchases. Lands' End has developed a Web site that enables the customer to enter measurements and create a custom computer mannequin that models different outfits in three dimensions. Further, customers can call in and talk to a "personal shopper" at Lands' End who can manipulate the contents of the screen that the customer is using. Also, two customers located in different locations, looking at different screens can "shop on line" together. Online auctions, virtual malls, and shipping "track and trace" capabilities are additional commercial uses of Web sites.

Inspired by the success of the e-retailers, many organizations have adopted Internet strategies to improve business-to-business (B2B) interactions. Valuable information and transaction activities are commonly available. Commercial Web sites that are designed for existing customers and suppliers are known as extranets. Access requires a password because relationship-specific information is accessible. For example, Office Depot has built Web pages for over 35,000 corporate customers. Each customized page is designed "with parameters that allow different employees various degrees of freedom to purchase supplies. Customers can also use the Internet to check up-to-the-minute inventory at the nearest store or warehouse to see what's available for delivery the next day."[8] Wal-Mart's "Retail Link" provides suppliers with access to three-year historic usage data and 18-month forecast on a product specific basis. Rockwell Collins has essentially posted its materials requirements plan on its extranet so that suppliers can make better decisions about their own production plans.[9] Other information that is often found on extranets includes product design information, materials specifications, training manuals, supplier scorecards, and virtually any other information that suppliers and/or customers might find useful. Similar to the extranet is the intranet, which is an in-house Web page that serves employees. While these pages may be linked to the public Web site, they require a password to be accessed. Any information that the organization wants to disseminate to employees worldwide can be posted on the organization's Intranet.

Another business-to-business application is the development of online catalogues. For instance, Intel has created a catalogue for its routinely purchased items. Internal users simply pull up the catalogue and with a simple click, place an order for the desired product or service. Use of the online catalogue provides two key benefits. First, because only approved suppliers are listed on the catalogue, greater purchasing control is established. Second, purchasing professionals can dedicate their time to more important activities than performing routine purchases. Purchasing's role is to identify good suppliers, build solid relationships, enter into volume contracts, and help design the catalogue. They are not involved in specific transactions, which are all handled automatically via the online catalogue. Both General Motors and Ford announced in November 1999 that they planned on taking the online catalogue a major step forward by creating a "virtual marketplace" where they would not only conduct business with their first-tier suppliers but where suppliers could do business with each other. GMs purchasing chief, Harold Kutner, noted that GM's site, called TradeXchange, would be operational by 2001 and that "we're going to expect all of General Motors' purchases to go through this site, and we would expect all of our suppliers to be as actively engaged." He forecasted that within a few years, TradeXchange could handle up to $500 billion in sales - a dollar value more than five times greater than GMs' annual purchases of about $87 billion.[10] It is interesting to note that by February 2000, GM, Ford, and DaimlerChrysler had announced that they would all work together to build a single automotive e-network.[11] "Web Exchanges" are also being developed in non-manufacturing industries. For example, Sears and Carrefour announced in February 2000 that they would jointly develop a retail network called GlobalNet Exchange, and that they would invite other retailers to participate.[12] The competitive promise of the Internet combined with the fact that "B2B" applications are in their infancy and enter uncharted territory means that organizations' Internet strategies are very fluid and likely to evolve dramatically over the next several years. Other current uses of the Internet by purchasing professionals include participation in online auctions, competitive bidding, and searches for unique products or suppliers.

The Internet will play a much larger role in the future business activities. E-commerce opportunities are in the early stage of development. Many organizations are experimenting with what are being called "click-and-mortar" strategies that combine an Internet interface with the customer and "back office" logistics required for rapid and reliable product or service delivery. Amazon.com added nine new warehouses in 1999 specifically to control the "customer satisfaction aspect of e-commerce." Other organizations like Office Depot and Toys R Us are encouraging Web customers to return unwanted items to the organizations' traditional "bricks and mortar" stores. While these commercial activities are being developed, the Web is finding a home as a substitute for EDI in several industries where the expense or the lack of a standard has limited EDI adoption. For example, in the electrical parts industry, EDI costs of $10,000 or more a month led the National Association of Electrical Distributors and the National Electrical Manufacturers Association to work together to develop IDxchange, a Web-based database and communication system. Using IDxchange, "a distributor can now send an order at 9:00 a.m. and have it received by 9:03 a.m. Then, the order can be packed, shipped, and delivered the same day.[13] Some managers believe that the Internet will replace EDI within five years; others believe that a more likely scenario will be the hybridization of the two systems.

Technology as an Enabler

The development and implementation of purchasing information systems can dramatically improve the efficiency and effectiveness of the purchasing process, making it possible for purchasing professionals to assume a more strategic role within the organization. However, exceptional purchasing information systems take time to design and can be difficult to implement. They also represent a costly investment. Without adequate planning and commitment, expensive information systems that fail to meet purchasing's needs can be implemented. Many organizations underestimate the cost of information system development and implementation. Many organizations implementing sophisticated information systems have exceeded the planned budget by more than 100 percent in terms of both time and money. Boeing's Phil Condit noted that companies have literally invested billions of dollars in the latest information technologies with no measurable productivity gains for many years. Until recently, both IT's proponents and its skeptics were asking the question, "Where did all that investment go?" He further suggested that managers are beginning to manage information technology better and the productivity gains "are now starting to come."[14] To more readily attain the benefits of systems investments, senior purchasing managers must support systems development efforts from the start. They must likewise recognize that short technology life cycles require on-going hardware and software upgrades. The decision to pursue a technology-enhanced purchasing strategy is a serious, long-term commitment that often involves significant capital investment, dedication and commitment throughout the design and implementation process, and specific, sustained training. Despite the challenges and costs of design and implementation, most purchasing professionals view advanced information technology systems as indispensable. To minimize technology disruptions and frustrations, purchasers should take a balanced approach that recognizes three realities regarding information technology:

- **Information technology is not a panacea** – too often, technology is identified as the cure to a problem that has not been fully understood or correctly diagnosed. Technology by itself is often the wrong prescription. Many organizations invest heavily in technology and simply end up automating existing processes. Such implementations fail to take advantage of information technology's greatest benefit – allowing managers to design better processes.
- **The "shiny hardware syndrome" must be avoided** – a frequent rationale for adopting a given information technology is the perception that other organizations are "doing it." Likewise, many organizations overspend in order to acquire the most advanced "shiny hardware" on the market, even when their needs are more modest. While benchmarking other implementation efforts can indeed be useful, the fact that a leading rival is implementing a given technology is seldom an adequate justification for adopting that technology.
- **Technology is an enabler** – the role of information technology is to enhance managerial decisionmaking, not replace it. When human and technology systems work well together, higher levels of performance are achieved. The director of supply chain management at a leading processed food manufacturer has consistently emphasized the linkage between people and technology, noting, "Technology is simply an enabler, people are either the bridge or the barrier to process integration."

Information technology will continue to alter purchasing practice. As e-commerce matures, it will help improve purchasing efficiency and lead to more streamlined purchasing processes. Purchasing professionals who undertake a balanced approach to information technology, recognizing its enabling role will make progress toward the development of the "ideal" information system discussed at the beginning of the chapter. These purchasers place substantial emphasis on IT training because they realize that the success of any IT strategy depends on the abilities and attitudes of the people who operationalize it on a day-to-day basis. Technology savvy purchasing professionals armed with well-designed communication and decision-support systems are fundamental to future purchasing success.

Key Points

1. The appropriate use of advanced information technology provides the following benefits to purchasing: better alignment, enhanced coordination, diminished uncertainty, reduced inventory levels, shorter cycle times, greater productivity, and more competitive decisionmaking.
2. Purchasers need to be conversant in basic hardware and software terminology because they not only need to use these technologies, but they also have to purchase them for use throughout the organization.
3. Technology has helped standardize and automate the purchasing process, allowing routine purchases to be handled automatically. Purchasers can use their time to develop greater strategic advantage.
4. Data warehousing and data mining technologies help purchasers gain a better understanding of the competitive supply environment. Purchasers can track and manage purchased goods and services as well as suppliers much more effectively when they use the knowledge gained via database analysis.
5. The Internet can reduce the costs of supply chain communication by speeding data transmission and providing much greater transaction visibility.
6. Great efforts need to be undertaken to establish appropriate technology policies, implement sound purchasing procedures, streamline the purchasing process, train people, and get them excited about technology applications. Technology can then enable greater purchasing efficiency and effectiveness.

Question For Review

1. Identify the primary areas where information technology has been used to change purchasing practice at your organization.

What successes have been enjoyed? What challenges have you encountered?

2. Describe your view of the ideal computerized purchasing information system. How does your organization's current system measure up to the ideal? What improvements need to be made?

3. What are the files contained in almost all computerized purchasing and materials systems? What are the basic materials modules used to create a computerized purchasing system?

4. Does computerization represent a threat or an opportunity for purchasing professionals? Why? What is the role of the purchaser in an automated purchasing environment?

5. In what ways does the use of computerized purchasing systems increase purchaser productivity and effectiveness? What are the long-term opportunities for computerization?

6. What are the primary caveats that you would explain to someone looking at information technology applications for purchasing and materials management?

Endnotes

1. CNN Moneyline, Interview with Phil Condit, December 13, 1999.

2. Monczka, R., R. Trent, and R. Handfield. *Purchasing and Supply Chain Management*, South-Western College Publishing, Cincinnati, OH, 1998.

3. Nelson, E. "Why Wal-Mart Sings, 'Yes, We Have Bananas!'" *Wall Street Journal,* October 6, 1998, pp. B1, B4.

4. Jacob, R. and B. Maddux. "How One Red Hot Retailer Wins Customer Loyalty," *Fortune*, July 10, 1995, pp. 72-79.

5. Coleman, C.Y. "Finally, Supermarkets Find Ways to Increase Their Profit Margins," *Wall Street Journal*, May 29, 1997, pp. A1, A6.

6. Brooks, R. "Alienating Customers Isn't Always a Bad Idea, Many Firms Discover," *Wall Street Journal*, January 7, 1999, pp. A1, A12.

7. Raedels, A. *C.P.M. Study Guide*, National Association of Purchasing Management, Tempe, AZ, 2000.

8. Rocks, D. "Why Office Depot Loves the Net," *Business Week*, September 27 1999, pp. EB 66-EB 68.
9. Robinson, D. "Supply Base Management," presented at the June 12, 1999 APICS –The Educational Society for Resource Management, Toronto, Canada.
10. White, G. "How GM, Ford Think Web Can Make Splash On the Factory Floor," *Wall Street Journal*, December 3, 1999, pp. A1, A8.
11. Simison, R.L., F. Warner, and G.L. White. "Big Three Car Makers Plan Net Exchange," *Wall Street Journal*, February 29, 2000, pp. A3, A6; Gomes, L. "Traditional Companies Grab a Piece of the 'B2B' Pie," *Wall Street Journal*, February 29, 2000, pp. B1, B4
12. Colemen, C.Y. "Sears, Carrefour Plan to Create Web Exchange," *Wall Street Journal*, February 29, 2000, p. A4.
13. Crockett, R. O. "A Neanderthal Industry Smartens Up," *Business Week*, September 27 1999, pp. EB 60-EB 64.
14. CNN Moneyline, 1999.

APPENDIX 7-A

GLOSSARY OF INFORMATION TECHNOLOGY TERMS

Advance Shipping Notice (ASN): A standardized EDI form detailing an inbound shipment to a receiving location.

Aggregator: A Web site that contains product catalogs from many suppliers in one place as a convenience to purchasing organizations.

American National Standards Institute (ANSI): Umbrella organization that issues national standards based on consensus by all stakeholder organizations.

ANSI X.12: A set of standards promulgated by the American National Standards Institute for use in formatting and handling purchasing-related documents transmitted by electronic data interchange (EDI).

Application Service Provider (ASP): An organization that provides software applications over the Internet.

Applications Package: A system of programs designed to assist in specific applications.

Artificial Intelligence: The ability of a computer to perform actions that would be perceived as intelligent if performed by human beings.

Bar Coding: Inventory control system that involves the use of machine-readable codes on packages and products for easy identification and computerized record keeping. In addition to materials inventories, bar coding can also be used for keeping records of tools, furniture, and equipment.

Batch Processing: The gathering together of transactions into batches before performing system updates. Such updates are usually performed at regular set days and times.

Bit: The smallest amount of data. One binary digit.

Byte: A group of eight bits. Also termed a character.

Central Processing Unit (CPU): This is the centerpiece of the computer system or, strictly speaking, the computer itself. It is composed of the control unit (which decodes program instructions and directs other components of the computer to perform the task specified in the program instructions), the arithmetic-logic unit (which does multiplication, division, subtraction and addition; and compares the relative magnitude of two pieces of data), and the primary storage unit (which stores program instructions currently being executed and stores data while they are being processed by the CPU).

Computer-Aided Purchasing: The use of computer technology in automating many purchasing activities.

Controller: A special computer used to ease the burden of a host CPU in communicating with several external peripheral devices.

Data: Data represents the basic facts and figures that constitute inputs to the computer.

Data Administrator: An individual responsible for the management of enterprise-wide databases.

217

Data Dictionary: A collection of definitions pertaining to a particular application or database. It is used to get detailed information about what goes into specific elements of a database or process.

Data Processing: The method of transforming data from an unorganized state to a form usable by end-users.

Database: A collection of data in an organized accessible form.

Database Management System (DBMS): A software system that creates, accesses, and controls a database. The interface between the programs and users needing to access the data.

Data Warehouse: A collection of data received from various transaction systems, which are accessible to many people at varying levels within an enterprise.

Decision-Support System (DSS): Models and applications that are designed to improve decisionmaking.

Dedicated Terminal: A computer terminal entirely dedicated to only one activity, such as EDI.

Demand Flow Technology: Linkages between buyers and sellers that enable efficient sharing of demand data for the purposes of reducing costs in the chain.

Digital Certificate: A security attachment to an electronic message to verify the identity of the sender and enables the receiver of the message to reply

Digital Signatures: Short units of data bearing mathematical relationships to the data in the document's content that are transmitted using public key cryptography programs. These programs create a pair of keys (one public key and one private key) and what the public key encrypts only the private key can decrypt. Alternatively what the private key encrypts only the public key can decrypt. This assures confidentiality of information and the digital signature allows the receiver to verify the sender of the data.

Digital System: A digital system is a computer system which uses the 0,1 binary digits to represent data.

Diskette: A small disk with a magnetizable surface upon which computer data can be stored.

Distributed Architecture: A system containing many components (computer systems, databases, workstations, etc.) in different locations that are interconnected.

Distributed Data Processing: A system in which data resources are accessible at many locations. The user has access to data regardless of his location. Data can be stored at several locations that are connected by a data communications network of terminals and computers that interface via phone or cable lines. If a centralized mainframe is used for this type of processing the organization usually will have a central data processing center where documents are sent for data entry then distributed to user sites.

E-Business: A means of doing business which uses electronic technologies, such as EDI, the Internet, and Web-based supply chain integration, to the benefit of an organization.

EDI: See: **Electronic Data Interchange**

EDIFACT: See **European Electronic Data Interchange for Administration, Commerce, and Trade**.

Electronic Agent: Defined by the UCITA as a "computer program or electronic or other automated means used to initiate an action or to respond to electronic messages or performances without intervention by an individual at the time of the action or response." These are often used to search the Internet for particular terms of information. See also: **Uniform Computer Information Transactions Act (UCITA)**

Electronic Bulletin Board: A Web-based bulletin board that brings people together in order to discuss topics of common interest.

Electronic Commerce (EC): Business activities of an enterprise that utilize the technology of the computer, including such tools as EDI, the Internet, Intranets, and/or Extranets to streamline and enhance commercial transactions of both private and public sector entities. See also: **Electronic Data Interchange, Internet, Intranet, Extranet**

Electronic Data Interchange (EDI): The computer-to-computer exchange of business information in a standard format. Transaction documents, such as purchase orders, invoices, and shipping notices, are transmitted electronically and entered directly into a supplier's (or purchaser's) computer or into a third-party network for processing.

Electronic Data Processing: The processing or manipulation of data by electronic means, such as word processing or transaction processing.

Electronic Funds Transfers (EFT): The electronic transmission of funds from one party (purchaser) to another (supplier).

Electronic Mail (E-mail): A system that allows the sending of letters, memos, and other documents between computer systems.

Electronic Requisitions: Purchase requisitions generated and transmitted by computer, replacing paper forms.

eMarketplace: New market models for conducting eCommerce, including aggregators, auctions, bid systems, and exchanges. Also called Net Markets. (Source: Forrester Research, Inc.)

Encryption: A process of transforming data such that it cannot be deciphered during transmission without specific translation software. This is a method of securing transmitted information.

End User: Any person who uses information technology in his or her job.

Enterprise: An entire business organization, from front line employees to top management, and all functions in between.

Enterprise Resource Planning (ERP): This usually refers to a particular type of computer software package that integrates various functions within an organization. It may be used for activities such as forecasting, materials management, or purchasing.

European Electronic Data Interchange for Administration, Commerce and Trade (EDIFACT): The most commonly used standard for electronic purchasing forms used in international commerce.

Executive Support System (ESS): A decision- support system tailored specifically for executive level managers. This may also be referred to as an Executive Information System (EIS).

Expert System: A computer system that provides an employee with a knowledge base of industry experts in any given field at their finger-tips. It may contain program goals, a consensus of facts by experts, rules of thumb used by experts to help them arrive at decisions, etc. This is interactive in the sense that the program asks the decisionmak-er questions regarding a situation and makes recommendations using the available expert information.

Extranet: An organization's Web site that provides a limited amount of accessibility to persons outside the organization. Often used to link with actual and potential suppliers.

File: A file is a set of related records. For example, a supplier file would contain records with information on each supplier.

Firewall: Protective software used to prevent unauthorized access to confidential records.

Forecasting/modeling: Data and infor-mation are secured from previous-ly acquired data processing opera-tions and manipulated by applica-tion software for output into reports or displays. Such output is used as a decision- support tool for management.

Functional Acknowledgement: A stan-dardized EDI form that indicates the receipt of a shipment. It is automatically generated and sent back to the shipping organization.

Hub: An organization that encourages and sponsors its paper-based busi-ness partners to utilize electronic commerce for trade.

Input Device: Devices including key-

boards, touch screens, scanners, voice recognition instruments, and readers of magnetically coded tape or disk drives which are used to feed information into a CPU. Some of these devices also operate as output devices.

Information Technology (IT): A set of electronic tools used by world class purchasers to generate, process, transfer, interpret, and uti-lize information. These tools include state-of-the-art hardware, software, databases, and networks.

Internet: Electronic network that links businesses and individuals all over the world.

Intranet: A secure part of the Internet, used by organizations for internal communications between their dif-ferent units around the country or the world.

Local Area Networks (LAN): An inter-connection of a group of personal computers and terminals within a defined area or location such as a department or office. The server permits a sharing of software and information between multiple users. This system's architecture is referred to as "client server" sys-tem. See also: **Wide Area Network (WAN)**

Mainframe: A very large computer that may accommodate several hundred users on connected terminals at any given time. The mainframe was for years the computer of choice for day-to-day transaction processing as well as large batch updating.

Management Information System (MIS): A system providing infor-mation processing and manipula-tion to support management in daily operations and reporting activities.

Microchip: A small hardware component that is affixed to a CPU. This is the component that carries bits of information.

Minicomputer: A computer that is larger in size than a PC, but not as large as a mainframe computer. The DEC VAX and the IBM AS/400 are both examples of minicomputers. They may take up the better part of a small room. This functions as a multi-user system for several hundred users.

Modems (modulators/demodulators): Devices used for converting data into formats for transmission over telephone and cable lines and then converting them back again for computer use. Modem capabilities are expressed in "baud" rates which means bytes per second (bps) or the speed at which data can be transmitted.

Modules: A standalone portion of an enterprise system that performs specific functions such as payroll, e-mail, or warehouse management. These modules can be linked together with an integrated system like an ERP.

Mouse: An input device attached to a CPU that can be used alone or in conjunction with a keyboard.

Multi-Tier Transaction Processing: Some systems allow transaction processing within more than one tier of an organization or supply chain.

Network: A group of physically connected computers (or workstations) that are attached to a file server. It allows users to share software and some hardware thus reducing costs while providing the user more applications.

Online Bidding: A process where organizations invite or require suppliers to submit their Bids over the Internet.

Open Buying on the Internet (OBI): Standard for business-to-business electronic commerce in which Web catalogs of suppliers are able to interact with the buying systems of their customers.

Open System: A system that allows the running of applications on more than one type of hardware or software, without changing the usability or appearance of the application.

Online Analytical Processing (OLAP): The performing of analysis interactively. OLAP allows users to gather data from various sources and to analyze it in many different ways in order to help in the decision-making process.

Output Devices: Devices that convey useful information to the computer user such as magnetic tapes and discs, printers, laser imaging devices, computer output microfiche (COM) cards, voice output devices, and terminals. Some of these devices will also operate as input devices.

PC (Personal Computer): A standalone computer system that can be used separately or in a network with other computers. It consists of a CPU, an input device (typically a keyboard and/or mouse), and a display monitor.

Paperless Office: A vision by some of an office environment virtually devoid of hardcopies – the trend toward EDI, computer databases and blanket purchase orders – this encourages such a vision of the future.

Part File Database: An electronic collection of basic information about parts including part numbers, costs, prices, etc.

Payment Authorization: A standard electronic authorization which is transmitted to an organization's Accounts Payable department.

Purchasing Information System (PIS): A computer system used to assist in the purchasing functions of an organization. The advantages of such a system may be improved productivity, improved accuracy of information, ability to easily handle complex scenarios, etc.

Real-Time Online Processing: This system handles transactions at the time they occur and provides output directly to users. It avoids delay and provides users complete and up to date information.

Record: Means of information storage. Their purposes are to provide: actionable information to enable better decisions; a knowledge base for sharing and transferring information; and complete documentation for legal and audit purposes. Purchasing is responsible for maintaining records for bills of sale, titles, warranties, and other purchase-related documents.

Scanning: Machine-reading of bar codes upon receipt of goods and withdrawal from inventory enables an organization to keep perpetual (real time) inventory records.

Shipping Notice: A notice created by a selling organization indicating the release of a shipment of goods to a purchasing organization. This is then transmitted electronically.

Smart Card: A plastic card resembling a credit card that includes an embedded chip that stores information in encrypted form.

Spreadsheet: Usually computerized today, a spreadsheet contains any number of cells of information that can be manipulated and calculations can be performed automatically by the computer program in which it resides.

Standard: An agreement on definite characteristics of quality, design, performance, quantity, or service. In the Internet world, a standard usually applies to an industry-wide agreement of code or hardware linkages such as a hypertext markup language (HTML) or ANSI-X12. See also: **American National Standards Institute (ANSI), Open Buying on the Internet (OBI)**

Status Request: A standardized EDI form generated by a purchaser requesting information on the status of a given order. The supplier's system should automatically reply with the requested information.

Storage: Media used for both the long- and short-term storage of data including mass storage devices, tape, and discs.

Third Party Network: In EDI operations, a third-party network organization functions as a central communications clearinghouse. It accepts the purchaser's purchase orders, separates them by supplier, and at the appropriate time, transmits them to the suppliers. In addition, the organization can provide format translation and other value-added functions.

Transactional System: A system that performs specific day-to-day business tasks such as generation of purchase orders or receipt of payments.

Transportation Data Coordinating Committee (TDCC): A committee developed by the transportation industry charged with the task of developing industry EDI standards.

Uniform Computer Information Transactions Act (UCITA): Act approved in July 1999 by the National Conference of Commissioners on Uniform State Laws (NCCUSL) and expected to be enacted by several states to govern electronic commerce transactions. Formerly known as Uniform Commercial Code (UCC) Article 2B, UCITA would apply to computer software, multimedia products, computer data and databases, online information, and other such products.

Uniform Electronic Transactions Act (UETA): List of guidelines adopted in a number of states that requires commercial or government contract agreement on automated transactions, electronic signatures, electronic agents, electronic records, and security. UETA was adopted in 1999 by the National Conference of Commissioners on Uniform State Laws (NCCUSL). See also: **Uniform Computer Information Transactions Act (UCITA)**

Value-added Network: A central communications clearinghouse that receives purchasing forms from organizations and then distributes them to receiving organizations in a timely manner and in the appropriate format. They may provide other similar services as well. Also known as a third-party network.

Vertical Market Community: A group of individual professionals and companies in the same vertical market that trade information,

advice, goods, and services online.

Virtual Private Network (VPN): Technology that uses encryption to allow secure transmission of private network information over the Internet.

Wide Area Network (WAN): An interconnection of personal computers and/or LANs across a business unit, division, or organization on a worldwide basis. The communication interface is accomplished via use of fiber optic cables, telephone lines, or satellites. Some people refer to these as intranets.

Word Processing: The creation, modification and editing of text material in various formats exemplifies the use of word processing by computers.

Workstation: A workstation is a PC-based setup that integrates personal processing applications with a network of PC's or with a mainframe computer. A workstation allows a user access to very large mainframe databases otherwise inaccessible.

World Wide Web (WWW): Electronic network that links businesses and individuals all over the world. Also referred to as Internet.

XML (Extensible Markup Language): A set of guidelines for designing text formats that allow flexibility in the creation of information formats for the Internet. The markup symbols (or tags) used in XML are unlimited and self-defining. XML was developed by the World Wide Web Consortium (W3C).

CHAPTER 8

THE ART AND SCIENCE OF NEGOTIATION

What does it take to be a great negotiator?

Chapter Objectives

This chapter is designed to help the purchaser:

- Identify when negotiation is the appropriate method for acquiring a good or service.
- Understand the importance of planning, and recognize the 10 steps in the planning process.
- Be able to develop an appropriate negotiation strategy and employ sound negotiation tactics.
- Recognize the need to develop key negotiation skills through training and practice.

Modern Negotiation

Today's supply environment places a premium on excellent supply relationships. Whether the organization is establishing a just-in-time replenishment program or building a world-class global supply base, success depends on the quality of the supply relationships that are put in place. Negotiation has always been an important part of purchasing and a valued skill for a purchasing professional to develop. Since the mid-1980s the role of negotiation has changed. The traditional role of negotiation was to determine the specifics of an important contractual relationship. Price, quality, delivery, and compliance were the critical issues. Today, one of the most important issues driving negotiations is the desire to build stronger, more competitive partnership relations. Determining the nature of the contractual relationship is still important, but achieving high levels of trust and synergy are often the primary objectives of modern negotiation.

What is Negotiation?

Negotiation is the formal communication process where two or more individuals meet face-to-face (or increasingly via electronic means) to discuss issues and come to a mutually satisfactory agreement. Negotiations take place in many aspects of our daily lives. Families negotiate issues such as whether to eat out or cook at home, where to go on vacation, and how to allocate responsibility for household chores. Work colleagues negotiate such issues as team roles and responsibilities, day-to-day work assignments, or who will drive to lunch. Everyone who has ever been in the job market has negotiated starting salary, vacation time, and perhaps even career paths. While these situations generally lack the preparation and organization found in negotiating most supply relationships, they do involve the basics of the negotiation process. In each case, individuals involved in the negotiation have specific goals they are pursuing. They communicate desires, listen to counterproposals, participate in a give-and-take concession process, and ideally arrive at a conclusion both sides find acceptable. Purchaser/supplier negotiations include all of these elements, but the process is more structured and formal.

From a purchasing viewpoint, negotiation is the process where "purchasers and suppliers attempt to arrive at an agreement about technical and quality specifications, price, delivery, service, and other issues essential to conducting business in a profitable manner."[1] While price, quality, and service are the topics most frequently discussed in negotiations, any issue that affects the performance of the purchase agreement and relationship can be negotiated. Some additional topics, which demonstrate the range and diversity of issues that should be discussed, are listed below:

- Confidentiality, especially with respect to cost structure and proprietary information
- Continuous improvement expectations in quality, cost, and other relevant areas
- Contract duration and volumes
- Delivery schedules
- Joint research and development

- Nonperformance definitions and penalties/legal recourse for non-compliance
- Ownership and use of intellectual property that is jointly developed
- Provisions for terminating the relationship
- Shared resources including capital, personnel, and technology
- Technical assistance and support

Successful negotiations require the careful management of information, personal relationships, time, and power as the two sides of the negotiation work out a mutually beneficial arrangement. In most negotiations, neither side obtains all of its desired objectives. Instead, considerable give and take occurs as the two sides define the relationship and establish performance expectations. It is important to recognize that mutual benefit does not necessarily imply equality of benefits. Seldom do both sides of a negotiation come to the table with equal power and influence. The key for negotiation success is for both parties to improve their position, and hopefully their competitiveness, through the negotiation process. When this is not possible because of philosophical differences or simple operational logistics, then both sides are probably better off walking away from the process than accepting an agreement that is detrimental to either side's competitiveness. While there are some managers who believe that failing to reach an agreement represents a negotiation failure, no agreement is better than a bad agreement.

When is Negotiation Appropriate?
Negotiation is a time and resource intensive activity. The time and expense incurred in traveling to and from the negotiation site and in the negotiation itself can be substantial. However, this expense represents only a small fraction of the total cost of negotiation. Preparation can represent up to 90 percent of a successful negotiation.[2] Negotiation is often the most sophisticated and expensive approach to meeting a purchase requirement and should only be used when off-the-shelf purchasing and competitive bidding are inappropriate or insufficient. For routine purchases or small-dollar buys, the expense of negotiation is prohibitive. Negotiation is used primarily for large, specialized, or technologically complex purchases where the value of the purchase or the risk of the purchasing scenario justifies the cost of the negotiation process. Because relationship building is an uncertain

process requiring extensive give and take, negotiation is also the preferred approach when an alliance relationship is desired.

It is not uncommon for competitive bidding and negotiation to be used in a sequential supplier selection and development effort. Competitive bidding is used to identify the best candidate for sourcing a product or service. Negotiation is then employed to create a foundation for a relationship that will yield significant value above and beyond the simple purchase of a product and establish the parameters of the contract. Through the competitive bid process, the forces of competition are brought to bear to determine an appropriate price point as well as to identify attractive proposal elements. In most cases, the bid proposal becomes a key input into the negotiation planning and a central discussion item in the actual negotiation. Negotiation provides an opportunity to probe for unique value-added opportunities that might involve specialized capital investment, shared resources, or the shifting of specific roles and responsibilities. For example, a large candy manufacturer provides capital to build dedicated warehouses that are then operated by third-party distributors. Negotiation is used to establish performance expectations as well as other aspects of the long-term relationship. An element of brainstorming often accompanies such negotiations. Mutual benefits often arise from shared learning that begins in the negotiation process. When appropriately pursued and executed, negotiation can lead to outstanding value creation. In these cases, the expense of negotiation should be viewed as an investment in future competitiveness. As organizations pursue tighter supply chain relationships, negotiation will become a more frequent and vital purchasing practice. The following are conditions that favor the use of negotiation.

- **The value of the contract is substantial** – Large dollar values often justify the cost of negotiation.
- **There is a lack of supplier competition** – Without multiple interested and capable suppliers competing for the purchaser's business, negotiation becomes the best route to obtaining a satisfactory outcome - competitive price with high quality and service.
- **The existence of special price, quality, and/or service needs** – When special needs exist, the purchaser must make sure that they are clearly communicated and understood. Negotiation provides an added opportunity to ensure that the supplier is capable of meeting the special requirements.

- **The contract is for specialized production/service capabilities** – When the purchasing organization is really interested in customized capabilities, it is important for the purchaser and supplier to spend time working out the details, especially when investments in specialized capital equipment are needed. Some questions to ask include, "Is the purchaser willing to share development costs?"; "Are both sides willing to share the needed information and resources?"; "Who assumes the risk if the effort does not work?"
- **The contract is for technically complex products** – Sometimes, the technical requirements of a product are sufficiently complex that negotiation is required to define both process and performance specifications. This is particularly true when the design is either brand new or under development.
- **A high degree of uncertainty exists** – When a purchaser deals with a new supplier, a degree of uncertainty regarding managerial philosophy or supplier capability might exist. This is particularly true when the supplier operates in an industry or country with which the purchaser is unfamiliar.
- **The contract is non-standard** – When the purchaser requires unique services or a high degree of flexibility that is not standard, a customized contract must be negotiated. All of the details should be spelled out and reviewed by both parties' legal counsel.
- **The supply relationship is a partner-style arrangement** – A desire to establish synergistic partnerships with the best suppliers begins with the negotiation of an up-front contract that denotes specific roles and responsibilities. The negotiation must clearly define performance criteria, expectations, and measurement issues. Non-performance issues as well as exit contingencies should be agreed on.

Negotiation Philosophies

For many years, purchasers pursued an adversarial or competitive negotiation philosophy. The best negotiator was the one who could extract the lowest price and as many concessions as possible from the supplier. This adversarial approach is known as the win-lose philosophy. When the win-lose approach is followed, negotiations become competitions in which a clear winner and a clear loser emerge. Purchasers who pursue the win-lose approach view the purchaser/supplier relationship as a zero-sum game. A fixed amount of value exists in the relationship, and the goal is to capture as much of the value as possible. Win-lose negotiating pits the purchaser and the supplier against each other, both sides pursue a hard line with fixed negotiating positions and a determined resistance to compromise. Leverage determines who wins and loses.

A deficiency associated with the win-lose philosophy is that the loser (usually the supplier) leaves the negotiating table not only beaten but also lacking any real commitment to the purchaser's success. In fact, suppliers have been known to retaliate by sharing their best technologies or allocating scarce capacity to less hostile purchasers. Suppliers can also tend to have long memories. For example, in the early 1990s, General Motors developed a reputation as a tough negotiator and a brutal customer. Jose Ignacio Lopez de Arriortua, General Motor's purchasing czar, broke the tradition of renewing one-year contracts with established supply partners. Lopez opened these contracts to competition, fiercely pitting suppliers against one another in an effort to obtain the lowest possible price. While suppliers who had made extensive investments to develop new products for GM were irate, the strategy appeared to work. In two short years, General Motors reduced its annual materials costs by $4 billion.[3] However, over time, General Motors has discovered that this approach has reduced suppliers' commitment to GM. By the late 1990s, many auto suppliers reserved their best ideas and highest level of support for more loyal customers. Others removed GM entirely from their preferred customer list. Based on this long-term perspective, there are no winners in win-lose negotiations.

Today, most purchasers recognize that win-lose negotiation and adversarial purchaser/supplier relations may result in immediate cost reductions, but they seldom help the organization beat growing, and often fierce, global competition over the long haul. Suppliers that are constantly on the defensive are generally reluctant to enter into truly creative, long-term relationships. As a result, cooperative, win-win negotiating philosophies have become more popular. The fundamental tenet of win-win negotiating is that by working closely together, both the purchaser and supplier can improve their competitiveness and profitability. Cooperation creates value while competition dissipates resources. Cooperation allows both sides to bring more energy and creativity to the table. Openly shared information, brainstorming, and resources lead to the discovery of many "hidden" options. Author Steven Covey discusses the win-win philosophy: "It is a belief in the

"Third Alternative". It's not your way or my way; it's a better way, a higher way."[4] Win-win negotiators believe that it is possible to grow or expand the pie. With a larger pie, both sides can have a bigger piece. Several conditions must be present for win-win negotiation to be successful.

- **Both sides must adopt a win-win mentality** – When one side behaves opportunistically, long-term dissatisfaction with the relationship occurs. Because negotiation strategies are seldom disclosed verbally, negotiators must carefully evaluate the behavioral signals sent by the other side.
- **Both sides must have a vested interest in a successful outcome** – Typically, this occurs when the product or service is strategically important to the purchaser, the value of the contract represents a significant portion of the supplier's business, or unique value can be created through cooperation.
- **Both sides must have a the negotiation as part of a larger or longer-term relationship** – If one or both sides of the negotiation view the negotiation as a one-time event, there is no reason not to approach the negotiation from a win-lose approach.
- **Both sides must recognize and understand the other's needs and wants throughout the negotiation process** – The ultimate measure of success is the perception that the process has been fair and everyone's objectives have been met.
- **Both sides must work jointly to create value not available through other forms of negotiation** – They share information during the negotiation and resources to build the relationship. When difficulties arise, cooperative efforts are undertaken to find an accommodating and creative solution.
- **Both sides must approach the negotiation with an attitude of trust** – For negotiations between existing business partners, trust is built on previous experience. For new relationships, trust is based on reputation, declared intentions, and behavioral clues.

To summarize, two negotiation philosophies dominate purchasing practice, cooperative and competitive. From the purchaser's perspective, neither philosophy is appropriate 100 percent of the time. When the purchasing organization's competitiveness depends on obtaining a disproportionately large piece of a truly fixed pie or when the purchase involves a one-time transaction, a win-lose approach might be in the interest of the purchasing organization. However, even when the decision is made to pursue a win-lose approach, the purchaser should still treat the supplier fairly. While the current situation might not call for a cooperative agreement, future circumstances might require a stronger, cooperative relationship between the purchaser and supplier. Purchasers have alienated suppliers that they later needed because of changes in technology or market structures.

Preparing for a Successful Negotiation

Negotiation success is built on the foundation of preparation. Most negotiation experts concur that preparation is the single most critical step in the negotiation process. Negotiators that most thoroughly do their homework by determining objectives, collecting information, analyzing strengths and weaknesses, or anticipating the other side's objections almost always achieve superior outcomes. Having a well thought-out plan allows successful negotiators to argue positions persuasively, respond to the tough questions, recognize the tactics employed by the other side, and know when to conclude a good agreement or walk away from a bad one.

Unfortunately, many negotiators make too many assumptions and fail to adequately prepare for the actual negotiation. These purchasers believe that bravado, cleverness, and/or eloquence can effectively substitute for the "dirty work" of analysis and preparation. However, this is simply one of several mistakes that negotiators commit in the negotiation process. In their book on negotiation, Lewicki and Litterer[5] identify several "failings" common to negotiation preparation.

- **Failure to plan** – Negotiators fail to invest sufficient time in the planning process. Planning takes time, especially for complex negotiations, and the time must be committed well before the actual negotiation. It is impossible to effectively "cram" for an important negotiation.
- **Failure to establish objectives** – Negotiators fail to establish clear objectives. Without clear objectives, negotiators really do not know what they are trying to achieve, what their position on specific issues should be, or when a good arrangement has been reached.
- **Failure to consider needs** – Negotiators fail to consider their counterpart's needs. Regardless of negotiation philosophy, a

good negotiator should understand what the other side hopes to achieve via negotiation. By knowing what issues are of greatest importance to the supplier, a purchaser can determine what concessions need to be made on both sides to achieve a satisfactory agreement.

- **Failure to formulate arguments** – Negotiators fail to formulate sound and convincing arguments for their positions. It is vital that negotiators understand the strengths and weaknesses of not only their position but also the position of their counterpart. Only then can negotiators understand the source of their negotiating power and anticipate the ebb and flow of the actual negotiation.

Effective negotiators avoid these mistakes. They develop detailed plans, analyze the strengths and weaknesses of their position, and know where and when concessions are acceptable. They have done their homework to find out who their counterparts are and what their negotiation philosophy is likely to be as well as what tactics they are likely to employ. And they are lucky, but they define luck as the meeting point of preparation and opportunity. Great negotiators are not born; they are great because they prepare meticulously and they develop the skills needed to achieve superior outcomes. Successful purchasers use a systematic approach that consists of the following negotiation planning steps:[6]

- Develop specific objectives
- Establish an effective negotiating team
- Gather relevant information
- Analyze the strengths and weaknesses of the supplier's position
- Analyze the strengths and weaknesses of their own position
- Recognize the supplier's needs
- Determine the facts of the situation
- Determine the issues to be discussed
- Establish the purchasing organization's position on each issue
- Plan the negotiation strategy
- Select appropriate tactics
- Practice the negotiation

Develop Specific Objectives

The first step in the planning process is to establish objectives for the negotiation. Objectives specify what the purchasing organization desires to achieve during the actual negotiation process. Is the goal a lower price, shared resources, more frequent deliveries, greater after-sales support, or, as is the case in most negotiations, some combination of these issues? The more specific the objectives, the more focused and better prepared the organization will be when the negotiation begins. It is important to note that the establishment of objectives begins long before most purchasers seriously begin to think about the actual negotiation. Purchasing professionals should initially consider key objectives as the request for proposal is put together. The RFP determines the nature and content of the proposals received from potential suppliers and sets the general parameters for the negotiation. Therefore, purchasers should develop the RFP with the negotiation process already in mind. Close scrutiny of the winning proposal can help frame and prioritize the negotiation objectives. Some issues previously thought to be important may be resolved in the proposal. Also, issues not previously considered may be raised by the proposal.

One objective of any negotiation should be to reach a satisfactory agreement. Negotiations are too expensive to undertake without a commitment to find a common ground that meets both sides basic wants and needs. Of course, from time to time, proposals are misinterpreted and the distance between a purchaser and supplier are greater than initially believed. When this occurs, a satisfactory outcome might not be obtainable and it would be preferable to look for a new supplier than to enter into a bad agreement. Five additional and fundamental objectives common to most purchaser/supplier negotiations are briefly discussed below.

1. To obtain a fair and reasonable price for the desired quality and service. Cost control is always a priority. However, purchasers recognize that cost is only one criterion that must be met. The notion of fair and reasonable should be considered from both the purchaser and supplier points of view.
2. To assure on-time delivery and reduce order cycle times. Historically, the most frequent supplier failure has been the inability to meet delivery schedules. Time-based expectations should be clearly stated, with measures and penalties agreed upon.
3. To exert some control over the manner in which the contract is performed. All performance issues should be discussed early in

the negotiation. Expectations should be clearly discussed, cancellation clauses spelled out, improvement clauses detailed, and renewal conditions carefully worded.

4. To persuade the supplier to give maximum cooperation to the purchasing organization. Ideally, the purchasing organization would like the negotiation process to foster relationships that achieve higher levels of support than are provided to competitors.

5. To develop sound and continuing relationships with world-class suppliers. Many organizations seek to become preferred customers to the best suppliers in their industries. The way in which negotiations are conducted influences the suppliers' desires to help the purchaser achieve greater success.

Establish an Effective Negotiating Team

Negotiation success hinges on the individual or team that is selected to conduct the negotiation. A single negotiator who has developed a personal relationship with the supplier's representative can often handle straightforward or routine negotiations, especially with partner suppliers. For more complex negotiations, it is often better to establish a dedicated negotiation team. Complexity can come from two sources: the type of product or service being purchased and the nature of the purchaser/supplier relationship that is being developed. The greater the complexity, the less likely it is for a single negotiator to possess all of the knowledge, experience, and skill necessary to conduct the negotiation. Bringing the right technical expertise to the team is also vital. Including experienced negotiators to either lead the negotiation or coach the lead negotiator is also a good idea. Finally, each department affected by the negotiation outcome should be represented on the team.

Once team composition has been determined, a team leader who will direct the negotiation should be selected. Team leaders are chosen based on their product/process knowledge, negotiating skill, or personal relationship with the supplier. The ideal team leader qualifies in all three areas. Each team member should be able to support the team leader and be willing to sacrifice personal opinions and goals to help achieve the specific objectives of the negotiation. Further, negotiating teams should get along well and be able to resolve disagreements quickly and in private. Demonstrating a lack of unity in the presence of suppliers is usually detrimental and should be avoided. To assure proper team chemistry, the team members should be brought together early in the planning process to give them time to bond as well as to provide an opportunity to contribute throughout the planning process. Team members must also understand and agree to their specific roles and responsibilities both during the preparation period and the actual negotiation. Well-designed and rigorously prepared teams give the organization the best opportunity for negotiation success.

Gather Relevant Information

A simple fact of negotiation is that the side with the best data is the one in the strongest position. The supplier often begins the purchaser/supplier interaction with the advantage because of its intimate knowledge of production costs, quality levels, and other performance issues. The reality that the supplier typically has an information advantage regarding costs and other issues places a special research burden on the purchaser. A major reason organizations perform serious preparatory research is to work up a detailed price analysis that breaks the product's cost down into specific elements (see Tables 8.1 and 8.2); however, good research helps the negotiating team answer several other key questions including,

- What are the supplier's actual production costs? What should they be?
- What are the pricing trends in the industry? For this supplier?
- What is the quality history for this supplier?
- How has the supplier performed in other vital areas such as delivery or cycle time?
- Does the supplier have adequate capacity to meet our current needs or future needs?
- What are the strengths and weaknesses of each party?
- What issues are important to the supplier in the negotiation?
- Who will negotiate on the supplier's side? What are their personalities and negotiating styles?
- What is the supplier's financial position?
- If the two organizations have a business track record, what has happened between them?
- What is the market structure? What are the sources of power today and in the future?

TABLE 8.1
Price Analysis Techniques

Method	When to Use	How to Use
Comparison with Published Price	When prices of items are publicly available without formal requests (i.e., off-the shelf or regulated items).	Purchaser obtains prices from sources such as trade journals, newspapers, published catalogues, or the Internet.
Competitive Proposals	When the supply market is highly competitive.	Requests for Quote can be sent out to several qualified suppliers and the most competitive supplier is selected.
Historical Comparisons	When the item has been purchased in the past and the market is fairly stable over time.	Past prices are tracked and current price is compared to them. Regression analysis can be a useful tool to estimate current or future prices.
Internal Cost Estimates	When the item is new and no history exists.	See three methods below.
Roundtables	When a quick estimate is needed and the organization has had experience with similar items.	Managers from engineering, manufacturing, purchasing, and finance come together to estimate the price based on their experience product knowledge, and market knowledge. This approach is highly subjective.
Comparison with Similar Products	When the organization has had experience with similar items or services.	Mathematical models (such as multiple regression) are established to estimate the cost of a new item based on the element costs of previously purchased items. This approach assumes comparability and relative market stability.
Detailed Analysis	When the organization has the time and resources needed to develop a detailed cost estimate. This approach can yield the best information for use in negotiating important purchases.	A thorough review of materials, components, and processes is performed. Estimation errors tend to cancel out when the cost of individual elements are estimated. This approach is knowledge intensive, requiring specifications, delivery quantities, bills of materials, material prices, drawings, understanding of the manufacturing process, quality requirements, time standards, overhead, and profit estimates.

TABLE 8.2
Discounts that Affect Pricing

Discount Type	Description
Volume Discounts	Reductions offered in recognition of the lower unit costs associated with larger order price breaks. Volume discounts can be based on specific order sizes, the total dollar value of a given order, or the total dollars spent by a customer over a specified period of time.
Trade Discounts	Reductions from a list price that are allowed to various classes of purchasers and distributors to compensate them for performing certain marketing functions. These may be stated in the form of "25-10-5" which translates to the retailer receiving a 25 percent discount off the list price, the wholesaler receiving a 10 percent discount off the retailer's price, and the manufacturer's price is 5 percent below the wholesaler's price.
Cash Discounts	Price reductions offered in order to encourage payment within a specified period of time. These are typically stated in the form of "2-10/net 30" which means that a 2 percent discount is offered if payment is made within 10 days, otherwise the full payment is due within 30 days.
Seasonal Discounts	Savings offered to induce purchasing organizations to purchase items during the product's off-season. A variation of this is when the purchaser takes delivery of the goods during the off-season but does not pay for them until much later, which effectively translates to a cost savings for the purchaser and a sharing of inventory carrying costs by both organizations.

Because information is power, successful negotiators take the research responsibility seriously and begin their quest for insight by carefully examining the supplier's proposal. The goal is to know the proposal as well as or better than the supplier's negotiator. After dissecting the proposal, the research often turns to an examination of previous transactions between the two organizations. If a long relationship exists, the research burden is diminished because the purchaser is familiar with the supplier's "hot buttons," production capabilities, and negotiating style. If the purchaser has no track record to rely on, other members of the purchasing organization including engineers and sales people might have some familiarity with the supplier. Outside sources of information such as business publications, commercial databases, trade associations, financial statements, and Dun & Bradstreet reports should also be evaluated. The purchaser might also directly ask personnel at the supplier for relevant information. Finally, a tour of the supplier's operations is often a vital part of the pre-negotiation investigation. Negotiation success often depends on the quality of research that has been done.

Analyze the Strengths and Weaknesses of Each Party

Before the actual negotiation begins, the purchaser must understand the relative positions of the purchasing and supplying organizations. Purchasers must not assume that the purchasing organization always negotiates from a position of strength - sometimes the supplier enters the negotiation in a position of strength. Much of the information gathered in the research stage is used to correctly assess the parties' relative strengths and weaknesses to improve negotiation outcomes. Knowing thoroughly the strengths and weaknesses of each side enables the purchaser to enter the negotiation with realistic expectations. This knowledge helps the purchaser develop an appropriate strategy and select winning tactics. Some of the specific issues that should be analyzed to understand the bargaining position include:

- **The supplier's desire to win the contract** – If the supplier holds a patent, has developed a unique process capability, or operates in a supplier's market, negotiating power is likely to favor the supplier. By contrast, if several competing suppliers are vying for market share, the supplier is likely to be more anxious to win the contract, placing the purchaser in the position of strength.
- **The supplier's certainty of getting a contract** – If the supplier is certain to receive the contract, as is often the case in today's partnership-oriented supply environment, the nature of the negotiation changes dramatically. The threat of using an alternative supplier no longer carries much weight. The purchaser must convince the supplier that it is in the supplier's best interest to create new value and perform at outstanding levels to assure future profitable business.

- **The amount of time available for negotiation** – The party operating under the greatest time constraint generally concedes power. It is best to negotiate without an externally imposed deadline. When time is available, more alternatives can be considered and both sides can participate in creative brainstorming. Time management is more critical in global negotiations because various cultures value time very differently. Global negotiators must understand how their counterparts measure time.

- **The adequacy of the purchaser's price analysis** – Entering a negotiation with confidence in the price analysis that has been performed makes it is easier to press for a fair and reasonable price. Supplier's quotes, price histories, and the purchaser's own analysis of production costs, direct labor, overhead, administration expenses, and shipping costs are the inputs to an accurate price analysis.

- **The options available to the purchaser** – The existence of multiple qualified suppliers strengthens the purchasing organization's leverage. When other suppliers do not exist, the purchasing organization may gain leverage by analyzing alternative products or by considering in-house production.

- **The supplier's competitive position** – Sometimes, a given supplier simply outperforms other sources. When a supplier makes a higher quality product, is more innovative, provides superior customer service, delivers more responsively, or offers better technical support, its bargaining position is improved. The purchaser must decide what it is willing to do to work with the best source available.

- **The skill and authority of the negotiators** – Including recognized technical experts, senior managers, and experienced, skilled negotiators on a team can shift the balance of power in a negotiation, especially if the other side lacks negotiation resources. Some organizations stack their negotiating teams with extra engineers or technical experts simply to overwhelm the other party.

- **The financial position of each party** – A purchaser in strong financial condition gains leverage because it can offer training, engineering support, better payment terms, and capital investment. Suppliers with strong finances are less likely to agree to unfavorable conditions but are likely to live up to negotiated commitments. While a supplier in weak financial condition is often willing to offer favorable prices, the purchaser must make sure that the supplier can fulfill quality, quantity, and delivery requirements.

Recognize Supplier's Needs

Just like purchasing organizations, suppliers enter negotiations with the expectation that a mutually beneficial agreement can be worked out. They also come to the negotiating table with a set of objectives that they hope to achieve. As purchasers prepare for the negotiation, it is paramount that they differentiate between the supplier's absolute needs and the items on the supplier's wish list. By conceding a point that is important to the supplier but not particularly vital to the purchaser, the purchaser can build good will without much cost. This good will can then be expended on those issues viewed as critical to the purchasing organization. A primary reason organizations negotiate is to determine where the give and take in the relationship will take place. By weighing carefully the supplier's needs, the purchasing negotiator can manage the give-and-take process to the mutual benefit of both parties.

Determine the Facts and Issues

An important aspect of negotiation planning is to identify the facts and issues that surround the situation. Facts are those items about which agreement is expected; they are the realities of the negotiation. By contrast, issues are those points about which disagreement is expected and which the negotiation is supposed to resolve. For example, when the purchasing organization prepares an RFQ, it includes a set of technical specifications that are usually accepted by the competing suppliers as facts. Suppliers rarely come back to the purchaser and argue that a particular product or service is not needed. Once the purchaser and supplier agree on the basic facts of the situation, time and effort can be dedicated to resolving the key issues such as what constitutes a fair and reasonable price or a late delivery. The number and types of issues can vary considerably based on what is being purchased and the type of purchaser/supplier relationship that already exists, but they should always be directly related to the negotiation objectives. While the majority of actual negotiating time should be spent narrowing the distance on key issues, the initial discussion of facts can help establish rapport and build the foundation for open and honest negotiations.

Establish a Position on Each Issue

After identifying the key issues to be negotiated, the purchasing organization needs to not only establish its own position on each issue but also estimate the supplier's positions. The position expresses the desired outcome the purchaser hopes to achieve. For most positions, a range of acceptable outcomes should be identified. Most negotiators establish a target position that they believe is realistically achievable. Based on this target, they then work out pessimistic and optimistic scenarios. Next to the target position, the pessimistic position is the most important point that must be decided upon before the negotiation. If the range of acceptable positions is not determined prior to the negotiation, poor decisions and buyer's remorse are probable outcomes. Fixing a pessimistic position is equivalent to a homebuyer deciding the upper limit of what they are willing to pay for a house. Certainly the buyer would like the seller to accept her first offer, but ultimately they need to know just how much they can afford to pay. If the home owner's and the potential buyer's positions overlap, then counteroffers can eventually lead to a price that is agreeable to both.

Finding an acceptable middle ground is the essence of negotiation (see Figure 8.1). If there is no overlap between the purchaser's and the supplier's positions, it is highly unlikely that an agreement can be reached, especially if the issue is viewed as critical to both parties. Failure to find a common ground on a critical point can undermine the entire negotiation. When positions overlap, a little give and take by both parties can usually lead to a mutually acceptable arrangement. Neither side should expect to achieve optimal results on every important issue. Establishing a range of positions before the negotiation increases the confidence of the negotiators and enhances the likelihood of negotiation success. However, legitimate occasions arise when the negotiator should consider modifying or abandoning a given position. For example, the supplier might bring new and relevant information to the negotiation. It is not unheard of for a supplier to make product design suggestions that require a modification in position regarding pricing or development leadtime. Other reasons for modifying a position include a concession by the supplier on an important issue, an overriding desire to finalize the contract, technological change, and unexpected changes in economic or political environments.

FIGURE 8.1

Negotiating Positions

Scenario #1

A puchaser and supplier are negotiating the unit price per pair of safety goggles.
- The purchaser has established a target price of $4.50, but would be willing to pay as much as $4.80.
- The supplier has set a target price of $5.25, but is willing to accept for as little as $5.00.

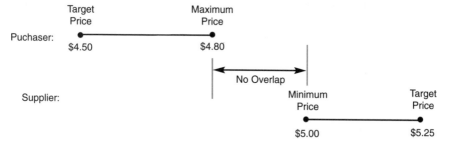

Outcome: Since there is no overlap in their acceptable positions, agreement is unlikely.

Scenario #2

- The purchaser has established a target price of $4.70, but would be willing to pay as much as $5.00.
- The supplier has set a target price of $5.10, but is willing to accept for as little as $4.85.

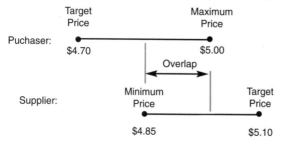

Outcome: Since the acceptable positions overlap, a negotiated agreement is likely.

Develop the Negotiating Strategy and Tactics

The negotiation strategy directs the organization's use of resources as it seeks to achieve desired objectives through a mutually beneficial agreement with the supplier. The strategy answers the overarching questions associated with the negotiation: Who will do the negotiating? Which issues should be discussed and in what sequence? Where is compromise acceptable? Where and when will the negotiation take place? How much of the organization's position should be revealed and when? How will the execution of the agreement be managed? The strategy provides guidance as the negotiation unfolds and provides the means by which progress is measured.

The tactical plan, by contrast, choreographs the actual negotiation process, arranging and directing the details required to get to a satisfactory agreement. It is the action plan. The tactics selected depend on the organization's negotiating philosophy, the negotiation objectives, and the strategy for the specific negotiation. Successful negotiators understand the importance of identifying the best tactics for a given situation and are able to execute them with skill and confidence. To do this well, negotiators must be dedicated to hard work, careful analysis, and hours of practice. The entire process should be thought out ahead of time with specific tactics selected and contingency plans in place. A large variety of tactics are available, some of which are well suited to all negotiations, while others are best used in collaborative negotiations, and still others apply only to adversarial settings. Some tactics are unethical and should be avoided. However, the experienced negotiator should recognize when the other party is using them. Common tactics include:

- **Argue based on facts** – Use facts and sound analysis to establish and back up key positions. Arguments that cannot be factually supported damage credibility.
- **Answer questions carefully** – Experienced negotiators know when to answer, when to leave a question unanswered, when to answer with precision, and when to be vague. They know that the proper answer to a question is the one that is truthful while advancing the negotiators tactical plan and better discerning the supplier's objectives.

- **Be considerate of suppliers** – Treating counterparts with respect and dignity almost never costs the purchasing organization the advantage in a negotiation. While aggressive and highly competitive negotiations might occasionally be justified and successful, a more reasoned and considerate approach that recognizes the emotional needs of the supplier often provides better long-term results.

- **Be wary of deadlines** – An effective negotiator does not let deadlines force bad decisions. It is preferable to let a supplier-imposed deadline pass than to agree to an unsatisfactory contract. Likewise, in setting a deadline, the purchaser must know ahead of time what consequence will be imposed. The use of arbitrary or meaningless deadlines diminishes credibility.

- **Best and final offer** – The take-it-or-leave-it approach signals the end of the discussion and the need for a decision on a specific point. While this tactic can help move the negotiation forward to the next issue, it should not be used as a bluff. If the negotiator is not prepared to end the negotiation and the supplier calls the bluff, then the purchaser loses credibility.

- **Do not be afraid to say no** – It is better to say no than to agree to an unsatisfactory position. While it is important not to rely excessively on saying no, being candid has merit.

- **Foot in the door** – Suppliers occasionally offer an unusually low initial price in an attempt to win business, establish switching costs, and then raise the price. Whenever an exceptional quote is received the purchaser should examine the supplier's motivation and capabilities to determine whether the offer represents a significant long-term benefit.

- **High ball** – Purchasers and suppliers sometimes begin a negotiation with extreme offers, expecting to make concessions. The goal is to contrast the "unreasonably high" offer with lower offers that are still quite favorable to the negotiator's position. This tactic is used mostly in adversarial negotiations where getting the biggest piece of the pie is important.

- **Honesty and openness** – Win-win negotiations emphasize free, honest, and open sharing of information. A high level of trust and a strong focus on "growing the pie" are needed for this tactic to be successful.

- **Keep the initiative** – Aggressive negotiators believe that the "best defense is a good offense." They establish the initiative early and maintain it by constantly probing the supplier's position, asking for justifications and requiring supporting documentation. When the supplier effectively supports a position, the initiative-driven purchaser has a counterproposal ready to maintain momentum. This tactic is employed most frequently in win-lose or adversarial negotiations.

- **Listen effectively** – Effective negotiators are great listeners. They listen not only to the words but also to the tone of voice and to the pauses. They pay close attention to the supplier's body language. Careful observation provides insight to the supplier's position and real objectives.

- **The missing person** – The deliberate absence of the person with the decisionmaking authority gives the negotiator extra time or an opportunity to escape negotiations that are not going well. Some negotiators refuse to begin a negotiation if the decisionmaking authority is not present. This is another tactic more frequently employed in win-lose negotiations.

- **Never give anything away** – Negotiators in a win-lose setting believe strongly that the other side should make more and larger concessions. For every concession the purchaser makes, equal or greater concessions are expected from the supplier. This exchange process usually leads to a mutually beneficial but not equally advantageous outcome. The willingness of the purchaser to make concessions often dictates whether a negotiation is win-lose or win-win.

- **Phantom quote/offer** – Deliberately attempting to mislead the other side into believing that "a better quote (or offer) is waiting from another supplier (or purchaser)" is unethical and risky. Effective win-win negotiators do not use this tactic.

- **Prioritize issues** – Two basic philosophies exist: discuss the most difficult issues first assuming that the other issues will fall into place and discuss the "easy" issues first to get a feel for the other side's style and establish a basic sense of trust that will help resolve more difficult issues.

- **Schedule breaks** – Scheduled breaks give the negotiator an opportunity to evaluate how things are going, discuss any surprises or areas of disagreement, gather additional information, and discuss negotiation strategies or tactics. It is a common practice to allow either side to call for a break whenever needed even if one is not scheduled. A negotiating team should call for a caucus immediately if a misunderstanding or disagreement among team members arises. A caucus can likewise be used to slow down momentum if the negotiation is moving in the wrong direction. The routine use of scheduled and unscheduled breaks makes it difficult for the other party to draw meaning from a team's decision to call for a caucus.

- **Security** – Experienced negotiators pay close attention to negotiation security. Occasionally, unethical behavior ranging from the use of hidden microphones to the copying of work notes occurs. Purchasers should be conscious of this possibility and careful in their discussions as well as with confidential material. It is easier to ensure a secure and ethical negotiation when the negotiation is conducted on-site at the purchaser's location.

- **Site selection** – Most negotiators prefer to host the negotiation to avoid travel and have access to needed information and support. When the home location is used, purchasers can arrange the physical facilities to their preference. Some negotiators prefer round tables while others are most comfortable using a rectangular table. Likewise, some negotiators prefer rooms with windows while others endeavor to avoid distractions by holding the negotiation in an interior room. The primary advantage of holding the negotiation at the supplier's site is that the purchaser can exercise the option to "walk away" from negotiations that are not going well. Regardless of specific preferences, most experts agree that informal and comfortable settings are best for win-win negotiations.

- **Strong initial offer** – Making a strong initial offer signals a desire to do business with the counterpart organization. It can also be an attempt to create a sense of indebtedness that is used to gain concessions throughout the negotiation.

- **The threat** – A tactic often used in win-lose negotiations is the threat. Suppliers threaten an imminent price increase or limited availability. Purchasers threaten to take the business elsewhere. It can be very difficult to determine whether the threat is legitimate or simply a bargaining tactic. Frequent threats greatly reduce the trust in a relationship.

- **Use diversions** – When negotiations grow excessively tense, as they occasionally do, the experienced negotiator diverts attention away from the problematic issue using a joke, an anecdote, or a well-timed break.
- **Use positive statements** – During most negotiations, the supplier's representative makes statements and argues positions that the purchaser disagrees with. To argue every point often leads to defensive behavior. It can be much more rewarding to respond with a positive statement like "I see your point." or "Your point is well taken."
- **Use questions effectively** – Well-positioned and well-phrased questions can be used to control the basic flow of the negotiation. The right question can undermine an unacceptable position held by the supplier or deflect criticism away from the purchaser's own position.
- **Use silence** – Because silence is not a normal part of the U.S. business culture, it can be effectively used to avoid difficult questions, make the other side nervous, seek concessions without specifically asking for them, and redirect the discussion tactfully.

Practice the Negotiation

The final step in effective negotiation preparation is to anticipate potential problems that might arise during the actual negotiation. One technique is for the negotiating team to present its negotiation plan (objectives, strategy, tactics, and agenda) to an internal panel of executives from purchasing, finance, manufacturing, engineering, and other relevant areas. The assembled panels, sometimes called a "murder board", aggressively dissects the plan, pointing out weaknesses and making suggestions for improvement.[7] Another popular approach is to conduct a mock negotiation. This dress rehearsal helps the negotiators simulate what might actually occur in the real negotiation. The team representing the supplier generally consists of marketing and other managers likely to be on the supplier's team. Both sides in a mock negotiation need to play their roles as realistically as possible in order to uncover flaws in the analysis, positions, or execution of the negotiating plan. The more realistic the mock negotiation, the better prepared the negotiator will be for the actual negotiation. A third method is to use a computer-based negotiation support system to critique the negotiating plan and test alternative scenarios. Of course, the amount and nature of practice should be driven by the importance of the negotiation. Because the organization will have to live with the negotiated outcome, strategically important negotiations should be thoroughly practiced before the real event.

Conducting Successful Negotiations

Negotiation is a very dynamic process. Even the best preparation and planning cannot guarantee success without careful execution. Professional negotiators recognize the need to effectively manage negotiation dynamics and possess the skills to do so. Purchasers need to recognize that while successful negotiations provide benefits to both the purchaser and the supplier, few negotiations conclude in a 50-50 sharing of benefits. It has been estimated that approximately 60 to 70 percent of the benefits of the typical negotiated contract go to the side with the more skilled negotiator.[8] Purchasers therefore need to understand those factors that determine whether or not a negotiation is conducted successfully.

The Four Phases of Negotiation

There are four phases to most negotiations: fact finding, the recess, narrowing the differences, and hard bargaining. Fact-finding brings the purchaser and the supplier together to clarify and verify the information provided by the other party. An important role of the fact-finding session is to build rapport between the negotiators. In many countries, serious negotiations do not begin until the two sides have spent considerable time getting to know each other. In addition to building trust, the purchaser uses this first meeting to confirm its understanding of the supplier's strengths, weaknesses, and interests. As soon as the facts are established, a recess should be called. Experience suggests successful negotiations are facilitated when the initial face-to-face meeting is limited to fact finding.

The recess is used to reassess relative strengths and weaknesses, review and revise objectives if necessary, and reevaluate key issues and the purchaser's position. The negotiation agenda is then organized to guide discussions once the negotiation reconvenes. Most experienced negotiators prefer to address specific issues in order of perceived difficulty, starting with the easiest, least controversial issues. This approach builds on the rapport established in the fact-finding session.

When the two parties next meet, the objective is to narrow the differences that exist with each issue on the agenda. Typically, the purchaser defines each issue, reiterates the facts, and justifies the purchasing organization's position. The supplier is likely to also present its position with supporting arguments. At this point, brainstorming, problem solving, and compromise are used to find a position that is mutually agreeable. Perhaps the use of a different material, a modified process, or slightly less restrictive tolerances might bridge the gap between the two positions, leading to an acceptable agreement. When the discussion on a specific issue deadlocks, the negotiation should move on to the next issue. Subsequent discussions on other issues can help break an earlier impasse. Effective negotiators use several practices to narrow distances and promote creative and cooperative agreements:

- **Effective negotiators do not make it personal** – Effective negotiators separate people from positions and are careful never to attack the individual. Every effort is made to assure a positive experience. Negotiations can become emotional; therefore, wise purchasers do not take offense when the supplier's representative voices frustration. They are also quick to compliment their counterparts throughout the negotiation and congratulate them on a job well done at the conclusion of the negotiation. They realize that future negotiations depend on everyone leaving the table with a sense of satisfaction and accomplishment.
- **Effective negotiators keep an open mind** – Revising objectives and positions when new information becomes available moves negotiations more quickly to successful conclusions. Thoughtful negotiators also recognize that good ideas often emerge during discussions and use the negotiation to enhance organizational learning. They are also willing to work closely with suppliers to invent new options for mutual gain. In fact, skilled negotiators

evaluate twice as many options per issue compared to average negotiators.[9]

- **Effective negotiators refer frequently to common ground** – They view issues independently and with an overall sense of give and take. They avoid the mentality that concessions must be made on a one-for-one basis and do not keep score. To promote common understanding, key positions and points of agreement are summarized throughout the negotiation.
- **Effective negotiators never negotiate beyond their physical and mental endurance** – They recognize that fatigue slows thinking and clouds judgment and arrange agendas to provide for sufficient rest before and during the negotiation, especially when international travel and unfamiliar surroundings are involved.

Hard bargaining is the final phase and should only be used when more cooperative efforts have failed. Because hard bargaining employs win-lose tactics and market power to get to a satisfactory deal, it should not be used when long-term partnership relationships are the goal. For example, the best-and-final offer is commonly used once a negotiation reaches this stage. The purchasing team carefully reevaluates its needs and positions in order to present a final offer. The supplier is then given the opportunity to accept or reject the offer. Take-it-or-leave-it propositions can easily antagonize or alienate suppliers. The purchaser should work to make sure that the supplier does not feel abused.

The Use of Power

The use of power in a negotiation can help an organization achieve important goals. The abuse of power can damage long-term relationships and even lead to future retaliation. Skilled negotiators recognize that different types of power exist and use them as needed to achieve desired outcomes. Six types of power have been identified:[10] informational power, reward power, coercive power, legitimate power, expert power, and referent power. Informational power is the use of facts and analysis for persuasion. Negotiation planning is performed to enhance informational power. Reward power involves the promise of value in return for a certain concession and is frequently used in purchasing negotiations. For example, many organizations promise larger contracts or future business to suppliers who are willing to offer favorable prices. Coercive power is the threat of punishment. A purchaser who threatens to shift business to a competing supplier is using coercive power. Because the use of coercive power can alienate business partners, it should be used sparingly. Legitimate power emerges from an individual's position of authority. Purchasers from well-known, prestigious organizations can sometimes use the opportunity to do business with their organization as a stimulus for a better agreement. Expert power comes from an individual's reputation for having accumulated specialized knowledge. Including experts on the negotiating team can lend force to the team's arguments and diminish challenges from non-experts representing the other party. Finally, referent power stems from personal attributes or characteristics that lead others to want to emulate an individual. A purchaser's charisma, integrity, or sensitivity can influence a supplier's negotiator to be less aggressive or more agreeable. In planning for a negotiation, purchasers should carefully analyze existing power relationships and determine when and how power should be used to influence the outcome of a negotiation. Expert, informational, and legitimate power can generally be used without risk to a relationship. The other types of power should be used cautiously and with an understanding of the affect that their use will have on the continuing relationship.

Negotiation Documentation

Meticulous and accurate notes should be taken throughout every negotiation. Personnel turnover and the limitations of human memory make documenting negotiations essential. Today's legal environment also enhances the value of an accurate record. The notes should be complete enough either to reconstruct the negotiation and the resulting agreement or to enable someone who was not involved in the negotiation to understand exactly what happened and why it happened. Another use of the notes is to debrief or review the negotiation to determine how successful the negotiation actually was as well as what could have been done differently to improve the outcome.

Someone whose sole responsibility is to document the negotiation needs to ensure that sufficiently detailed notes are taken. Taking complete notes and negotiating a great contract at the same time is difficult. The individual responsible for taking notes should capture what is said, who said it, reactions to discussion, significant body language, and even lengthy periods of silence. Specific details regarding the supplier's name and location, the contract number, and a description of the item should be included in the documentation file. A copy of the supplier's proposal, the organization's negotiation plan, and the final contract might also accompany the notes. Keeping accurate records can be very beneficial in future negotiations and in case non-performance or other unexpected problems arise.

Becoming a Great Negotiator

Purchasers need to be effective negotiators. Strong purchaser/supplier relationships and successful contracts are built on the judgment and negotiating skill of purchasing professionals. Much of the organization's success depends on outstanding supplier cooperation and performance. Experience suggests that while some individuals possess a quicker wit, more charisma, or stronger verbal aptitudes, almost anyone can improve their negotiating ability. Table 8.3 lists some of the characteristics and skills possessed by outstanding negotiators. It is interesting to note that all of these abilities can be developed or enhanced through training and practice. No one is born with negotiating knowledge and skills. Equally important, as previously noted, up to 90 percent of the negotiation process occurs before the two parties enter the same room. A thorough understanding of the organization's negotiation philosophy combined with the superior preparation that comes from hard work can help any purchaser become a more successful negotiator. Ultimately, successful negotiators are characterized by three common attributes, each of which should give confidence and provide motivation to the aspiring purchasing negotiator.[11]

1. They recognize that specialized training and practice are required to become an effective negotiator.
2. They enter negotiations with high expectations, which they generally achieve. Their negotiating goals consistently exceed the goals of their counterparts.

3. They become among the most highly valued professionals in their organization.

TABLE 8.3
Characteristics of an Effective Negotiator

Ability to gain respect	Persistence
Ability to listen	Personal integrity
Analytical ability	Planning ability
Competitiveness	Problem solving ability
Decisiveness	Quick, agile thinking ability
Desire to achieve	Self-control
Flexibility	Tact
Insight	Tolerance for ambiguity
Intelligence	Verbal clarity and language skill
Knowledge of human nature	Willingness to listen to other's ideas
Patience	Willingness to study and practice

Key Points

1. Off-the-shelf purchasing or competitive bidding are often the best approaches for acquiring a good or service. However, excellent supply relationships often involve negotiated agreements. As a result, negotiating skills are more important to purchasing success than ever.
2. Negotiation is the formal communications process where two or more individuals discuss an issue or issues and come to a mutually satisfactory agreement.
3. Negotiation is the most expensive approach used to purchase a good or service. Therefore, it is most applicable when large or complicated contracts are involved, the supplier provides truly specialized services, or long-term relationships are being established.
4. In recent years, the win-win or cooperative negotiating philosophy has become more popular, largely because of the desire to build continuing purchaser/supplier relationships. The win-lose or adversarial approach may still be called for in selected situations such as a one-time purchase.
5. Negotiation planning is the most critical part of the negotiation. The party that is best prepared almost always gains the most from

a negotiated contract. Key steps in the planning process include developing specific objectives, establishing an effective negotiating team, gathering relevant information, analyzing bargaining positions, recognizing the supplier's needs, determining the facts and issues, identifying the purchasing organization's position on each issue, developing the negotiation strategy and tactics, and practicing the negotiation.

6. Effective negotiators know how to manage the basic phases of negotiation, understand when and how to use power to influence negotiation outcomes, and carefully design negotiating scenarios to facilitate success.

7. Great negotiators are individuals who develop key skills through training and practice. They recognize the importance of preparation and generally work smarter than their counterparts.

Questions For Review

1. What forces have made negotiation a vital purchasing skill for today's supply environment?

2. Discuss the basic negotiating philosophies. When would each be appropriate? How would a negotiating team change its preparation to achieve success using each philosophy?

3. Identify the critical issues that might be discussed in a negotiation. Why are these issues important to the purchaser? The supplier?

4 Why is planning the most important part of the negotiation process? What are the key planning steps? Why is minimizing the planning effort a risky approach?

5. Discuss three factors that influence the purchaser's negotiating position. Discuss three factors that influence the supplier's negotiating position.

6. During preparation, the effective negotiator selects the tactics that are likely to lead to favorable results. Which tactics are most applicable to all negotiations? Why? Which tactics should only be used in win-lose negotiations? Why? Which tactics are unethical? Why?

7. Discuss the role of power in negotiation. What are the pros and cons of using each type of power? Should some types of power be avoided altogether? Why?
8. What are the characteristics or attributes of an effective negotiator?

Endnotes

1. Raedels, A. *C.P.M. Study Guide*, National Association of Purchasing Management, Tempe, AZ, 2000.
2. Dobler, D.W. and D.N. Burt. *Purchasing and Supply Management*, McGraw-Hill, New York, NY, 1996.
3. Tully, S. "Purchasing's New Muscle," *Fortune*, February 20, 1995, pp. 75-83.
4. Covey, S.R. *The Seven Habits of Highly Effective People*, Simon & Schuster, New York, NY, 1989.
5. Lewicki, R. J. and J.A. Litterer. *Negotiation: Readings, Exercises and Cases*, Irwin/McGraw Hill, Homewood, IL, 1993.
6. Leenders, M.R. and H.E. Fearon. *Purchasing and Supply Management*, Irwin/McGraw Hill, Chicago, IL, 1997; Dobler, Op. Sit; Monczka, R., R. Trent, and R. Handfield. *Purchasing and Supply Chain Management*, South-Western College Publishing, Cincinnati, OH, 1998.
7. Dobler, 1996.
8. *Ibid.*
9. Monczka, Trent, and Handfield, 1998.
10. Lewicki, and Litterer, 1993.
11. Dobler, 1996; Monczka, Trent, and Handfield, 1998.

CHAPTER 9

PURCHASING'S ROLE IN THE LEARNING ORGANIZATION

What skills will I need to succeed in the future?

Chapter Objectives

This chapter is designed to help the purchaser:

- Identify important changes that are likely to occur in the supply environment over the next decade.
- Encourage purchasing managers to be involved in their organization's strategic assessment process.
- Understand the need for continuous improvement and life-long learning.

Value-Added Purchasing

The future of purchasing depends entirely on its ability to create measurable value. Fortunately, forces that have made today's supply environment complex and challenging promote purchasing as a competitive weapon. For example, the move to global marketing and manufacturing networks – which needs to be supported by more proactive and sophisticated purchasing practices – has raised the visibility of purchasing. Other competitive practices including cycle-time reduction, integrated product development, process integration, and supply chain management all draw on the expertise of the purchasing function. The convergence of these practices with purchasing's ability to respond effectively to the challenges confronting modern business has elevated purchasing to a new and unprecedented

257

levels of strategic relevance. The opportunity is now for purchasing to build on this momentum and provide cutting-edge solutions to tomorrow's challenges. To do this successfully, purchasers must:

- Understand and adapt to a constantly changing and increasingly complicated supply environment.
- Find ways for purchasing to help the organization achieve its most important strategic objectives.
- Establish an attitude that unlocks the creativity and the passion of the purchasing professional.

Ten Trends of Tomorrow's Supply Environment

Organizations that are adept at anticipating future trends, understanding their implications, and formulating an appropriate plan of attack tend to succeed. The value of this forward vision was once described by retired hockey great Wayne Gretsky. When asked what made him "The Great One," Gretsky replied, "Most people skate to where the puck is. I try to skate to where the puck will be." Combining this attitude with his knowledge of the game, experience, and relentless practice Gretsky became one of the game's most feared offensive weapons. Organizations do not operate with a crystal ball. They rely on experience, effort, a willingness to be wrong on occasion, and an undeviating focus on anticipation instead of reaction. As a result, they arrive at the competitive junction before the competition.

Purchasers who possess this same trait of foresight are always scanning the environment for clues regarding the next opportunity or signs of imminent, as well as eventual threats. They have already identified where they believe the supply environment is heading over the next decade.[1] The following 10 trends are likely to shape the environment in which purchasers make decisions:

1. **Intense competition** – The competitive challenge is already fierce in almost all industries. Even so, excess global capacity, the emergence of competitors from newly industrializing countries, and dramatically shorter innovation cycles promise to further intensify competition.
2. **Globalization** – Barring a severe economic downturn that could revive protectionist sentiment, global economic integration will

continue. Many organizations have discovered that global markets are the source of the majority of their sales and profit growth.

3. **Customer sophistication** – Customer empowerment is a trend that must be taken seriously. The arrival of competitive options from around the world coupled with customer's increasing access to accurate information will truly shift channel power downstream. Organizations must prepare to meet the demands of a more sophisticated customer.

4. **Mass customization** – Advancing technology continues to propel mass customization. The ability to capture economies of standardization while customizing products to specific customers' preferences will create tremendous pressure to enhance flexibility and responsiveness. True mass customization may be several years away, but leading organizations are inching closer to this goal.

5. **Virtual integration** – Emphasis on supply chain management and strategic alliances will continue as organizations opt for the flexibility of virtual integration. Managers will try to reap the expertise and global reach of collaboration while relying on the ability to "walk away" from one relationship in search of an opportunity made more attractive by the dynamics of a global market. Finding the balance between integration and flexibility will be a great challenge for purchasers over the next several years.

6. **Network rationalizations** – The exigencies of tomorrow's supply environment will increase the pressure to simplify whenever and wherever possible. Supply-base reduction near 80 to 90 percent has been used to focus resources and reduce complexity. Managers will increasingly look for opportunities to reduce network complexity including SKU reduction, customer-base optimization, and logistical network rationalization.

7. **Outsourcing** – Competitive dynamics are likely to force a continued drive toward specialization and core competence. Any activity that does not affect the customer's ultimate satisfaction is likely to be outsourced so that organizations can focus on providing a remarkable customer experience.

8. **Electronic channels** – The Internet is changing the way organizations communicate with each other, greatly enhancing the visibility of the entire supply chain. Multiple channels that include traditional "brick-and-mortar" options as well as "click-and-mortar" options are emerging. In an e-commerce world, private and public sectors will have to use diverse channels to deliver incredible value.

9. **The dominant organization** – The last 10 years have witnessed a quest for the cash flow and the economies of scale needed to do battle with global industrial behemoths. Participating in a supply chain dominated by a behemoth will be an ever-present challenge in the near future.

10. **Constant dynamism** – The only constant in tomorrow's supply environment will be change, and it is a safe bet to say that the rate of change will only increase. Agility, learning, and relationships will be needed to deal with challenges presented by constant change.

Purchasing and the Assessment Process

There are three simple but powerful questions that purchasing professionals must constantly answer to help their organizations compete in tomorrow's dynamic supply environment: "Where are we?", "Where do we want to be?", and "How do we get there?". These questions emerge from the four elements of strategy discussed in Chapter 1. Asking the question "Where are we?", involves understanding how purchasing resources are employed to create value. The question "Where do we want to be?", focuses the purchaser's attention on customers' needs and competitors' capabilities. Finally, the question "How do we get there?", emphasizes the fact that strategic purchasing is a feedback-dependent process. Rigorous assessment requires information on customer characteristics and desires, competitors' capabilities, and the organization's own practices and performance. These three assessment questions promote a creative and rigorous thought process.

"Where are we?" – Answering the question "Where are we?", requires a review of all of the organization's key value-added processes. Such an encompassing examination of how the organization's resources are used to create value is seldom performed because knowledge is typically dispersed among many individuals who work in a variety of functional areas. While top managers possess a vision of the organization's strategy, they seldom see the details of value addition. While line managers intimately understand the details, they may not see broader interactions. Much of the value-added process is hidden from view and poorly understood. Yet, for purchasers to contribute to organizational success, they must understand the entire value-added process and how they can support value creation at each step.

The key to understanding value-creation is to make the process visible. This can only be done by carefully tracing the process from beginning to end. This is true for both production and service processes. For example, a creative consultant charged with the task of helping an organization get its order processing system under control arrived on site and said, "I'm an order, process me." With management in tow, the consultant moved through the organization just as if he were an order. By the time he had been "processed," a first-hand perspective of how the system worked had been gained. Becoming an order provided managers with their first view of the process as a value-added system. Making a process visible allows for thoughtful analysis and provides a focal point for discussion, communication is enhanced, and problems can be worked through on a realistic basis. To gain visibility of its order fulfillment process, one organization constructed a "war room" with walls made of poster board "coated with color-coded sheets of paper and knitting yarn that graphically charted the order flow from the first step to the last."[2] This understanding helps purchasers highlight problems and identify opportunities for purchasing to make a difference.

"Where do we want to be?" – Positioning purchasing to help meet customers' real needs better than the competition is the objective of answering this question. Traditional questions that emphasize product characteristics and competitors' offerings seldom yield the insight needed to understand the product/customer interaction. The right questions are those that help purchasers understand why the customer purchases the product or service in the first place. Asking questions that are overlooked by competitors allows purchasers to change competitive rules and avoid costly head-on competitive battles.

As purchasing managers learn what customers value, they must design purchasing processes that close the gaps between the organization's capabilities and customer expectations. Competitors' performance should also be evaluated because competitors' actions and reactions affect customer perceptions. A simple matrix can be used to develop and organize information during this assessment. For the example in Figure 9.1, quality is evaluated at the level of overall perceived quality and in more specific terms such as percent of internal defects, frequency of field failures, and response time of after sales/service personnel. The use of an assessment matrix helps an organization benchmark its practices and processes against both customer requirements and competitors' capabilities. Better customer focus and constant learning are two benefits of answering the question, "Where do we want to be?".

FIGURE 9.1
The Assessment Matrix

Competitive Dimensions	Self	Competitors			Customer Valuations			
		#1	#2	#3	#1	#2	#3	Overall Market
Quality								
% Internal Defects								
Field Failures								
After Sales Response								
Cost								
Dependability								
Flexibility								
Innovation								

© Stanley E. Fawcett, Ph.D., C.P.M.

"How do we get there?" – Purchasing managers are involved in a diversity of value-added initiatives ranging from cycle time reduction to Internet sourcing. Each initiative targets enhanced purchasing contribution. However, scarce resources make it dangerous to undertake too many initiatives at the same time. The third question, "How do we get there?" emphasizes the issue of prioritization. Purchasers must quantify the affect of each initiative on critical processes and the organization's ability to deliver value to key customers. Purchasing initiatives that enhance those value-added capabilities that most close-ly align with market requirements receive the highest priority. Because the supply environment is so dynamic with both customer expecta-tions and competitors' capabilities constantly evolving, a well-designed feedback system is essential. Accurate, relevant, and timely feedback allows purchasers to evaluate the competitive status of each endeavor while making adjustments to both priorities and programs. Excellent feedback promotes continual improvement and will make or break purchasing's ability to effectively use the assessment process.

Purchasing Improvement Through Personal Initiative

Becoming best-in-class requires that every purchaser bring expertise, creativity, and passion to work every day. Three practices underlie this goal: a leadership style that encourages personal initia-tive; aggressive measurement and goal setting; and a program that draws on individual participation. A leadership style that emphasizes getting the right people in the right place and then getting out of their way so that they are free to perform begins to unlock the potential of the human resource. This style requires a shared vision, clearly com-municated expectations, skill enhancement through targeted training, consistent and fair performance measurement, and aligned incentives. Purchasers who possess a desire to learn, thrive within this environ-ment and contribute the ideas and energy needed for innovation.

Second, one manager, referring to her organization's attitude toward goal setting noted, "We don't accept mediocrity; we set goals." With this attitude in place, change at this organization is no longer viewed as a threat, but as an opportunity to excel. For each vital program or activity, specific goals are set and performance benchmarked. Likewise, goal setting extends down to each individ-ual. Workers meet with their immediate supervisors in a mentoring or coaching setting. Together, each worker/supervisor team identifies and assesses the competencies that the worker needs to excel. This process helps identify what the worker does well and where opportu-nities for improvement exist. Annual goals are then set with specific timelines for important milestones. Quarterly reviews are held to dis-cuss progress and assure that the resources are available to facilitate success. For this approach to work, failure cannot be punished. Purchasing managers must recognize that when people try new things and establish goals, desired outcomes are not always achieved. The vital question when failure occurs is, "Did you learn something?"

Finally, a program that gives structure to the continuous improvement initiative must be established. A leading company in the mineral extraction industry experienced tremendous success with an initiative known as the "Pet Project Program Three."[3] The program asks the question, "What are the problems that need improving but that we haven't gotten around to yet?". With this theme in mind, a simple matrix guides the selection of potential projects (see Figure 9.2). The matrix weeds out low payoff projects while encouraging individual initiative. The basic process consists of the following seven steps:

1. Group leaders and individuals generate the pet project list
2. List refined to top 20 (must be in final set)
3. Each individual selects a pet project
4. Each individual enrolls team members
5. Team submits project proposal with milestones, individual responsibilities, and completion date
6. Proposals reviewed by group leaders
7. Final project list reviewed by purchasing director

FIGURE 9.2
The Pet Project Selection Matrix

	Low Payoff	High Payoff
Low Effort	Tasks that are easy to do, but are of minimal value. Should not be the focus of effort.	Tasks that are easy to do and yield immediate, visible payoff. Target these first. Relatively rare after first round.
Big Effort	Tasks that are hard to do and offer little payoff. Should be avoided.	Tasks that are hard to do but have a high payoff. Require a plan, a team, and concerted effort.

Each employee is expected to be a project leader and to take ownership for purchasing improvement. When assembling a project team, members must be enrolled, not enlisted. Individuals should be free to decline participation and encouraged to participate only if they are truly interested and can contribute in a meaningful way. Finally, the project proposal must include the goal, a plan of action with specified activities, important milestones, and a targeted completion date (see Figure 9.3). Each action is directly tied to a team member to assure personal ownership.

FIGURE 9.3
Sample Pet Project Proposal

Pet Project Name_____

Goal   Completion Date

Project Leader_____   Team Members_____

Milestones	Completion Date
1.	
2.	
3.	

Promised Actions	Who's Responsible	Promised Date	Completion Date
1.			
2.			
3.			

Pet project programs tap into pent up creativity and has in practice yielded strong buy-in. The example purchasing group, which consisted of 67 employees, successfully completed 96 of 102 approved pet projects in the first year of the program. Many high-value projects have been completed. For example, the "inventory reduction through consignment" pet project produced consignment and stockless inventory arrangements that have streamlined operating processes, shortened replenishment leadtimes, and reduced total inventory costs (18 percent of all on-site inventory is now on consignment). The pet project program has unleashed the passion for excellence held by this organization's purchasing professionals.

The Need for Constant Purchasing Education

A world characterized by constant change demands continual education. Back in 1990, Bernard J. La Londe[4] identified two fundamental long-term propositions regarding life-long education and the need for materials managers to stay current:

- Despite the rapid changes in the materials profession, the burden for skill building would shift away from formal, organization-sponsored training to the individual.
- Supply managers would need to spend 10 percent of their time acquiring new skills to avoid obsolescence in five years.

The experience of the past decade has substantiated these two propositions. The purchasing and supply management profession has changed at an incredible pace. Ten years ago, almost no one talked about supply chain management, third-party logistics, or supplier-managed inventory. As recently as five years ago, Web pages, relational databases, and e-commerce were largely unknown.

Few organizations have established training programs to keep pace with the rapidly changing supply landscape despite the fact that investments in education often provide double the return of investments in technology. A few organizations like Motorola, McDonalds, and Modus Media International sponsor their own corporate universities. Others like Deere & Company have established extensive in-house training programs. The National Association of Purchasing Management has also made continued education a key part of its professional certification program, for the Certified Purchasing Manager (C.P.M.). Additional certifications such as becoming a "black belt" in six sigma or going through SAP's enterprise resource planning training greatly increase the marketability of today's purchasing professional. Important skills for tomorrow's purchasing manger will include negotiation and supplier management as well as database design and management and Internet purchasing. The fact that purchasers are pursuing professional development is vital since

Professor LaLonde has recently updated Proposition 2, predicting that by the year 2002, successful supply managers will need to spend 20 percent of their time building new skills to avoid obsolescence in a scant three years.

Key Points

1. Purchasing has become a legitimate competitive weapon in many organizations because progressive purchasers have leveraged opportunities created by today's evolving supply environment.
2. The supply environment will continue to change at a rapid pace over the next 10 years with continued emphasis on globalization, product/service customization, network rationalization, outsourcing, and supply chain integration. New forces will arise from advances in information technology and emergence of "click-and-mortar" distribution channels.
3. Purchasing managers will need to more actively participate in their organization's competitive assessment process to establish purchasing processes that can turn the threats of the new supply environment into opportunities.
4. Purchasing organizations must cultivate an environment where the creativity and passion of every purchaser is used to promote continuous improvement.
5. Purchasing professionals will quickly lose relevance without constant and life-long dedication to professional development.

Questions for Review

1. What changes in the supply environment will have the greatest affect on your organization over the next five years and over the next 10 years?
2. What are your organization's most important resources (core competencies)? What are your organization's most important objectives? How are resources used to help meet critical objectives? What affect is a changing supply environment having on your resource use and development and on key objectives?
3. Does your organization have the right feedback mechanisms in place? Are strategic objectives and specific roles easily commu-

nicated throughout the organization? Is an appropriate performance measurement system in place?
4. Does your organization have a formal continuous improvement
program in place? What needs to be done to establish such a program?

Endnotes

1. Carter, P. L., J.R. Carter, R.M. Monczka, T.H. Slaight, and A.J.
Swan. *"The Future of Purchasing and Supply: A Five- and Ten-
Year Forecast,"* National Association of Purchasing Management
and the Center for Advanced Purchasing Studies, Tempe, AZ,
1998.
2. Shapiro, P., V. Rangan, and J. Sviokla. "Staple Yourself to an
Order," *Harvard Business Review*, (70:4), 1992, pp. 113-122.
3. Fawcett, S.E. "Purchasing Innovation through Pet Projects,"
*Praxis: Best Practice in Purchasing and Supply Chain
Management*, (1:2), 1997, pp. 1-4.
4. La Londe, B. "Trends in Logistics and Materials Management,"
presented at the 1990 Council of Logistics Management Annual
Meeting, Anaheim, CA.

Author Index

B

Bhote, Keki, 114, 127
Birou, L.M., 27, 58, 127
Blackwell, R.D., 27, 126
Bleakley, F.R., 190
Bourner, T., 157
Bower, J.L., 126
Bowersox, D.J., 27, 126, 189
Brooks, R., 215
Bucklin, D., 127
Burt, D.N., 27, 58, 256

C

Calantone, R.J., 27, 126, 189
Carter, J.R., 268
Carter, P.L., 268
Clark, K.B., 27
Clausing, D., 127
Clinton, S.R., 27, 126, 189
Closs, D.J., 27, 126, 189
Coleman, C.Y., 215-216
Condit, Phil, 191, 212
Cooper, M.B., 27, 126, 189-190
Covey, Steven, 230, 256
Crockett, R.O., 216
Crosby, Philip, 11, 27, 113, 127

D

Deming, W. Edwards, 100, 102, 109
    110, 127
Dobler, D.W., 58, 256
Droge, C.L., 27, 126, 189
Drucker, P.F., 126

E

Ellif, S.A., 189
Evans, P., 27, 126

F

Fairclough, G., 57
Fawcett, S.A., 126
Fawcett, Stanley E., 14, 27, 39, 44,
    57-58, 62, 86, 94, 99, 111, 116,
    126-127, 140, 168, 189-190, 262,
    268
Fearon, H.E., 27, 256
Feigenbaum, A.V., 102, 127
Ford, Henry, 60
Frankel, R., 27, 126, 189
Frayer, D.J., 27, 126, 189

G

Galle, W.P., 58
Garvin, D.A., 100, 127
Ginsburg, I., 126
Giunipero, L.C., 58
Grove, Andrew S., 32, 57
Gryna, J.F.M., 126

H

Hadjian, A., 86, 157
Hall, G., 156
Hamel, G., 156
Handfield, R.B., 27, 58, 189, 215, 256
Hayes, R., 27
Henkoff, R., 27, 127, 189
Hoole, R., 27
Hout, T.M., 126
Hymowitz, C., 157

I

Isikawa, Kaoru, 110

J

Jacob, R., 156, 215
Jensen, M., 157
Juran, J.M., 95, 102, 126

K

Kahl, Jack, 92
Kolb, David, 149
Kolbe, Kathy, 149, 156
Krause, D.R., 189
Kutner, Harold, 211

L

La Londe, Bernard J., 266, 268
Lawson, J., 157
Leenders, M.R., 27, 256
Levitt, Theodore, 30, 57
Lewicki, R.J., 232, 256
Litterer, J.A., 232, 256
Loeb, M., 127
Lopez, Jose Ignacio, 79, 230

M

McDonald, A.L., 58
McGrath, M., 27
Maddux, B., 215
Magnan, G.M., 189
Miller, N., 126
Min, H., 58
Monczka, R.M., 27, 58, 74, 87, 215, 256, 268
Morash, E.A., 27, 126, 189
Murphree, J., 190
Murray, M., 157
Musi, V.J., 156

N

Naj, A.K., 86
Nelson, E., 190, 215

O

Ohmae, Kenichi, 12, 27

P

Porter, Michael, 27, 95, 126
Prahalad, C.K., 156

R

Raedels, A., 215, 256
Ramstad, E., 190
Rangan, V., 268
Rao, R.M., 156
Rinehart, L.M., 27, 126, 189
Robinson, David, 135, 190, 216
Rocks, D., 216
Rosenthal, J., 156
Row, A., 157, 190

S

Salk, G., 86
Schmitz, J.M., 27, 126, 189
Schonberger, R.J., 86
Schulman, L.E., 27, 126
Scully, J.I., 57
Senge, Peter, 67
Shapiro, P., 268
Sherman, S., 86, 157
Shirouzu, N., 86
Simison, R.L., 57, 87, 216
Siqueira, M., 190
Sirkin, Harold, 19, 159
Slaight, T.H., 268
Stalk, G., 27, 126-127
Stallkamp, Thomas, 43
Stewart, T.A., 86, 127
Sviokla, J., 268
Swan, A.J., 268

T

Taguchi, Genichi, 103, 127
Taylor, Frederick, 60
Taylor, J.C., 86
Trent, R.J., 27, 58, 74, 87, 215, 256
Tuckman, B., 157
Tully, S., 27, 58, 256

U

Upton, D.M., 86

SUBJECT INDEX